Immersion Education

D1452493

MIX
Paper from
responsible sources
FSC® C014540
www.fsc.org

BILINGUAL EDUCATION & BILINGUALISM
Series Editors: Nancy H. Hornberger, *University of Pennsylvania, USA* and Colin Baker, *Bangor University, Wales, UK*

Bilingual Education and Bilingualism is an international, multidisciplinary series publishing research on the philosophy, politics, policy, provision and practice of language planning, global English, indigenous and minority language education, multilingualism, multiculturalism, biliteracy, bilingualism and bilingual education. The series aims to mirror current debates and discussions.

Full details of all the books in this series and of all our other publications can be found on http://www.multilingual-matters.com, or by writing to Multilingual Matters, St Nicholas House, 31–34 High Street, Bristol BS1 2AW, UK.

BILINGUAL EDUCATION & BILINGUALISM
Series Editors: Nancy H. Hornberger and Colin Baker

Immersion Education
Practices, Policies, Possibilities

Edited by
Diane J. Tedick, Donna Christian and
Tara Williams Fortune

MULTILINGUAL MATTERS
Bristol • Buffalo • Toronto

Library of Congress Cataloging in Publication Data
A catalog record for this book is available from the Library of Congress.
Immersion Education: Practices, Policies, Possibilities/Edited by Diane J. Tedick,
Donna Christian and Tara Williams Fortune.
Bilingual Education & Bilingualism: 83.
Includes bibliographical references and index.
1. Immersion method (Language teaching) 2. Language and languages--Study and
teaching. 3. Education, Bilingual. I. Tedick, Diane J. II. Christian, Donna. III. Fortune,
Tara Williams
P53.44.I44 2011
418.0071–dc22 2011015597

British Library Cataloguing in Publication Data
A catalogue entry for this book is available from the British Library.

ISBN-13: 978-1-84769-403-4 (hbk)
ISBN-13: 978-1-84769-402-7 (pbk)

Multilingual Matters
UK: St Nicholas House, 31–34 High Street, Bristol, BS1 2AW, UK.
USA: UTP, 2250 Military Road, Tonawanda, NY 14150, USA.
Canada: UTP, 5201 Dufferin Street, North York, Ontario, M3H 5T8, Canada.

The policy of Multilingual Matters/Channel View Publications is to use papers
that are natural, renewable and recyclable products, made from wood grown in
sustainable forests. In the manufacturing process of our books, and to further
support our policy, preference is given to printers that have FSC and PEFC Chain
of Custody certification. The FSC and/or PEFC logos will appear on those books
where full certification has been granted to the printer concerned.

Typeset by Techset Composition Ltd, Salisbury, UK.
Printed and bound in Great Britain by Short Run Press Ltd.

Dedicated to the memory of
Wallace (Wally) E. Lambert
Immersion Pioneer
1922–2009

Contents

Introduction to the Volume

Part 1: Practices in Immersion Program Design

Part 2: Program Outcomes and Implications for Practice

Acknowledgements

Since we began our work on this edited volume, the demand for immersion education has grown, and new immersion programs have been launched around the world. In many ways immersion appears to be experiencing a renaissance, and the timing seems appropriate for a volume that offers new research and perspectives in the field and that invites readers to 'dwell in possibility,' to imagine ways that immersion can reach its full potential. It was with this spirit in mind that we began this project, and the many authors who have contributed to the volume embraced that spirit and imagined possibilities with us. We are deeply grateful to them for contributing their work and insights to this volume. Throughout the process they have collaborated generously with us on the preparation of their chapters, responding swiftly and carefully to every request and question sent. Few edited book projects go as smoothly as this, and that is thanks to the diligence, attention and responsiveness of our wonderful roster of contributors.

We especially thank Merrill Swain for agreeing to write the foreword. Merrill has been and continues to be an exceptional mentor, and this volume would not have been complete without her voice. We are indebted to Fred Genesee for his comprehensive grasp of the field and willingness to write the concluding synthesis chapter – a tall order that required reading the entire volume and offering his perspective on overarching themes and future directions within a very short time frame. The volume is much richer because of Fred's insights. We further thank our colleagues Roy Lyster, Stephen May and Kim Potowski for reading the final manuscript and offering comments for the book's cover.

Working with Multilingual Matters is a true pleasure. We thank Tommi Grover for believing in the project from the start and for his support throughout the process. We are also grateful to the series editors, Colin Baker and Nancy Hornberger, for their support and to the staff members who worked behind the scenes to bring the book to fruition and market it – Sarah Williams, Elinor Robertson and Hannah Turner at Techset Composition Limited.

We would also like to acknowledge the University of Minnesota's College of Education and Human Development, which granted Diane a sabbatical for 2009–10, allowing her to devote much of her time and energy to this book project.

Finally, we thank Wallace (Wally) Lambert, to whom this volume is dedicated, for envisioning the promise of immersion education, and for his pioneering work in exposing its possibilities.

Diane J. Tedick
Donna Christian
Tara Williams Fortune

Contributors

Carol Bearse is currently Associate Professor of Educational Leadership and Literacy at Touro College. In this capacity she has taught courses both in literacy and English Language Acquisition. With over 25 years of experience in public schools, including urban areas, Carol brings to her research the seasoned leadership of a teacher practitioner in the areas of literacy and English Language Learners (ELLs). She designed the curriculum for the recently US federally funded Language Development in the Context of the Disciplines (LDCD) program, working intensively with New York City high-school teachers in the content areas. Her research interests include dual-language education, literacy for adolescent ELLs and teacher preparation.

Siv Björklund is Professor of Swedish immersion and head of the Centre for Immersion and Multilingualism, which is a subdivision under the Unit of Scandinavian languages at the University of Vaasa, Finland. Her PhD thesis on second-language lexical development among immersion students was published in 1996 and is a pioneer study on Swedish immersion education in Finland. Her main research areas are language acquisition, bi- and multilingualism and language pedagogy. She has a great deal of experience with bi- and multilingual issues and has been involved in both national and international in-service professional development for immersion teachers since 1991.

Maggie Broner is Associate Professor of Spanish and Hispanic Linguistics in the Department of Romance Languages at St Olaf College in Northfield, Minnesota. She has published on Spanish and English language use and language play in full K-6 Spanish immersion settings and on content-based instruction at the college/university level. She is currently studying how foreign/second-language learners process full-length literary and nonliterary texts and the effect of reading for pleasure on student engagement and life-long learning in the undergraduate setting.

Sandra Burger, recently retired from the Institute for Official Language and Bilingualism, University of Ottawa, is now a visiting professor there. She has been involved in content-based language teaching and immersion teaching since the early 1980s. She was pedagogical co-coordinator of the 'Regime d'immersion en français' from 2005 to 2007. Her articles on immersion have been published in *The Canadian Language Review*, *The TESL Canada Journal*, *Cahiers de l'ILOB* and *Contact, Research Symposium*.

Donna Christian is a Senior Fellow at the Center for Applied Linguistics in Washington, DC (www.cal.org). Her work focuses on the role of language in education and society, with special interests in dual-language education, second language learning, dialect diversity and public policy. She has published extensively on those topics, including coauthored or coedited publications such as *Educating English Language Learners: A Synthesis of Research Evidence* (Cambridge University Press), *Bilingual Education* (TESOL), *Dialects, Schools, and Communities* (Routledge/Taylor & Francis) and *Profiles in Two-Way Immersion Education* (CAL/Delta Systems).

Ester de Jong is Associate Professor in ESL (English as a Second Language)/ Bilingual Education at the University of Florida, Gainesville, Florida. A native of the Netherlands, she held the position of Assistant Director for Bilingual Education for the Framingham Public Schools in Massachusetts, working closely with teachers in three different programs: two-way immersion, general bilingual education and ESL. Her work has focused on issues of teacher preparation for linguistic diversity, as well as additive bilingual programs for all children. Another area of interest is language policy and its impact on teachers and teacher practice.

Lisa Dorner is Assistant Professor at the University of Missouri-St Louis. Her research examines immigrant childhoods, second language learning and educational policy, especially the politics of implementing immersion programs. Currently, she is documenting the development of a network of language immersion schools in the Midwest, and studying how the adolescent children of immigrants perceive their opportunities for civic engagement. She has published in the *American Journal of Education, Educational Policy, International Journal of Bilingual Education and Bilingualism, Journal of Adolescent Research* and *Journal of Educational Change*.

Tara Williams Fortune is Immersion Teaching Specialist and Coordinator of the Immersion Projects at the Center for Advanced Research on Language Acquisition at the University of Minnesota. She is founding editor of *The American Council on Immersion Education (ACIE) Newsletter*, a publication written for and by immersion practitioners that is currently in its 14th year of dissemination. Her professional and research interests focus on struggling immersion learners, K-8 oral proficiency development of immersion students and language and literacy development in early total Chinese immersion programs. Recent publications include *Pathways to Multilingualism: Evolving Perspectives on Immersion Education* (Multilingual Matters, 2008) and *Struggling Learners and Language Immersion Education* (2010, University of Minnesota).

Fred Genesee is Professor in the Psychology Department at McGill University in Montreal. He has carried out extensive research on alternative approaches to bilingual education, including second/foreign language immersion for language majority students and alternative forms of bilingual education for language minority students. His current work focuses on simultaneous acquisition of two languages during early infancy and childhood, language development in international adoptees and the language and literacy development of children at risk for reading and language impairment in immersion programs.

Carla Hall has been working at the University of Ottawa since 1994. In addition to teaching English as a Second Language and second language teacher training courses, she is the Test Development Coordinator for the Official Languages and Bilingualism Institute. She also does test development and language testing for the Federal Government of Canada and the British Council.

Tracy Hirata-Edds teaches in the Applied English Center at the University of Kansas. She was a Fulbright Scholar in Nepal where she worked on issues related to second language acquisition, curriculum design and classroom teaching. She works with Native American tribal organizations on language and culture maintenance and revitalization, providing workshops and teacher trainings. She has worked closely with the Cherokee Nation's revitalization efforts for 10 years, and serves as an advisor to their immersion school documenting the children's developing language, assessing their linguistic skills and designing approaches to enrich language learning.

Philip Hoare was until recently an Associate Professor in the Department of English in the Hong Kong Institute of Education. Over a 39-year career he taught English in many parts of the world and spent 23 years in teacher education in Hong Kong, specializing in English immersion and content-based language teaching (CBLT). He also worked with immersion teachers in mainland China and undertook a number of research projects on classroom practice in immersion and CBLT both in China and Hong Kong.

Amelia Kreitzer Hope is Head of Language Testing Services at the University of Ottawa, Ontario. She manages test development and test administration for French and English tests for a widely varied clientele: students, professors, employees, foreign-trained professionals, foreign students and federal civil servants. In addition, she trains pre-service and in-service teachers in methods of language assessment.

Kauanoe Kamanā is the Director of Laboratory School Programs for the State of Hawai'i Hawaiian Language College, Ka Haka 'Ula O Ke'elikōlani, located at the University of Hawai'i at Hilo. She is responsible for the overall development and administration of programs at P-12 Nāwahīokalan'i'ōpu'u School. Her current research focuses on utilizing traditional Hawaiian conflict resolution in maintaining student discipline at the school. She is also president of the statewide 'Aha Pūnana Leo language nests organization, the organization that initiated Hawaiian medium education in Hawai'i.

Kathryn Lindholm-Leary is Professor Emerita of Child and Adolescent Development at San Jose State University, where she has taught for 22 years. At San Jose State, Kathryn received a Teacher-Scholar award, was a finalist for the President's Scholar award, and was a San Jose State nominee for the prestigious Wang Family Excellence award. She has worked with over 50 two-way and developmental bilingual programs over the past 25 years and has written books and journal articles, and given presentations to researchers, educators and parents on the topics of two-way immersion education and child bilingualism.

Karita Mård-Miettinen is Senior Lecturer at the Centre for Multilingualism and Language Immersion at the University of Vaasa in Finland. She has worked with research, development, and teacher preparation and professional development in Swedish immersion in Finland for 20 years. Her research interests include early second language acquisition, teaching strategies and multiple languages in immersion. She has been involved in immersion projects both on the national and international level.

Parvin Movassat is a language professor at the University of Ottawa. She has been teaching French as a second language in Canada since 2000 and she is currently the test development coordinator for the Official

Languages and Bilingualism Institute (OLBI). Her research interests include teaching methodology and pedagogy of immersion courses, pedagogical grammar and language testing and assessment.

Pádraig Ó Duibhir is Lecturer in St Patrick's College, Dublin City University, Ireland where he teaches a range of pre-service and in-service courses for teachers on language teaching methodologies for Irish as a first and second language. Prior to that he worked in the area language in-service education for primary school teachers and was principal of an Irish-immersion school. His research interests include language teaching and language learning, particularly for young learners. He is currently completing an analysis of the oral language of Grade 7 students in Irish-immersion schools in Northern Ireland.

Lizette Peter is Assistant Professor of second language studies in the Department of Curriculum and Teaching at the University of Kansas. Her primary area of research and advocacy for the past decade has been the revitalization of the Cherokee language, with a focus on preschool through upper elementary Cherokee language immersion. With her colleagues, she has worked to identify both the morphological features of children's interlanguage and the pedagogical implications of information generated by assessment instruments. Her current project is an ethnographic investigation of language ideologies and practices of Cherokee Nation tribal members in northeastern Oklahoma.

Gloria Sly works in Education Services of Cherokee Nation (www.cherokee. org) in Tahlequah, Oklahoma. Her work focuses on language revitalization through the development and implementation of programs to serve all segments of Cherokee citizens. The major focus for the past 10 years has been staff development for teachers of Cherokee language immersion.

Merrill Swain is Professor Emerita in the Second Language Education Program at the Ontario Institute for Studies in Education, University of Toronto, where she has taught and conducted research for 40 years. Her present research focuses on the role of collaborative dialogue and 'languaging' in second language learning within a sociocultural framework. She was President of the American Association for Applied Linguistics (AAAL) in 1998–1999, and a Vice President of the International Association of Applied Linguistics from 1999 to 2005. She is a recipient of the 2003 Canadian Robert Roy Award and AAAL's 2004 Distinguished Scholarship and Service Award. She has authored books and many book chapters, as well as over 160 refereed articles.

Diane Tedick is Associate Professor of Second Languages and Cultures Education at the University of Minnesota. For over 20 years she has worked in the preparation of pre-service teachers and ongoing professional development of in-service teachers representing a variety of language teaching contexts: immersion and bilingual programs, world languages and ESL. Her professional and research interests focus on the pedagogy required for successful integration of language and content instruction, student oral language proficiency development in immersion programs and language teacher development. Her edited, coedited and coauthored volumes include _Second Language Teacher Education: International Perspectives_ (Routledge); _Pathways to Multilingualism: Evolving Perspectives on Immersion Education_ (Multilingual Matters); and _Teaching Foreign Languages: Content-Based Instruction for Social Justice_ (forthcoming, Routledge).

Alysse Weinberg is Associate Professor at the Official Languages and Bilingualism Institute at the University of Ottawa. She has been a language teacher of immersion courses since the inception of the 'Regime d'immersion en français' and was pedagogical co-coordinator of the Regime from 2005 to 2010. She has published articles on immersion in the _Cahiers de l'ILOB_ and _Contact Research Symposium_ as well as giving presentations at the Canadian Association of Applied Linguistics, Teaching English as a Second Language (TESL) Ontario, immersion conferences hosted by the Center for Advanced Research on Language Acquisition (CARLA) at the University of Minnesota and The Computer Assisted Language Instruction Consortium.

William H. Wilson is the Academic Programs Division Chair of the State of Hawai'i Hawaiian Language College, Ka Haka 'Ula O Ke'elikōlani, located at the University of Hawai'i at Hilo. His interests include early literacy development in Hawaiian and third-language teaching in immersion. He is also a historical linguist focusing on Polynesian languages. Wilson and Kauanoe Kamanā are married with two children educated through Grade 12 in Hawaiian immersion.

Gary Zehrbach is currently Principal of a dual language (two-way) school in Phoenix, AZ. He was the founding principal of Nuestro Mundo Community School, a two-way Spanish/English charter immersion elementary school in Madison, WI. He has a PhD from the University of Wisconsin-Madison in Educational Leadership and Policy Analysis. His dissertation focused on two-way immersion charter schools.

Foreword

Dedicating this book to Professor Wallace Lambert feels wonderfully right. Wally was one of the most important persons in my graduate student life, and an always-there-when-you-need-him friend during his lifetime. He was a playful and charming scholar who never missed an opportunity to advocate for bilingualism and bilingual education. Honoring Wally as an 'immersion pioneer' pays tribute to a wonderful human being who researched and talked endlessly about the promises and possibilities of immersion education for all children. He did so at a time when the dominant thinking was that the cognitive, social and emotional consequences of bilingualism were negative. Dedicating this book to Wally shows the deep understanding the three editors have of immersion education: of its history, of the way it has diversified to meet local needs and contexts and of its future possibilities.

From those exciting, heady days of envisioning, implementing and researching early French immersion programs back in the 1960s, who would have thought the ideas generated and outcomes produced would have had such far-reaching effects? Goals set then of bilingualism, biliteracy and high academic achievement, which many educators and parents at that time considered impossible to attain, have been reached over and over again across programs and languages and countries.

Perhaps most remarkable of all is that the goals have held steady and immersion has diversified to meet the widely varying populations who wish to attain them. Thus, we now have one-way immersion programs originating with Wally's St Lambert experiment (e.g. English-speaking children learning Chinese); two-way immersion programs (e.g. English-speaking children learning Spanish alongside Spanish-speaking children learning English); and language revival immersion programs (e.g. English-speaking children learning a heritage (Irish) and/or indigenous (Hawaiian) language). In the case of language revival, across one generation, we see examples of non-speakers of the heritage language learn it as a second language, subsequently passing it on to their children who learn it as a first language. And in the case of indigenous languages, we are often seeing the rescue of the language itself, and with it, a distinctive world-view and epistemology. Transformative indeed!

Goals for immersion education have expanded to include biculturalism, and most recently, multilingualism and multiculturalism. Biculturalism and multiculturalism are difficult concepts to operationalize and measure. Efforts have been made to do so using questionnaires and interviews to elicit learners' attitudes toward ethnolinguistic groups other than their own. But just what do we mean by bi- and multiculturalism? Do our expectations relate to students' appreciation and knowledge of other cultures, or do they relate to the affective aspects of cognition – about students' feelings toward members of other cultures and identification with them? A full discussion on what we mean by biculturalism and multiculturalism will invoke competing beliefs and ideologies. Disagreements and disputes are inevitable. But it is a much needed discussion, if for no other reason than to determine whether our expectations are appropriately set. The implications of such a discussion, however, are much broader. They range from making choices about curriculum development and teacher education to relevant research methodology. Quasi-experimental, quantitative research might be appropriate to respond to questions about cultural knowledge whereas qualitative, ethnographic research will more likely help us to understand identity issues.

Multilingual immersion programs, while perhaps not a recent phenomenon, are currently attracting attention as the impact of globalization on education, commerce and national and international economies dramatically increases the need for additional language learning. Multilingual immersion education can take at least two forms. In one form, a relatively homogeneous linguistic population may add an additional target language to the existing one (e.g. the addition of German or English to the curriculum of Finland's Swedish immersion program). In a second form, a relatively heterogeneous, multilingual population is present in the existing immersion program, and through curricular and pedagogical innovation, the acceptance and use of the first languages of all children are promoted. For example, many French immersion programs in Canada now include speakers of other first languages than English. However, to date, those languages remain unacknowledged and the resources they provide to learners remain unused. This need not be the case, as some scholars have argued and demonstrated. Accepting other home languages in immersion programs will allow multilingualism to flourish, adding affective as well as academic value. It also points to new directions in language immersion practices of the 21st century.

A key issue for the long-term development and maintenance of the additional languages learned through immersion is the continuity and coherence of programs across all levels of education, from preschool to university graduation. Articulation of programs is a significant challenge that will involve the cooperation and collaboration of policy makers, school and university administrators, teachers and parents. As we continue to modify and improve programs based on both formative and summative assessments, advice from educators and the first-hand experiences of teachers and parents, we must continuously consult and seek the views of the students themselves. It is for the students that such extraordinary efforts are being made, and it is the students to whom we must turn for advice on what to do, and how to do it better.

This book brings together a stimulating and exciting set of chapters about the practices and policies of a wide variety of immersion programs. In common to them all are their goals and commitment to a pedagogy that integrates language and content learning. The chapters inform us of current immersion practices; they raise issues concerning the impact of policies at government and local school levels; they make suggestions for pedagogical and curricular changes; and they offer ideas for teacher education innovation. In their totality, they, and the editors, ask us to 'dwell in possibility' by being open to new challenges and new possibilities that will strengthen even further the extraordinary impact immersion has had to date.

Merrill Swain
The Ontario Institute for Studies in
Education of the University of Toronto

Chapter 1

The Future of Immersion Education: An Invitation to 'Dwell in Possibility'

D.J. TEDICK, D. CHRISTIAN and T.W. FORTUNE

Introduction

In *Pathways to Multilingualism: Evolving Perspectives on Immersion Education*, Fortune and Tedick (2008) argued that the three immersion program types – one-way (foreign language), two-way (bilingual) and indigenous language immersion – have much in common despite their different contexts. They proposed that there is much to be gained from 'cross-fertilization' of ideas and practices across program types and social contexts. This volume builds on those themes by describing the practices and policies that characterize a variety of immersion programs. In this introductory chapter, we reiterate the definition of immersion, describe the three program types and offer a brief overview of the volume's chapters. We then speak to the continued growth of immersion worldwide, acknowledge that many challenges persist and conclude with a call for immersion scholars and practitioners to imagine and embrace possibilities for strengthening immersion education to increase its impact and better achieve its goals.

Defining immersion

Language immersion education falls within the more encompassing category of bilingual education when referred to from the international perspective. In the United States, we have adopted the term dual language education to describe programs that adhere to the principles of additive bilingualism and biliteracy and cultural pluralism. The three immersion programs identified above comprise three of four dual language program types. The fourth is developmental/maintenance bilingual education, that parallels one-way foreign language immersion in that it targets learners with similar linguistic and cultural backgrounds, in this case language minority learners.

Originating in Canada in 1965 and now found worldwide, one-way (foreign language) immersion programs enroll linguistically homogeneous students who are typically dominant in the majority language and have no or minimal immersion language (IL) proficiency on program entry. One-way programs aim to (1) develop additive bi/multilingualism and bi/multiliteracy, (2) ensure that learners achieve academically and (3) foster the development of intercultural understanding.

Two-way (bilingual) immersion (TWI) programs, initiated in the early 1960s (Ovando, 2003) and predominantly found in the United States, differ from one-way immersion primarily in the student population. They bring together language minority and language majority learners to be instructed in and to learn each others' languages (e.g. Spanish/English or Chinese/English) and work toward immersion goals of additive bi/multilingualism and bi/multiliteracy, academic achievement and cross-cultural understanding.

Indigenous language immersion programs are designed to revitalize endangered indigenous cultures and languages and promote their maintenance and development. They typically enroll children with indigenous heritage, though increasingly attracting some nonheritage learners. These programs are one-way or two-way depending on their student population. Besides reclaiming Native peoples' cultural identity, they strive for academic achievement and additive bi/multilingualism and bi/multiliteracy. Indigenous immersion is becoming increasingly common around the world, notably in Oceania, Scandinavia, North America and South America. Just as indigenous communities have embraced immersion to restore Native identity and reverse language shift (Baker & Jones, 1998; Fishman, 1991), so too have autochthonous minority language communities such as the Basque, Irish and Welsh, to name a few.[1]

At least 50% of subject-matter instruction must be taught through the IL for the program to qualify as immersion, and some immersion programs maintain or surpass 50% of IL instructional time from elementary through the end of secondary school. In the United States, secondary continuation programs offering a minimum of two year-long subject-matter classes in the IL still receive the immersion designation, however (Fortune & Tedick, 2008; Met & Lorenz, 1997). While some postsecondary programs exist (e.g. Burger *et al.*, Chapter 7 and Wilson & Kamanā, Chapter 3), there are as yet no guidelines to specify how much time the IL must be used for subject-matter instruction in order for a program to be considered immersion at this level.

Overview of the volume

This volume showcases the immersion program types described above (Table 1.1). It is divided into four sections, each providing studies, literature reviews or descriptions of at least two of the three program types. The first section, *Practices in Immersion Program Design*, includes descriptions of

Table 1.1 Overview of the volume's chapters

Chapter/ Authors	*Language(s), (Context) and Program Variation*	*Student and Language Characteristics*
One-Way Immersion Programs		
Chapter 2: Björklund and Mård-Miettinen	*Swedish* (Finland) PreK–9, early total	Language-majority students; minority (official) language
Chapter 7: Burger *et al.*	*French* (Canada) Postsecondary continuation	Language-majority (Anglophone) students; minority (or second majority) language
Chapter 8: Ó Duibhir	*Irish* (Republic of Ireland) PreK–12, early total	Language-majority (English) and heritage learners; minority (official) autochthonous language
Chapter 9: Broner and Tedick	*Spanish* (US) K–5, early total	Language-majority (English) learners; international (foreign) language
Chapter 11: Hoare	*English* Hong Kong: Late immersion Xi'an, China: Middle-school continuation (linked to early partial program)*	Language-majority students; international language
Two-Way Immersion Programs		
Chapter 4: Zehrbach	*Spanish/English* (US) K–8 charter programs, varying from 90:10 to 50:50	Language-minority (heritage) students; native language and majority language Language-majority (+heritage) students; minority (international) language

(Continued)

Table 1.1 (*Continued*)

Chapter/ Authors	Language(s), (Context) and Program Variation	Student and Language Characteristics
Chapter 5: Lindholm-Leary	*Chinese/English* (US) K–8, 80:20 and 70:30[†]	Same as above
Chapter 6: de Jong and Bearse	*Spanish/English* (US) Middle/high-school continuation (linked to 50:50 program)[†]	Same as above
Chapter 12: Dorner	*Spanish/English* (US) K–5, 50:50	Same as above
Indigenous Immersion Programs		
Chapter 3: Wilson and Kamanā	Hawaiian (US) PreK–12, early total	Heritage (+ some nonheritage) learners; language/culture revitalization and development of ethnic identity
Chapter 10: Peter *et al.*	Cherokee (US) PreK–4, early total	Heritage learners; language/culture revitalization and development of ethnic identity
Additional Chapters		
Chapter 13: Fortune	Not language- or context-specific	N/A
Chapter 14: Genesee	Concluding chapter	N/A

*As explained by Hoare, the program in Xi'an does not technically qualify as immersion.
[†]As explained by Lindholm-Leary and de Jong and Bearse, the middle and high-school continuation programs do not technically qualify as immersion.

Swedish immersion (Björklund & Mård-Miettinen), Hawaiian immersion (Wilson & Kamanā) and two-way Spanish/English immersion charter programs (Zehrbach). The second, *Immersion Program Outcomes and Implications for Practice*, summarizes research on Chinese/English two-way programs (Lindholm-Leary), a Spanish/English two-way secondary continuation program (de Jong & Bearse) and a French Immersion Studies postsecondary program (Burger *et al.*). The next section showcases studies on student *Language Use*, involving Irish immersion 6th graders (Ó Duibhir) and US Spanish immersion 5th graders (Broner & Tedick), and *Assessment Practices* as a means of impacting Cherokee immersion student language use (Peter *et al.*). The final section emphasizes *Policy and Practice in Immersion Education* with contributions that explore the impact of context on policies and practices in English immersion in Hong Kong and China (Hoare) and two-way Spanish/English immersion in the United States (Dorner). This section also includes a chapter that summarizes research and guides policy and practice related to struggling learners in immersion (Fortune). The volume closes with reflections on the current state and future possibilities for immersion (Genesee).

The Continued Expansion of Immersion Education

From Asia to Europe to North America and beyond, immersion programs are proliferating as more communities embrace the promise they hold for developing a bi/multilingual and bi/multicultural citizenry and for revitalizing and/or maintaining autochthonous and indigenous languages. Björklund and Mård-Miettinen (Chapter 2) indicate that the demand for Swedish immersion exceeds the places available in existing programs. Ó Duibhir (Chapter 8) explains that more 'all Irish' immersion programs are added each year. Hoare (Chapter 11) describes new legislation in Hong Kong that will lead to significant immersion growth. In the United States, the state of Utah has the goal of initiating 100 immersion programs within five years (Gregg Roberts, personal communication, February 9, 2010).

This impressive growth is undoubtedly due in large part to the strong research base that has consistently demonstrated the benefits of immersion education, including the development of functional proficiency in the IL at no expense to learners' first language (L1), and academic achievement and majority language development at levels that equal or surpass those of nonimmersion students (e.g. Genesee, 1987, 2004; Howard *et al.*, 2004). At the same time, many challenges that have plagued immersion programs from their inception persist.

Persistent Immersion Challenges

Just like the benefits, the challenges facing immersion programs have been well documented. Although a thorough discussion of these challenges is beyond the scope of this chapter, we briefly summarize several key issues here.

Achievement of the primary goals of immersion

IL development

Research on one-way immersion has established that language majority students do not acquire native-like levels of IL proficiency in the productive skills (e.g. Genesee, 1987, 2004). Underdeveloped productive skills persist even after students have been schooled in immersion throughout the entire K-12 sequence (Burger *et al.*, Chapter 7). Students' language lacks grammatical accuracy and lexical specificity, is less complex and is sociolinguistically less appropriate when compared with the language of native speakers (e.g. Harley *et al.*, 1990; Mougeon *et al.*, 2010). Students' use of English during IL instructional time increases as they progress through the grade levels in both one-way and two-way programs (e.g. Broner & Tedick, Chapter 9; Fortune, 2001; Potowski, 2007). Students tend to code mix somewhat frequently in upper elementary grades (Broner & Tedick, Chapter 9; Ó Duibhir, Chapter 8), and they struggle to produce extended discourse, often producing only sentence-level utterances even after six years in immersion (Broner & Tedick, Chapter 9; Fortune, 2001).

Recent research on two-way immersion (TWI) has shown that Grade 8 students who were English dominant on program entry performed significantly less well on grammatical and sociolinguistic measures than those who were Spanish dominant (Potowski, 2007). Even native Spanish-speaking students were unable to produce accurate forms all of the time. Howard *et al.* (2004) found that whereas Spanish speakers in TWI developed more balanced levels of bilingualism and biliteracy, English speakers continued to perform better in English than Spanish. Additionally, research has demonstrated that Spanish speakers accommodate to English speakers, become English dominant and often reserve their Spanish for other Spanish speakers (e.g. Fortune, 2001; Potowski, 2007).

Academic achievement

Academic achievement is touted as one of the consistently demonstrated benefits of immersion. Research has also shown that students from a range of socioeconomic and ethnic backgrounds as well as students with some learning disabilities are successful in one-way, two-way and indigenous immersion programs (e.g. Genesee, 2007; Holobow *et al.*, 1991; Lindholm-Leary, 2001, Chapter 5; Wilson & Kamanā, Chapter 3; Zehrbach, Chapter 4). However, studies typically compare immersion student performance to peers matched for linguistic/cultural background and socioeconomic status in nonimmersion programs. Studies showing achievement comparisons among 'at risk', ethnically diverse students and middle-class white students in the same program are rare. Do immersion programs hold promise for decreasing the achievement gap that persists in US schools between students of color and white students? Are immersion programs able to demonstrate success for children with autism, or other language and learning disorders?

Cultural understanding

Relatively little attention is given to the goal of intercultural understanding in one-way immersion programs (e.g. Met & Lorenz, 1997). In TWI, the goal of cross-cultural understanding or biculturalism appears to be achieved for native speakers of the minority language but not for language majority students (de Jong & Bearse, Chapter 6). In addition, although a goal of TWI is to *integrate* learners, some studies have shown that students more often choose to interact with members of their own cultural group, typically not with learners representing other cultural groups (de Jong & Howard, 2009).

Teacher development

It has been argued that less-than-optimal levels of student IL proficiency persist in part because immersion teachers lack systematic approaches for integrating language in their content instruction (e.g. Hoare, Chapter 11; Lyster, 2007; Ó Duibhir, Chapter 8; Swain, 1988). The weaker proficiency levels among learners make it difficult for teachers to promote content understanding and language production as academic demands (with accompanying linguistic demands) increase in upper elementary grades and beyond (e.g. Fortune *et al.*, 2008). A recent study revealed that immersion teachers may not understand the interdependence between academic learning and language learning and if they do, they have difficulty identifying language that should be taught and knowing how to teach language effectively as they teach content (Cammarata & Tedick, in press).

Current immersion teacher preparation is in many ways inadequate (Fortune *et al.*, 2008; Hoare, Chapter 11), as teachers are generally required to obtain 'generic' elementary- or secondary-level licenses and are not exposed to immersion-specific knowledge and teaching skills. Teachers are also not prepared to address the needs of the increasing number of struggling learners enrolled in immersion (Fortune, Chapter 13). The need for strong teacher preparation and development has long been recognized in the field and continues to expand (Broner & Tedick, Chapter 9; Hoare, Chapter 11, Lindholm-Leary, Chapter 5; Ó Duibhir, Chapter 8).

Program design and implementation

As immersion programs proliferate worldwide, we continue to find programs adopting the immersion label without adhering to critical design and implementation features. In China, for example, the so-called English 'immersion' programs are on the rise, though they often lack certain core features (Hoare, Chapter 11). In the United States, California, Arizona and other states apply the label 'structured English immersion' to programs for language minority students that do not support their native language (Rolstad *et al.*, 2005). This lack of fidelity to immersion principles risks compromising the robust research base that has developed over decades.

Another challenge is the scarcity of teachers with sufficient language proficiency to be effective. Although lack of proficient teachers is not likely as great a challenge in countries where the IL has official status [e.g. Canada, Finland (Björklund & Mård-Miettinen, Chapter 2), Ireland (Ó Duibhir, Chapter 8), etc.], it is a significant problem for indigenous immersion (where teachers are often nonnative speakers of the IL) and for programs in the United States where monolingualism remains pervasive. As a consequence, a major challenge facing US immersion program administrators is teacher recruitment and retention. Compromises on teacher language proficiency (or conversely on pedagogical skills when hiring occurs because of language proficiency) can undermine program goals. Similarly, developmentally appropriate materials and resources in the IL may not be as hard to find in countries with two or more official languages, but this is a significant challenge for indigenous immersion programs and US immersion programs.

Finally, myriad policy issues impact immersion programs (Dorner, Chapter 12; Hoare, Chapter 11). Among them is consistent inattention to systematic assessment of IL proficiency. Peter *et al.* (Chapter 10) describe the power of IL assessment in an immersion program. Also, articulation between elementary-level programs and offerings at secondary (and post-secondary) levels remains a thorny issue (de Jong & Bearse, Chapter 6; Burger *et al.*, Chapter 7).

This brief and incomplete review of challenges leads us to conclude that much work remains to be done in immersion education. It is time for us to bring to fruition the 'cross-fertilization' called for in 2008 and to welcome the limitless possibilities for continued advancement of the language immersion model.

Conclusion: An Invitation to 'Dwell in Possibility'[2]

A dictionary definition of 'possible' is: 'being within the limits of ability, capacity or realization' (www.merriam-webster.com). It is this notion, imagining the *possible*, that must lead immersion scholars and practitioners into the future. Consider the following examples: How might indigenous immersion program practices serve as models for strengthening program design and development in other program contexts? What can one-way and two-way programs in the United States (that overwhelmingly decrease IL instruction to 50% by upper elementary grades and even less at the secondary level) learn from programs that maintain maximum percentages of IL instruction through Grade 12 and beyond? How might programs emulate the practices of others that integrate multiple languages? How can all forms of immersion promote positive language policies and increased funding opportunities? The volume's contributors explore possibilities for improving practices, policies and outcomes in their own contexts, and some suggest ways in which their practices might apply to other programs.

'An open … mind allows us to be receptive to new possibilities and prevents us from getting stuck in the rut of our own expertise, which often thinks it knows more than it does' (Kabat-Zinn, 2005: 35). With this in mind, we invite readers to 'dwell in possibility' as you read these pages and allow this frame of yet-to-be-realized potential to inspire new practices and policies as together we strive for an ever stronger future for immersion education.

Notes

1. Autochthonous means native or original to a country. European autochthonous minority groups are not typically considered 'indigenous' because their cultural and socioeconomic features are similar to those of the country's language majority speakers (cf., Wilson & Kamanā, Chapter 3).
2. From Emily Dickinson's (1830–1886) famous poem: 'I dwell in Possibility' (Johnson, 1955: No. 657).

References

Baker, C. and Jones, S.P. (1998) *Encyclopedia of Bilingualism and Bilingual Education*. Clevedon: Multilingual Matters.

Cammarata, L. and Tedick, D.J. (in press) Balancing content and language in instruction: The experience of immersion teachers. *Modern Language Journal*.

De Jong, E. and Howard, E. (2009) Integration in two-way immersion education: Equalising linguistic benefits for all students. *International Journal of Bilingual Education and Bilingualism* 12, 81–99.

Fishman, J.A. (1991) *Reversing Language Shift*. Clevedon: Multilingual Matters.

Fortune, T. (2001) Understanding students? Oral language use as a mediator of social interaction. PhD thesis, University of Minnesota, Minneapolis.

Fortune, T.W. and Tedick, D.J. (2008) One-way, two-way and indigenous immersion: A call for cross-fertilization. In T.W. Fortune and D.J. Tedick (eds) *Pathways to Multilingualism: Evolving Perspectives on Immersion Education* (pp. 3–21). Clevedon: Multilingual Matters.

Fortune, T.W., Tedick, D.J. and Walker, C. (2008) Integrated content and language teaching: Insights from the immersion classroom. In T.W. Fortune and D.J. Tedick (eds) *Pathways to Multilingualism: Evolving Perspectives on Immersion Education* (pp. 71–96). Clevedon: Multilingual Matters.

Genesee, F. (1987) *Learning through Two Languages: Studies of Immersion and Bilingual Education*. Cambridge, MA: Newbury House.

Genesee, F. (2004) What do we know about bilingual education for majority language students? In T.K. Bhatia and W. Ritchie (eds) *Handbook of Bilingualism and Multiculturalism* (pp. 547–576). Malden, MA: Blackwell.

Genesee, F. (2007) French immersion and at-risk students: A review of research evidence. *The Canadian Modern Language Review* 63, 655–688.

Harley, B., Cummins, J., Swain, M. and Allen, P. (1990) The nature of language proficiency. In B. Harley, P. Allen, J. Cummins and M. Swain (eds) *The Development of Second Language Proficiency* (pp. 7–25). Cambridge: Cambridge University Press.

Holobow, N.E., Genesee, F. and Lambert, W.E. (1991) The effectiveness of a foreign language immersion program for children from different ethnic and social class backgrounds: Report 2. *Applied Psycholinguistics* 12, 179–198.

Howard, E., Christian, D. and Genesee, F. (2004) *The Development of Bilingualism and Biliteracy from Grade 3 to 5: A Summary of Findings from the CAL/CREDE Study of Two-Way Immersion Education*. Santa Cruz, CA: Center for Research on Education, Diversity & Excellence.

Johnson, T.H. (ed.) (1955) *Complete Poems of Emily Dickinson*. Boston: Little, Brown & Co.

Kabat-Zinn, J. (2005) *Full Catastrophe Living*. New York: Random House.

Lindholm-Leary, K.J. (2001) *Dual Language Education*. Clevedon: Multilingual Matters.

Lyster, R. (2007) *Learning and Teaching Languages through Content: A Counterbalanced Approach*. Philadelphia, PA: John Benjamins.

Met, M. and Lorenz, E.B. (1997) Lessons from U.S. immersion programs: Two decades of experience. In R.K. Johnson and M. Swain (eds) *The Development of Second Language Proficiency* (pp. 243–264). Cambridge: Cambridge University Press.

Mougeon, R., Nadasdi, T. and Rehner, K. (2010) *The Sociolinguistic Competence of Immersion Students*. Bristol: Multilingual Matters.

Ovando, C.J. (2003) Bilingual education in the United States: Historical development and current issues. *Bilingual Research Journal* 27, 1–24.

Potowski, K. (2007) *Language and Identity in a Dual Language School*. Clevedon: Multilingual Matters.

Rolstad, K., Mahoney, K. and Glass, G.V. (2005) Weighing the evidence: A meta-analysis of bilingual education in Arizona. *Bilingual Research Journal* 29, 43–67.

Swain, M. (1988) Manipulating and complementing content teaching to maximize second language learning. *TESOL Canada Journal* 6, 68–83.

Part 1

Practices in Immersion Program Design

Chapter 2

Integrating Multiple Languages in Immersion: Swedish Immersion in Finland

S. BJÖRKLUND and K. MÅRD-MIETTINEN

Finland: Language Situation and Education System

The language situation in Finland

Finland is officially a bilingual nation in Northern Europe. Finnish and Swedish are Finland's national languages as declared in the Constitution (1917/2000). This official bilingualism can be explained by Finland's history. During five centuries until 1809, Finland formed the eastern part of the Swedish Empire, and during this lengthy period Swedish language and culture were deeply rooted. When Finland became a Grand Duchy of Russia in 1809, the autonomy granted by the Russian Czar included retaining Swedish as the Grand Duchy's official language until the Language Decree of 1863 initiated the process of elevating the status of Finnish to an official language (Latomaa & Nuolijärvi, 2005).

Today the position of Swedish as one of two official languages in Finland is truly unique. Only 5.5% of inhabitants register themselves as Swedish-speaking Finns (for details, see Liebkind *et al.*, 2007), but the constitutional status of national languages gives Finnish and Swedish equal status throughout the nation. On the whole, the statistical data clearly show that in comparison with many other European nations Finland can linguistically be described as homogeneous. In 2008, Finland counted about 5.3 million inhabitants (Statistics Finland, 2009), of whom 91.7% had Finnish registered as their mother tongue, 5.5% Swedish, 0.03% the Saami languages and 2.7% other languages. However, official statistical data are based on registration of mother tongue and do not allow bilingual individuals to register several languages as their mother tongue. Thus, varying degrees of both individual and local/regional bilingualism exist within the nation, but they are not officially registered.

Today most Finland-Swedes are concentrated in Finland's western and southern coastal areas (Figure 2.1). Although the number of Finland-Swedes has remained almost the same for a century (approximately 289,000 speakers), their share of the population is decreasing. Their living conditions have changed considerably too. Some hundred years ago, most Finnish and Swedish speakers lived in predominantly monolingual areas, but by 1970 almost half of the Finland-Swedes lived in municipalities with Finnish dominance. This societal change has led to a clear minority situation for Finland-Swedes, who today are mostly highly bilingual. The number of mixed marriages (Finnish–Swedish) has increased radically, and each year almost 50% of all marriages among Finland-Swedes are linguistically mixed. Families in these mixed marriages can be described as potentially bilingual. Since the late 1970s, this potential has been realized, as an increasing proportion of the children in these families are registered as Swedish speakers (Tandefelt & Finnäs, 2007).

Figure 2.1 Map of Finland with neighbouring countries. The bilingual coastal areas appear in white
Source: Copyright Gnu Free Documentation Licensed map[1]

When bilingualism does not occur naturally within the family, expectations are directed towards the national school system. As schools in Finland are separated according to language of instruction (Finnish or Swedish speaking), the proficiency of the other national language by monolingual children does not equal the level obtained by simultaneous bilingual children. This fact, combined with an increasing awareness among parents that communicative competence in several languages is crucial for their children's careers, led to an increase in bilingual education programmes during the late 1980s and early 1990s. One of the pioneer bilingual education programmes is Swedish immersion, the focus of this chapter.

Education System in Finland

Compulsory education consists of nine years of basic education for children between the ages seven and 16. The municipalities are obliged to provide early childhood education and care (ECEC) for all children under school age. Compulsory education is followed by general and vocational upper-secondary education (2–4 years), and after that higher education in universities or polytechnics (Finnish National Board of Education – FNBE, 2009; Ministry of Social Affairs and Health, 2004).

Voluntary ECEC consists of day care for children under the age of seven and preschool for six-year-olds. About two-thirds of Finnish children under school age attend day care (63% in 2008, SVT Sosiaaliturva, 2009), and virtually all six-year-olds participate in preschool (99.2% in 2007; FNBE, 2009). The ECEC curriculum is guided by the National Curriculum Guidelines on ECEC and the Core Curriculum for Pre-School Education. Basic education curriculum is guided by the National Core Curriculum for Basic Education (FNBE, 2009). ECEC and basic school education are divided into Finnish-speaking and Swedish-speaking sections and target monolingual Finnish- and Swedish-speaking children. The aims of educational policy and the curriculum are similar for both Finnish-speaking and Swedish-speaking sections, the language of instruction being the only difference.

Teaching groups in basic education are formed according to year classes, that is grade levels. The first six years are offered in primary schools, and instruction is usually given by a classroom teacher, who teaches all or most subjects. The three highest grade levels are offered in secondary schools, and instruction is usually organized as subject teaching, where different subjects are taught by different teachers. Basic education also includes student counseling and special education as needed.

The school week consists of 19–30 one hour lessons (including a 10–15 minute break), depending on the school level and the number of optional

Table 2.1 Allocation of subjects in basic education by grade level according to number of weekly lessons per year

Subject/Grade level	1	2	3	4	5	6	7	8	9	Total
Mother tongue and literature	14		14				14			42
A-language			8				8			16
B-language							6			6
Mathematics	6		12				14			42
Environmental studies	9				5		17			31
Religion or ethics	6						5			11
History and social studies					3		7			10
Arts, crafts and physical education	26						30			56
Home economics							3			3
Educational and vocational guidance							2			2
Optional subjects							13			13
Voluntary A-language	6						6			12
Minimum number of weekly lessons	19	19	23	23	24	24	30	30	30	

Source: Finnish National Board of Education, 2010

subjects taken. A school day has at maximum five (lower primary grades) or seven (higher primary and all secondary grades) lessons. The weekly minimum number of teaching hours is set at 19–23 (primary school) or 30 (secondary school). The Government determines the overall time allocation by defining the minimum number of lessons for core subjects. As Table 2.1 shows, in Grades 1–6, pupils usually receive the same education, but schools may focus on different subjects in different ways due to the flexible time allocation (FNBE, 2009).

Swedish Immersion in Finland

Immersion: A part of European bilingual education

Bilingual education is described as a 'simple label for a complex phenomenon' (Baker & Jones, 1998: 464). One current example of this complexity is the rapid growth of different bilingual approaches both within and between European countries. This trend can be traced back to the mid-1980s when research on successful immersion programmes in Europe (such as those for Welsh and Catalan) was published. In a way, immersion programmes renewed hitherto existing bilingual programmes in Europe, since they showed that young language majority speakers developed functional mastery of a new language at no cost to first-language development. This new way of learning a language among students, who did not have the benefit of being raised bilingually, awakened the interest of other language majority monolinguals, such as parents and educational authorities. Consequently, European immersion programmes are today accompanied by many other approaches, such as content-and-language-integrated-learning (CLIL). The concurrent use of the labels 'language immersion' and 'CLIL' alongside other similar terms complicates the understanding of the current language teaching situation in European schools, and it is difficult even for specialists in the field to keep well informed. Even though there are similarities between European immersion and CLIL, immersion has rationales that diverge from many other CLIL-type provisions and that are essential for programme design and outcomes. Using immersion education in Finland as a case in point, these rationales are discussed in the next section.

The distribution of immersion education in Finland

Immersion was first introduced in the city of Vaasa/Vasa with 25 children in one preschool.[2] A national survey conducted in schools in 1999 revealed that immersion education spread fairly slowly during the first five years, but experienced explosive growth in the mid-1990s, as shown in Figure 2.2 (Buss & Mård, 2001).

In 1999, about 1900 children were enrolled in Swedish immersion, and the number of preschool children was estimated at 600. Immersion education has grown steadily during the 2000s, and the number of immersion students from preschool to secondary school is today (2009) estimated at 4500.[3] The number of immersion students will no doubt continue to grow in the future, since the demand for immersion education in many municipalities is greater than the number of places available in existing programmes. This pattern appears to be repeating itself worldwide, as briefly described in Tedick, Christian and Fortune (Chapter 1). Geographically, immersion programmes are concentrated along Finland's bilingual coastal area (see Figure 2.1).

On the national level Swedish immersion is a small educational option comprising about 0.5% of the school population in Finland. It is, however,

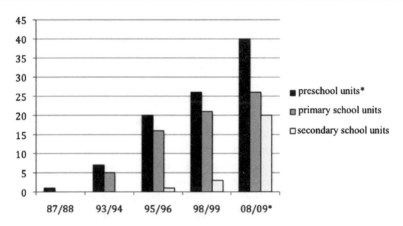

Figure 2.2 The number of preschool, primary-school and secondary-school units offering Swedish immersion in 1987–2009
*Estimated number of preschool units 1993–2009 and primary and secondary school units 2008–2009 based on the number of units sending participants for in-service professional development at the Immersion Centre, University of Vaasa. Primary and secondary school numbers for 1987–1999 are based on a national survey (Buss & Mård, 2001)

recognized nationally and mentioned in the national core curriculum as a programme option with specific language goals (National Core Curriculum, 2004). In some municipalities immersion students form 10–50% of the school population.

Programme design: An early introduction of several languages

The pioneer immersion programme in Finland was an early total Swedish immersion programme established in Vaasa/Vasa in 1987. This programme has served as a prototype for all immersion programmes in Finland. During the 1990s, an early partial Swedish immersion programme was offered in the capital city area, but it has since evolved into an early total programme, and thus today all immersion programmes in Finland are early total programmes.

The Swedish immersion programmes comprise three articulated school levels: preschool (ages 3–6), primary school (Grades 1–6) and secondary school (Grades 7–9). Children enrol in Swedish immersion typically at the age of 5, two years before compulsory education. Some preschools offer immersion for children 3–4 years of age. At the time of enrolment the children have no knowledge of Swedish. During preschool all instruction is given only in Swedish by native or near-native teachers.

Immersion students receive 80% of instruction in Swedish in Grades 1 and 2. Systematic teaching of reading and writing is provided initially in Swedish, the students' second language (L2). A feature that distinguishes Swedish immersion from most of the early total immersion programmes described in Swain and Johnson (1997) and Fortune and Tedick (2008) is that instruction in the students' first language (L1), Finnish, begins in Grade 1. This is similar to Irish immersion programmes (Ó Duibhir, Chapter 8) which introduce English (students' L1) early on, and contrary to some Hawaiian immersion programmes where L1 instruction is withheld until Grade 5 (Wilson & Kamanā, Chapter 3). Since the strategy of one person–one language is implemented, instruction in Finnish and Swedish is given by different teachers. The 1–2 weekly lessons in Finnish in Grade 1 focus on oral and receptive language competence, cultural aspects and general language awareness. Activities requiring more systematic reading and writing in Finnish are introduced gradually in the later stages of Grade 1 or in Grade 2. Finnish instruction already in Grade 1 was originally due to the requirements of national education authorities, who expressed concern about the development of mother-tongue skills. An early introduction of Finnish has since proved to be advantageous to the development of early biliteracy. One indicator of this are results on a national standardized reading test for primary schools in Finnish, which the city of Vaasa/Vasa administers to all students in Grade 3. The test measures three domains of reading: language awareness, technical reading skills and comprehension (Lindeman, 1998). The immersion students' results for the last seven years (2003–2009) are shown in Figure 2.3.

Figure 2.3 indicates that as early as Grade 3 immersion students do as well as, or better than the national norm, even though they are tested in their L1, Finnish. These results differ from those for early total programmes in Canada and the United States, where typically an initial 'lag' in English (L1) literacy development occurs until English is formally introduced. Genesee summarized results for Canadian French immersion:

> A lag in English literacy followed by parity within one year of having English language arts instruction characterizes the performance of students in all varieties of early total immersion, regardless of whether English language instruction begins in grade 2, grade 3, or even grade 4. (Genesee, 1987: 37)

It should be noted, however, that some early total programmes report similar findings to those presented here even though the students' L1 is not introduced formally in the curriculum until later. For example, Essama (2007) reports on a French immersion programme in the United States in

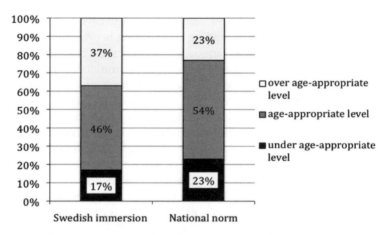

Figure 2.3 Results on a national reading test in Finnish, 2003–2009 (Lindeman, 1998)

which formal instruction in English is withheld until the second semester of Grade 4. Even by Grade 3, 62% of the students perform at or above grade-level norms in English reading based on standardized tests. Indeed, the results of Swedish immersion reported in this chapter are even more impressive, with fully 83% of Grade 3 immersion students performing at or above grade-level norms in L1 reading. Yet, it is unclear if these results can be linked exclusively to the early introduction of Finnish; other factors may be influencing these results.

In addition, early introduction of L1 literacy helps to identify whether possible problems in literacy development are learning problems, or problems related to L2 acquisition. The possible problems may also be addressed in both languages depending on their source and thereby be used as diagnostic tools by special education teachers (Eklund, 2007). Bergström (2002) discusses in depth issues related to language acquisition versus learning problems among immersion students as does Fortune (Chapter 13).

A major characteristic of Swedish immersion in Finland is its multilingual orientation, where four different languages are introduced within the programme. Thus, Swedish immersion belongs to programmes that orient towards multilingualism rather than bilingualism [e.g. Basque immersion in Spain (Cenoz, 1998), double immersion in Canada (Genesee, 1998), Hawaiian immersion at Nāwahī school (Wilson & Kamanā, Chapter 3), and some charter two-way programmes in the United States (Zehrbach, Chapter 4).

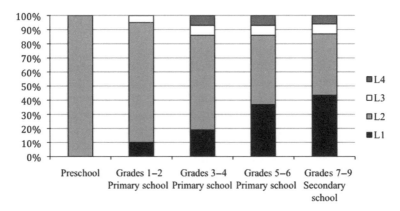

Figure 2.4 Allocation of instructional time according to language of instruction

In immersion programmes in Finland, the main immersion language, Swedish (L2), is introduced in preschool (Figure 2.4). Finnish (L1), and a third language (L3), most often English, are integrated in the programmes in Grades 1 or 2, and an optional fourth language (L4), for example German, in Grades 4 or 5. L3 and L4 are taught as foreign languages, explained further below.

This multilingual orientation is a natural feature stemming from Europe's long history of teaching several languages within one educational programme. It was taken for granted that immersion students would also have the opportunity to learn at least a L3, since studying three languages (mother tongue + Finland's other official language + a 'big' European language) during compulsory education constitutes the minimum criterion within the national language curriculum (Table 2.1).

Evaluating our multilingual orientation

When Swedish immersion was launched the primary interest in the community was focused on the relationship between Finnish and Swedish, and the impact of extensive instructional time in L2 on the development of students' L1 (cf. Björklund, 1997). The addition of other languages in immersion was never questioned, even though the introduction of Finland's first immersion programme was vividly debated nationwide.

In the late 1980s, during the early years of Swedish immersion, L3 and L4 were taught predominantly following a traditional foreign language syllabus. Many teachers of L3 and L4 used both the target language and students' L1 for instruction, and a textbook with supplementary material was used as the primary teaching source. The change to a more communicative approach in L3 and L4 teaching in the city of Vaasa/Vasa started when teachers noticed that immersion students seemed to be confused and even resistant to learning when teachers concurrently used two languages. In addition, teachers noted that immersion students wished to use more authentic and self-sourced material rather than textbooks (Björklund & Suni, 2000). These pioneer immersion student reactions encouraged L3 and L4 teachers to adapt their teaching strategies to a new kind of student population that did not seem to worry if they did not understand every single word in the target language and which was ready and willing to use that language in authentic communication even if their language proficiency was limited. The new strategies of the teachers were readily supported by immersion researchers at the University of Vaasa, who since the start had envisioned a multilingual orientation.

Once it was decided that teachers of additional languages in immersion were very much an integral part of the programme, the actual multilingual development within Swedish immersion began. In order to promote more authenticity and a more communicative approach, it was decided that L3/L4 teachers would implement the one-person–one-language strategy. Furthermore, immersion researchers at the University of Vaasa suggested that it would be beneficial to introduce an L3 when the students had not yet developed literacy skills and therefore could not be expected to use written material as their primary learning source. Accordingly, the introduction of L3 was lowered from Grade 5 to Grade 3 and from 1993 onward to Grades 1 or 2. The movement from Grade 5 to Grade 1 was gradual, as it had to be recognized and accepted by all partners involved. Subsequently, the introduction of L4 was moved from Grade 8 to Grade 4. Today in some secondary schools it is possible for immersion students to study an optional L5 in Grades 8 and 9.

Even though the time allotted to additional languages in Swedish immersion continues to be just a couple hours per week, the changes within these lessons strengthen the underlying features of immersion and enforce the programme's consistency. Because most content teaching is organized thematically and unit themes are collectively decided on by both Swedish teachers and Finnish teachers, it is easy for teachers of additional languages to follow the same themes and focus on the same content while teaching L3/L4. In this way, they further add a clearly content-based approach.

In the multilingual evolution of Swedish immersion, parents have also played a significant role. Since the start of immersion in Finland, they have commented on their children's willingness to use the target language when it is introduced at an early age and the teaching emphasizes authentic and communicative needs. In evaluation instruments directed at immersion parents about their reasons for choosing immersion, one of the main reasons emerging repeatedly is the programme's multilingual dimension. Common arguments put forth by parents are based on language similarities. The students' L1, Finnish, is a Fenno-Ugric language, whereas the immersion language, Swedish, is a Germanic language, as are English and German. The parents also understand that once children have learnt a new language it is easy for them to acquire additional languages.

Immersion with multiple languages: Responding to European calls for multilingualism

The multilingual orientation in Swedish immersion is today well in tune with the Framework Strategy for Multilingualism developed by the European Commission in 2005. The overall emphasis in the strategy is widespread individual multilingualism among European Union (EU) citizens. The strategy outlines key areas of action in education systems and practices, including early language learning. The long-term objective is that all citizens study at least two languages other than the mother tongue from a very early age. This goal is, of course, surpassed in Swedish immersion which introduces three languages in addition to L1 before the age of 10.

Among the key areas of the strategy is also an appeal for national strategies for the teaching of regional and minority languages, indicating the importance of gradually expanding language experience for all EU students. In Swedish immersion language experience starts at home with Finnish (L1); it expands in preschool with the other national language, Swedish, and in basic education with other languages. This language path gives the immersion students early experiences in using their languages in everyday communication inside school as well as the linguistic confidence to participate in Swedish and bilingual activities outside school.

A third key area in the strategy that is closely linked to Swedish immersion is the integration of language and content teaching. In immersion the integration is twofold: school subjects are taught in two languages and additional languages are taught through a content-based approach.

Results of a Swedish Immersion Programme with Multiple Languages

The change to a more multilingual orientation within Swedish immersion has been gradual, and we think that it has not yet reached its full potential, even though awareness of a multilingual approach among different immersion stakeholders has increased. Because immersion is optional in Finland, it is important to inform stakeholders that Swedish immersion in fact includes multiple languages, which adds value to the programmes. Therefore, it is of utmost importance to evaluate scientifically development in all programme languages and to identify crucial factors for successful programme design. This is an ongoing process in Swedish immersion. In the following section we briefly describe results of language assessments within the programmes. Some of the results are from projects conducted since the mid-1990s under our supervision by university students of English and German as well as immersion teacher trainees for their Masters' theses.

L3 and L4 outcomes: Process and product

The initial stages of L3 learning among immersion students have been documented by two experienced English teachers (Björklund *et al.*, 2000). The immersion groups in this study were situated in a dual-track school, where nonimmersion students with L1 (Finnish) were introduced to L2 (English) at the same time (Grade 1) as immersion students were introduced to English as L3. Since the two teachers taught English in both tracks, they decided to use the same communicative approach and the same content with all groups. In particular, the teachers observed if the communicative approach (exclusive use of English and rich use of authentic material) was more advantageous for immersion students, who already had experienced learning Swedish in the same way, or for nonimmersion students, who started foreign language learning with English.

Although the two groups were not strikingly different, the tendency was that immersion students were relatively more confident in learning English. Although nonimmersion students had not had previous experience learning a new language in school, their expectations about their own learning abilities were lower than immersion students' despite the fact that positive attitudes towards learning English were likely because English is by far the most common foreign language chosen by Finns. In addition, immersion students made full use of the learning approach and paid more attention to teachers' nonverbal strategies to enhance their comprehension. They were more willing to advance even if they did not understand everything the teacher said, whereas the nonimmersion students tended to expect word-for-word translations and were not willing to go on if they did not completely understand the teacher.

Observations during oral activities showed that immersion students were very determined to stick to their communicative intentions and used all the means they had (simplifications, other languages, etc.) to communicate their message in English. Nonimmersion students tended either to give up their original communicative intentions or to clearly show that they preferred to listen to the teacher. In sum, the immersion experience seems to give students confidence even when their proficiency is limited. As the study included only initial stages of L3 teaching, this pattern may not be notable in the long run.

There have been additional studies involving immersion and nonimmersion groups, where English is taught as L3 (immersion) and L2 (nonimmersion) to same-age students, beginning in the same grade, with the same instructional time and a similar teaching approach. Results of a study in Grade 5 ($n = 68$) showed that immersion students wrote longer essays than nonimmersion students (Björklund, 2001, 2005). The shortest essays of immersion students contained about 50 words, while one-third of the nonimmersion students wrote stories with only 15–48 words. In contrast, results of an orthographic analysis showed that immersion students spelled words incorrectly more frequently than nonimmersion students. This finding further underwent a content analysis, which showed that more than 12% of the nonimmersion students' texts (approximately 7% in immersion students' texts) consisted of proper nouns (Finnish names), which of course were not problematic to spell correctly. In addition, the content analysis showed that immersion students' texts were lexically more varied and contained, for instance, more low-frequency verbs. Thus, the results support a multilingual orientation, but the reasons behind these achievements are multifaceted. Are immersion students really more advanced learners of English than same-age nonimmersion students? Instead, are they perhaps more willing to take risks than nonimmersion students in both speaking and writing? Is it predominantly the immersion teaching approach that leads to these results, or is it mainly students' previous experience of learning Swedish, which is very similar to English?

A Masters' project on oral production of English in Grade 5 showed that nonimmersion students' ($n = 22$) speech flow was more fragmented than that of the immersion students ($n = 18$) (Lainas & Nurmi, 2002). In this oral production test, students were asked to look at a comic strip for a few minutes and then describe in their own words what was happening. The nonimmersion students produced more clause fragments partially because the researchers had to ask more questions to get them to sustain communication in English throughout the task. In addition, the immersion students used relatively more grammatical items to show relationships between lexical items, as the examples below illustrate.

Example 1. Indians sit. Indians go forest. (Nonimmersion, girl)

Example 2. Those is riding and/they can/they can't go over the river. And one of them go over the river and he jumping on the stone. Then he fall and everyone safe him. (Immersion, boy)

Example 1 scores the highest lexical density (1.00), whereas the lexical density of Example 2 is 0.27, indicating that the immersion student's utterance was more easily understood. For lexical density there was a statistically significant difference between immersion and nonimmersion students, with the average lexical density considerably lower among immersion students.

The productivity of immersion students and their eagerness to communicate are also documented in studies on how immersion students' language repertoire influences their language production. In a comparative study of 125 immersion and nonimmersion students in Grades 6, 7 and 8, the immersion students more readily used their knowledge of Finnish, Swedish and English in learning German (optional L4 for immersion; L3 for nonimmersion) than nonimmersion students (Havunen, 2001). Sometimes the use of all four languages even functioned as a communication strategy among immersion students. The strategy worked well in the classroom since both teachers and fellow students were acquainted with all four languages, but it would not, of course, work as well with nonimmersion counterparts. Lexical transfer from Swedish to German was most beneficial for the Swedish-speaking, nonimmersion comparison group, while lexical transfer from Swedish to German was not as evident as expected in the German lexicon of immersion students. Instead, the German lexicon of both groups was mainly influenced by Finnish (students' L1).

Another study on the relationship between the immersion students' languages shows somewhat contradictory results, as neither Finnish nor Swedish elements were used as much as expected in the writing of English in a Grade 4 immersion group (17 students, 47 essays) (Heinonen, 1996). However, this study does not compare immersion with nonimmersion, as it is longitudinal. As expected, the influence of other languages decreases over time. Interestingly, elements originating from Swedish dominate clearly over Finnish elements in the English production of the immersion students even though Finnish is the students' L1. Despite the small scale of these studies, they clearly show that more research of this type is needed to fully understand the relationship among different languages, language mastery and language teaching.

The inclusion of additional languages in immersion is further supported by studies on immersion students who participate in the national matriculation examination that Finnish students take at the end of their upper secondary education (beyond Grade 9). Because immersion in Finland ends at Grade 9 (the end of compulsory education), the matriculation examination is taken 2–4 years after finishing immersion. The examination consists, at minimum, of four tests that can be taken in any order between the second and fourth year of upper secondary school. The maximum number of tests is not restricted. The mother-tongue test is compulsory as well as three of the following: the test in the second national language (Finnish or Swedish), a foreign language test, the mathematics test and one general studies test (science and humanities) (Finnish Matriculation Examination, 2009).

Bergroth at the University of Vaasa has collected data on former immersion students' results on the matriculation examination in the city of Vaasa/Vasa (cf. Bergroth, 2006, 2007). By spring 2007, 75% (137) of the former immersion students in the city of Vaasa/Vasa had taken at least one test. The mother tongue (Finnish) test was taken by 102 former immersion students. The mother tongue test is a Finnish-as-a-first-language test based on the mainstream mother tongue curriculum. It consists of a textual skills section that measures analytical skills and linguistic expression, and an essay that measures general level of education, development of thinking, linguistic expression and coherence. The results clearly show that immersion has given the students a good basis for the mother tongue skills measured. None of the former immersion students failed the test, and 75% of the students earned a grade in the middle of the scale (C) or above (Grades M, E and L).[4] The former immersion students' distribution of middle and higher grades is about 10 percentage units higher than the standardized scale of normal distribution that the matriculation examination board uses (Figure 2.5).

By the year 2007, a total of 97 former immersion students had taken the test on the second official language (Swedish). The Swedish test is based on the mainstream Swedish language arts curriculum and consists of reading and listening comprehension and the production of written text (e.g. glossary on words and structures and a short essay), which is graded on its grammatical, semantic and stylistic accuracy. The test has two levels of difficulty: advanced and intermediate. All but a couple of former immersion students chose the advanced level. The former immersion students did very well. Most of the students (75%) scored the three highest Grades (L, E and M), representing 35 percentage units higher than the normal

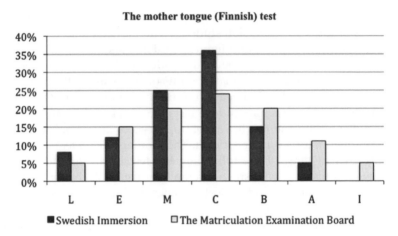

Figure 2.5 Comparison of 102 former immersion students' scores on the Finnish matriculation examination in 2000–2007 with the national distribution

distribution for the three highest grades on the scale the matriculation examination board uses (Figure 2.6).

All the former immersion students in Vaasa/Vasa (97 students) who participated in the compulsory foreign language test took the English test. It is based on the mainstream English language arts curriculum and consists of sections similar to those of the Swedish test. The English test is also

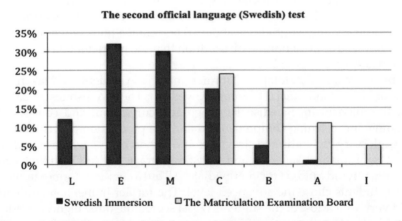

Figure 2.6 Comparison of 97 former immersion students' scores on the Swedish test in 2000–2007 with the national distribution

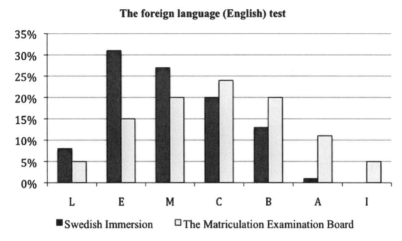

Figure 2.7 Comparison of 97 former immersion students' scores on the English test in 2000–2007 with the national distribution

graded on similar criteria and has two levels of difficulty: basic and advanced. Most of the former immersion students took the advanced level test. The English test results nearly parallel the Swedish test results (Figures 2.6 and 2.7). The three highest grades (M, E and L) were achieved by 66% of the former immersion students, representing 26 percentage units higher than the normal distribution for the three highest grades.

By 2007, 27 former immersion students had taken the optional foreign language test in German. It is structured and graded in the same way as the Swedish and English tests and also has two levels of difficulty: basic and advanced. Most of the former immersion students took the basic level test. As with the other language tests, the results on the German test are higher for the former immersion students (Figure 2.8). Over 70% achieved the three highest grades (M, E and L), representing about 30 percentage units higher than the normal distribution for the three highest grades. No former immersion student scored the lowest grade (A).

The results on the matriculation examination clearly show that immersion develops strong competence in students' L1, Finnish, as well as in Swedish. The results further show that early bilingualism in immersion also favours the acquisition of additional languages. The former immersion students' results on the English and the German tests are well above the average national results, although immersion students have experienced the same amount of instructional time in these languages as nonimmersion students.

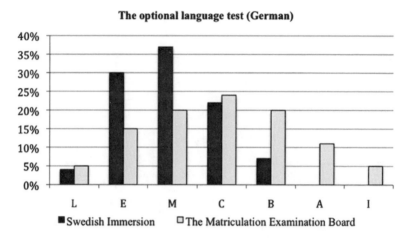

The optional language test (German)

■ Swedish Immersion   □ The Matriculation Examination Board

Figure 2.8 Comparison of 27 former immersion students' scores on the German test in 2000–2007 with the national distribution

The Interplay between Outcomes, Language Status and Programme Design

Our presentation of the linguistic outcomes of Swedish immersion in Finland clearly shows that with an early introduction and a more communicative and content-based approach, the time devoted to L3/L4 instruction does not necessarily have to be increased to give students a good mastery of multiple languages in immersion, at least in this northern European context. This issue appears to be crucial for future programme design and development and has to be evaluated more thoroughly. Because neither immersion classes nor schools in general are isolated from the surrounding language community, it is important to identify how immersion students make use of their languages, what their attitudes towards different languages are and what kind of motivation they have for learning multiple languages. In this section, we present some tentative results.

Immersion students' use of their languages has been studied to some extent in the city of Vaasa/Vasa, where the majority of the population is Finnish speaking (71%), but the Swedish-speaking minority is large enough (25%) to have a daily presence in the city and thereby to provide a genuine bilingual environment for those immersion students who wish to use Swedish outside school. In particular, the relationship between Swedish and English (as students' L3 but also as lingua franca) has been the focus of these studies.

In the 1997–1998 school year, a total of 119 immersion students in Grades 3–6 were given a questionnaire about their language use both within and outside school (Björklund, 2005; Björklund & Suni, 2000). Results of the questionnaire showed that students in Grades 4–6 (approximately 70% of the students in each grade) felt confident to use all their languages in the classroom. Only the youngest students (Grade 3) had a more bilingual (Finnish-Swedish) orientation, which may imply that they still did not find their L3, English, to be equally well developed as L1 and L2. Furthermore, students in Grades 3 and 4 reported that they used all three languages at home more than the bilingual L1 and L2 alternative, indicating that English must have a strong presence at home as the language of television, computer games and so on. In an explicit question about what languages are used in the TV programmes the students prefer, the most popular alternative among students in Grades 5 and 6 was 'Finnish and English'.

In another questionnaire distributed to 76 students in Grades 2 and 6 in school year 2002–2003, the status of Swedish and English was directly addressed in two questions. Students were asked what language they preferred to use. Almost 80% of the students in Grade 2 chose Swedish before English, whereas less than half of the group preferred Swedish in Grade 6. In another question, students were asked to judge which of these two languages they were going to use more in the future. In both grades almost half of the group was not able to rank the two options. Among those who ranked the two languages, the majority of students ranked English as more important than Swedish in both Grades 2 and 6 (Björklund, 2005).

These types of studies naturally depend heavily on how immersion students of different ages define their language use. They also indicate, however, that within the immersion context we need careful monitoring in order to identify the societal and psychological status of different languages, their interdependency and their combined effect on proficiency outcomes. In Swedish immersion careful attention must be paid in particular to language status and the relationship between Swedish (L2) and English (L3). Results of the studies summarized above suggest that English is perceived as more prestigious than Swedish among upper primary immersion students. In that sense it may be advantageous to devote more instructional time to Swedish as more instructional time in English may negatively affect Swedish language development. It is also important to replicate these studies with older and former immersion students to gauge their perceptions about Swedish and English.

A Multilingual Approach: The Possibility of Serving as an Immersion Prototype

As we have shown in this chapter, the interplay of multiple languages in Swedish immersion relies on three important cornerstones in programme design, that is separation of languages, integration of languages in the curriculum and teaching methods.

In a multilingual immersion approach separation of languages is actualized in time by allocating each language its share in the school schedule. The change in language of instruction is very clear for the students because each language is taught in a separate classroom and by a different teacher. Moreover, each subject is taught in only one language during a school year, but in both languages over the course of the programme (e.g. history in Swedish in Grades 5–6 and in Finnish in Grades 7–9).

The integration of languages in the programme is actualized in time by offering students' multilingual days in the school schedule. A primary school student might begin the day with a couple of lessons in Finnish, continue with some lessons in Swedish and finish the day with a lesson in English. Students are also active in integrating their languages. They are encouraged to use their multilingual competence and to use cross-linguistic comparisons a strategy for learning in all classes regardless of the language of instruction.

In addition, integration of languages is actualized in teaching methods. Each language to be learnt is used as the language of instruction in both content and language arts teaching. The immersion programme thus surrounds the students by natural, oral, written and contextual activities in each language. The teachers use similar communicative and more content-based teaching across languages, in contrast to how languages are traditionally taught in Finnish schools. The learning environment provides plenty of input with numerous opportunities for output.

As immersion researchers, we believe that the holistic design and evaluation (multiple languages, content teaching and learning) of our programmes point to exciting programmatic possibilities for immersion programmes around the world. Our programmes may serve as a prototype for other contexts to consider, as multilingualism and cross-cultural competence are being recognized as fundamental to a 21st-century global citizenry.

Notes

1. For information about Gnu licenses, see www.gnu.org. The map's source is: http://commons.wikimedia.org/wiki/File:Finland-swedish.jpg. Accessed 5.2.10.

2. In this chapter, we use the term 'preschool' for all early childhood education for children three to six years old.
3. Official national statistics are, unfortunately, not available on the spread of immersion education in Finland.
4. To interpret Figures 2.5 through 2.8, the Finnish grading scale is as follows: L (Laudatur) is the highest grade and A (Approbatur) is the lowest grade to pass the test. I (Improbatur) means a failing grade.

References

Baker, C. and Jones, S.P. (1998) *Encyclopedia of Bilingualism and Bilingual Education.* Clevedon: Multilingual Matters.

Bergroth, M. (2006) Immersion students in the matriculation examination. Three years after immersion. In S. Björklund, K. Mård-Miettinen, M. Bergström and M. Södergård (eds) *Exploring Dual-Focussed Education* (pp. 123–134). Vaasa: University of Vaasa.

Bergroth, M. (2007) Kielikylpyoppilaiden menestyminen ylioppilaskirjoituksissa [Immersion students' results on the matriculation examination]. In S. Björklund, K. Mård-Miettinen and H. Turpeinen (eds) *Kielikylpykirja – Språkbadsboken [The Immersion Book]* (pp. 126–134). Vaasa: Levón Institute, University of Vaasa.

Bergström, M. (2002) *Individuell andraspråksinlärning hos språkbadselever med skrivsvårigheter. [Individual Differences in Second-Language Learning of Immersion Pupils with Writing Difficulties.]* Vaasa: University of Vaasa.

Björklund, S. (1997) Immersion in Finland in the 1990s. A state of development and expansion. In R.K. Johnson and M. Swain (eds) *Immersion Education: International Perspectives* (pp. 85–101). Cambridge: Cambridge University Press.

Björklund, S. (2001) English as a second and as a third language; are there any differences. Paper presented at the *Second International Conference on Third Language Acquisition and Trilingualism*, Ljouvert/Leeuwarden.

Björklund, S. (2005) Toward trilingual education in Vaasa/Vasa, Finland. *International Journal of the Sociology of Language* 1/2005, 23–40.

Björklund, S., Still, E. and Suni, I. (2000, August 17–19) English as L3 in immersion in Vaasa/Vasa. Poster presented at the fifth European conference on immersion programmes, Vaasa/Vasa.

Björklund, S. and Suni, I. (2000) The role of English as L3 in a Swedish immersion program in Finland. Impacts on language teaching and language relations. In U. Jessner and J. Cenoz (eds) *English in Europe: The Acquisition of a Third Language* (pp. 198–221). Clevedon: Multilingual Matters.

Buss, M. and Mård, K. (2001) Swedish immersion in Finland: Facts and figures. In S. Björklund (ed.) *Language as a Tool: Immersion Research and Practice* (pp. 157–175). Vaasa: University of Vaasa.

Cenoz, J. (1998) Multilingual education in the Basque country. In J. Cenoz and F. Genesee (eds) *Beyond Bilingualism. Multilingualism and Multilingual Education* (pp. 175–191). Clevedon: Multilingual Matters.

Eklund, P. (2007) Poimintoja lukiopetuksen piirteistä kielikylvyssä [Aspects of teaching struggling learners in Swedish immersion]. In S. Björklund, K. Mård-Miettinen and H. Turpeinen (eds) *Kielikylpykirja – Språkbadsboken [The Immersion Book]* (pp. 144–150). Vaasa: Levón Institute, University of Vaasa.

Essama, L. (2007) Total immersion programs: Assessment data demonstrate achievement in reading and math. On WWW at http://www.carla.umn.edu/immersion/acie/vol11/BridgeNov07.pdf. Accessed 16.12.09.

European Commission (2005) Communication from the Commission to the Council, the European Parliament, the European Economic and Social Committee and the Committee of the Regions. A New Framework Strategy for Multilingualism. Brussels: Commission of the European Communities.

Finnish Matriculation Examination (2009) On WWW at http://www.ylioppilas-tutkinto.fi/en/index.html. Accessed 7.10.09.

Finnish National Board of Education (2009) Opetushallitus – Education. On WWW at http://www.oph.fi/english/education. Accessed 23.2.10.

Finnish National Board of Education (2010) Education. Online at: http://www.oph.fi/english/education. Accessed 21.10.10.

Fortune, T.W. and Tedick, D.J. (2008) One-way, two-way and indigenous immersion: A call for cross-fertilization. In T.W. Fortune and D.J. Tedick (eds) *Pathways to Multilingualism: Evolving Perspectives on Immersion Education* (pp. 3–21). Clevedon: Multilingual Matters.

Genesee, F. (1987) *Learning through Two Languages: Studies of Immersion and Bilingual Education*. Cambridge, MA: Newbury House.

Genesee, F. (1998) Case studies in multilingual education. In J. Cenoz and F. Genesee (eds) *Beyond Bilingualism. Multilingualism and Multilingual Education* (pp. 243–258). Clevedon: Multilingual Matters.

Havunen, L. (2001) Sind Immersionsschüler bessere Fremdsprachenlerner? Eine Fallstudie zum lexikalishen Transfer in Deutschaufsätzen finnishsprachiger Schüler in schwedishsprachiger Immersion [Are immersion students better foreign language learners? A case study of lexical transfer in written production among Finnish-speaking students in Swedish immersion]. Master's thesis, Tampere University.

Heinonen, P. (1996) Non-native language influence on foreign language learning. Swedish immersion pupils learning English in Keskuskoulu Comprehensive school. Master's thesis, University of Vaasa.

Lainas, A. and Nurmi, E. (2002) Study of fifth grade elementary students' spoken English: Differences between an immersion group and a regular teaching group. Master's thesis, University of Vaasa.

Latomaa, S. and Nuolijärvi, P. (2005) The language situation in Finland. In R.B. Kaplan and R.B. Baldauf Jr (eds) *Europe* (Vol. 1). *Hungary, Finland and Sweden* (pp. 125–232). Clevedon: Multilingual Matters.

Liebkind, K., Tandefelt, M. and Moring, T. (2007) Introduction: Why a special issue on the Swedish-speaking Finns? *International Journal of the Sociology of Language* 187/188, 1–11.

Lindeman, J. (1998) *Ala-asteen Lukutesti [Reading Test for Primary School]*. Turun Yliopisto: Oppimistutkimuksen keskus.

Ministry of Social Affairs and Health (2004) Early Childhood Education and Care in Finland. On WWW at http://pre20090115.stm.fi/cd1106216815326/passthru.pdf. Accessed 24.2.10.

National Core Curriculum (2004) *Basic Education*. Helsinki: National Board of Education.

Statistics Finland (2009) *Population Structure*. On WWW at http://stat.fi/til/vaerak. Accessed 24.2.10.

SVT Sosiaaliturva (2009) *Sosiaali-ja terveydenhuollon tilastollinen vuosikirja 2009 SVT Sosiaaliturva 2009* [*Statistical Yearbook on Social Welfare and Health Care 2009 OSF Social Protection 2009*]. Helsinki: National Institute for Health and Welfare.

Swain, M. and Johson, R.K. (1997) Immersion education: A category within bilingual education. In R.K. Johnson and M. Swain (eds) *Immersion Education: International Perspectives* (pp. 1–16). Cambridge: Cambridge University Press.

Tandefelt, M. and Finnäs, F. (2007) Language and demography: Historical development. *International Journal of the Sociology of Language* 187/188, 35–54.

Chapter 3
Insights from Indigenous Language Immersion in Hawai'i

W.H. WILSON and K. KAMANĀ

Introduction

Indigenous immersion is a distinct category of immersion education (Fortune & Tedick, 2008) and is especially well developed for Hawaiian. In this chapter, we provide some background information on immersion in indigenous languages, especially those of the United States. Specific attention will be given to Hawaiian and our P-12 laboratory school, Ke Kula 'O Nāwahīokalani'ōpu'u (Nāwahī for short). Nāwahī is a particularly well-designed and implemented school that offers a distinct perspective on immersion goals within its focus on restoring Hawaiian to first language status.

Hawaiian Immersion: Unique Contextual Factors

A unique historical context: Indigenous language repression and endangerment

Hawaiian is the sole indigenous language of Hawai'i, and, like all Native American languages, it is severely endangered. The current endangered status of Native American languages is relatable to a long history of US conquest of indigenous peoples and subsequent forced assimilation (Hinton, 2001b; McCarty, 2002). In addition, issues of discrimination and powerlessness have heavily impacted communities where revitalizing nearly exterminated languages is the goal of community activists (Hermes, 2006; Kipp, 2000; McCarty, 2002; Peter, 2007). Similar conditions exist for indigenous languages worldwide (Grenoble & Whaley, 2006).

While Native Hawaiians escaped the most horrific mistreatments of other indigenous groups, the extermination of the Hawaiian language proceeded quickly through the repression of childhood use of Hawaiian in English-only schools (Wilson & Kamanā, 2006). Within 25 years of annexation to the United States in 1898, the last group of Native Hawaiians to use Hawaiian as their peer-group language had been born in all Hawaiian communities, except for tiny, highly isolated Ni'ihau island.[1] By the end of the 20th century fewer than 700 Hawaiian-dominant native speakers remained out of a Native Hawaiian population of 401,162 (US Census Bureau, 2000a; Wilson & Kamanā, 2001).

Besides outright oppression, indigenous language endangerment is tied to the loss of traditional economies and autonomy based in hunting and gathering, fishing, subsistence agriculture and herding, all of which are conducted through the indigenous languages. Indigenous immersion has a number of parallels with immersion conducted in historically surpressed European autochthonous minority languages such as Welsh, Basque and Irish (Ó Duibhir, Chapter 8). While indigenous peoples are autochthonous, most European autochthonous minority peoples, other than Inuit Greenlanders and the Sámi, are not generally described as 'indigenous', because their cultural and socioeconomic features are quite similar to the surrounding majority language speakers.

A unique legal context: Hope for a linguistically intact future

Increasingly, the survival of minority autochthonous languages is supported through their recognition as 'official languages' in their regions. Indigenous languages are also receiving political recognition for official use by their speakers. Among them are Sámi within Scandinavia, Māori in New Zealand and Quechua in Peru (Baker & Jones, 1998; Hornberger & King, 1999; Todal, 1999).

While recognizing an indigenous language as official provides political support, language revitalization requires carefully ordered and strategically accomplished advocacy and actions to be effective (Fishman, 1991). Often an early action is to introduce the indigenous language as the medium of instruction in schools, especially where the majority of children are first language (L1) speakers of the language, as is the case in Greenland and the Northern Sámi area of Norway. Among international policy statements supportive of official use of indigenous languages in schooling are the Declaration on the Rights of Indigenous Peoples, adopted by the United Nations in 2007.[2] Within the United States the federal Native American Languages Act of 1990 provides broad legislation, but Hawai'i is unique among US states in granting official status to its indigenous language (Arnold, 2001; Lindholm-Leary, 2001; Wilson, 1999).

Using 'immersion' for language revitalization occurred with such languages as Hebrew and Welsh well before the initial Canadian French immersion program in 1965 (Baker & Jones, 1998; Fishman, 1991; Morgan, 2001). The purpose of Canadian French immersion is not language revitalization but rather improved proficiency for majority language (English-speaking) children in a minority official language (French). Nevertheless, once Canadian French immersion was initiated, it inspired indigenous communities to establish their own immersion programs, beginning with the Mohawks of Kahnawa:ke, Quebec in 1979 (Grenoble & Whaley, 2006).

Internationally, the largest efforts in endangered language immersion education have a European autochthonous language as their target, for example Welsh, Basque, Irish and so on (Fishman, 1991; Morgan, 2001; Ó Duibhir, Chapter 8). For indigenous languages, the largest immersion effort is in New Zealand's Māori language, with Hawaiian second. Indeed, Hawaiian is the third largest target language for immersion programs within the United States after Spanish and French (Lenker & Rhodes, 2007). Like those of most Native American language immersion programs, the Hawaiian sites tend to be small and enroll almost exclusively students of indigenous origin. An overall growth in use of Hawaiian has accompanied growth in immersion. Between the 1990 census and the 2000 census, those reporting some use of Hawaiian in the home grew from 14,315 to 27,160, a growth of almost 90% (US Census Bureau, 1990, 2000b).

Even though there is some confusion over the meaning of the term 'immersion' within Native American communities, with, for example, some using '... the term "immersion" to describe culture- and language-driven programs ...' rather than subject matter-driven programs (Fortune & Tedick, 2008: 8), interest among Native Americans in pursuing the revitalization of traditional languages through immersion has spread considerably in recent years (Pease-Pretty On Top, 2003). Among the other Native American languages with immersion programs that are truly 'immersion' (e.g. Fortune & Tedick, 2008; Swain & Johnson, 1997; Tedick *et al.*, Chapter 1) are Navajo, Mohawk, Ojibwe, Blackfeet, Arapaho, Montana Salish, Cherokee (Peter *et al.*, Chapter 10), Atsina (Gros Ventre), Central Alaskan Yup'ik, Inupiaq and Chinuk Wawa. Elsewhere internationally, there are fairly well-established indigenous immersion programs in Canada (Mohawk, Shuswap, Cree), Chile (Rapanui) and Finland (Inari Sámi).[3]

A unique implementation context: Challenges for indigenous language immersion

Use of an indigenous language as the medium of instruction faces huge challenges not experienced by one-way or two-way immersion

(TWI), even when the target language is lesser used. With no external country promoting them, and a long history of suppression in their own homelands, indigenous languages typically lack the resource of university-trained individuals fluent in the language to serve as teachers, administrators and curriculum developers (McCarty & Watahomigie, 1999). They also lack the vocabulary used in educational settings and children's books needed for academic learning and pleasure reading, and often even a comprehensive dictionary and grammar (Hinton, 2001a). Considerable progress has been made in addressing curriculum challenges for Hawaiian. For example, the consortium of the nonprofit 'Aha Pūnana Leo and University of Hawai'i at Hilo have a coordinated system that provides contemporary academic vocabulary and curriculum materials development for all grades, annual book distribution, online support, Hawaiian immersion-specific teacher certification and teacher professional development for all Hawaiian immersion programs (Kawai'ae'a *et al.*, 2007; Silva *et al.*, 2008; Wilson & Kamanā, 2001; Wilson & Kawai'ae'a, 2007).

The most important challenge is that indigenous language revitalization activists establishing immersion programs are constantly facing the diminishment of their fluent speaker base. The native speaker profile continually gets older, to the point that some Native American languages completely lack any remaining native speakers. This situation requires development of highly fluent and literate young adult L2 speakers who can become teachers, an area where Hawaiian is especially well resourced (Hinton, 2001a; Wilson & Kamanā, 2001).

The unique revitalization context: 'Primary' and 'auxiliary' languages

For indigenous immersion, the roles of the program languages are quite distinct from their roles in one-way (foreign language) immersion programs. At Nāwahī, the target language – Hawaiian – is considered the 'primary' language, that is the language that students are expected to use among themselves and then continue using as the language of their future families and communities. As part of a language revitalization effort, Nāwahī seeks for the community of Hawaiian language speakers what we call 'revernacularization', that is, the reestablishment of Hawaiian in the position of primary language with English as the auxiliary language (Wilson, 2008).

The additive bilingualism sought in immersion education involves maintaining age-appropriate proficiency in L1 while simultaneously adding L2 for other purposes. Nāwahī seeks these same goals, but, with the difference that the immersion language (IL), Hawaiian (L2 for most Nāwahī students) is seen as the language to be revernacularized as 'primary', while the nationally dominant language, English (L1 for most Nāwahī students) is seen as the language to be maintained as 'auxiliary', that is the language to be developed to a high level of proficiency for use with those outside the Hawaiian-speaking community.

For indigenous immersion programs, the IL is not fully available in the local community, having been marginalized through language shift to the dominant national language. Students thus do not have opportunities outside of school to regularly use the IL, especially with L1-speaking peers. The challenge of immersion education to fully transmit a language not actually used dominantly in the local society, has been highlighted by researchers (e.g. Broner & Tedick, Chapter 9; Tarone & Swain, 1995); yet, the typical indigenous community expectation of immersion is no less than full revitalization of the local indigenous language in all its highly distinctive registers and domains. Indeed, indigenous immersion is also typically expected to establish new registers and domains consistent with full official use of the indigenous language in contemporary society (Grenoble & Whaley, 2006). 'Revernacularization' immersion as practiced at Nāwahī, thus, requires intensive programming and planning to expand the language throughout the broader community.

Foreign language immersion programs in the United States also have 'primary' and 'auxiliary' language goals, but these are generally left implicit. In these programs, English (the students' L1) is implicitly the primary language and the IL the auxiliary language, the exact opposite of our goals at Nāwahī. Foreign language immersion programs, therefore, are not under the same intense pressure as indigenous immersion programs to produce native-speaker proficiency in the IL.

The unique academic context: Challenges of educating an 'at-risk' population

While focusing on an extraordinary level of proficiency in the IL, indigenous immersion also faces the extra challenge of serving academically 'at-risk' students. Throughout the US Native American students have a history of low academic performance in the nationally dominant language (their L1) relative to students from other ethnic groups – a common situation with forcibly incorporated minorities (Cummins, 2001b; Demmert & Towner, 2003; Ogbu, 2003). The situation is often further complicated by Native American student use of nonstandard dialects of English (Leap, 1982), with Hawai'i Creole English being among the most distant of these from standard American English.[4] Thus, relative to foreign language immersion, indigenous immersion faces a relatively larger gap between the starting point and desired end point both for L1 and L2 proficiency.

A unique ideological context: Ideological clarification and implementation

Fishman (1991: 394–396) describes 'ideological clarification' as a crucial feature of language revitalization. Ideological issues requiring attention in indigenous immersion go beyond those typical of foreign language immersion. Indigenous immersion must often address unique, and politically charged, organizational issues (tribal versus state versus language revitalizationist control of programs), dialect and orthographical issues, cultural issues (purism versus cultural synchritism) and participant selection issues (tribal membership, tribal descendant, commitment to program, etc.) (Hinton, 2001a).

Establishing an ideology is not sufficient to reach language revitalization. The ideology must be implemented. Our description of Nāwahī later in this chapter relates its success to a close relationship between ideology and implementation. Meek and Messing (2007) describe the opposite situation, where implementation does not reflect ideology. While the teaching of indigenous languages is frequently associated with community ideologies calling for use of indigenous languages as primary, Meek and Messing (2007) show that the materials and programs used to teach them, as well as the personal actions of administrators and teachers, often unconsciously emit an implicit message that the dominant national language is primary and the indigenous language is of minor importance. For example, they note how indigenous language teachers and program administrators frequently use the dominant language rather than the indigenous language with their indigenous peers and their own children. This sends an unspoken message that the indigenous language is not relevant for contemporary use. In addition, materials used in teaching indigenous languages and cultures commonly follow models for foreign language teaching materials, thus framing indigenous languages and cultures as subordinate to the national language and culture.

Indigenous immersion that follows too closely models designed for foreign language immersion also faces the danger of framing the indigenous language as subordinate. Such auxiliary-oriented framing includes the diminished use of the IL as students mature and progress through grades, and restriction of IL use to the classroom and school, rather than expanding it to the public arena.

The Hawai'i Context: Administration and Programming

The initiation of Hawaiian immersion education began in part as a reaction to language shift effects observed among Ni'ihau children enrolled in transitional bilingual education on Kaua'i Island (Wilson, 1999). The first Pūnana Leo language nest site was opened in 1984 in the main community of Ni'ihauans residing on Kaua'i and then rapidly spread to other islands around a small core of L2 speakers of Hawaiian raising their children as L1 speakers of Hawaiian at home (Wilson & Kamanā, 2001). Today, the privately run Pūnana Leo form the base of the statewide Hawaiian immersion educational system. Currently numbering 11 sites, the Pūnana Leo are 100% total immersion preschool programs. Every public school Hawaiian immersion site at the kindergarten level and above, except for one, developed from a core group of families whose children had attended a Pūnana Leo (Kawai'ae'a *et al.*, 2007).

All 22 Hawaiian immersion sites at the elementary level and higher are state funded and staffed with teachers who are primarily L2 speakers of Hawaiian. These sites are administered through standard public or charter schools (see Zehrbach, Chapter 4, for definition of charters). Within this administrative framework, there are two models in practice: one with Hawaiian immersion as a strand within an English-medium school, and the other a stand-alone Hawaiian immersion site. Various combinations of administrative and site configurations exist, that is stand-alone standard public schools taught through Hawaiian (two sites), a Hawaiian strand in an English-medium public school (14 sites), a Hawaiian strand in an English-medium charter school (one site), a separate Hawaiian immersion charter school sharing a campus with a standard English-medium school (one site) and stand-alone Hawaiian immersion charter schools (four sites).

All Hawaiian immersion elementary programs, except for one, are within one hour's drive from a secondary immersion continuation program to Grade 12. Seven middle- and/or high-school sites provide partial immersion programs. Six sites, all stand-alone or charter, include total Hawaiian immersion beyond elementary. In 2008–2009, the percentage of Hawaiian immersion students enrolled in total immersion models was 100% in preschool through Grade 5, 64% in Grades 6–12, and 88.3% overall ('Aha Pūnana Leo, 2008; Hale Kuamo'o, 2008).

Within the United States as a whole, partial immersion has been more common than total immersion, with 56% of US one-way programs reported as partial in 2006 (Lenker & Rhodes, 2007). Furthermore, in the United States early total immersion programs are considerably less L2 oriented than Hawaiian immersion programs. They commonly introduce English by Grade 2 or 3 and allow up to 50% of subject-matter instruction through English at Grade 5 or 6 (Fortune & Tedick, 2003; Genesee, 2008). In Hawai'i, total immersion typically entails teaching 100% of all subjects through Hawaiian, except English language arts, typically introduced at Grade 5. Partial immersion in Hawai'i at the secondary level typically involves teaching Hawaiian language arts and at least one other subject-matter course through Hawaiian.

Highly L2-oriented total immersion as with Hawaiian is practiced with some languages such as Blackfeet and Mohawk and is more common in some European models (see Ó Duibhir, Chapter 8 and Björklund & Mård-Miettinen, Chapter 2). Models similar to the developmental bilingual model are currently used for others, such as Navajo (Arviso & Holm, 2001; McCarty, 2002). However, most Native American language immersion programs are confined to elementary school and none, other than Hawaiian, as yet continue through high school.[5] At present, primary school is also the program limit for most indigenous immersion programs outside the United States.

Also distinctive of Hawaiian immersion and other indigenous programs is the role of culture. The Pūnana Leo language nest movement began with a strong base in Hawaiian traditions practiced by native-speaking elders who were the first Pūnana Leo teachers. These cultural practices and traditions then moved into the public school immersion programs.

The Nāwahī model: An integrated stand-alone PreK–12 total immersion program

A total immersion program that is especially strong in the use of Hawaiian language and culture is Ke Kula 'O Nāwahīokalani'ōpu'u, or Nāwahī. It includes a private infant/toddler and preschool program (the Pūnana Leo), a K–8 charter school, and a Grades 9–12 component affiliated with an English-medium off-site public high school. All three components of the program are coordinated as a single laboratory school. Instruction at Nāwahī is 100% Hawaiian at all levels. Introduced in Grade 5, English language arts is among the courses taught through Hawaiian. Nāwahī also includes programming for parents and staff.

Nāwahī has a history beginning in 1985 with the initiation of a Pūnana Leo in Hilo on the rural island of Hawai'i. Eventually it moved to the present 10 acre site to graduate the state's first class of Hawaiian immersion seniors in 1999 (Wilson & Kamanā, 2001). Table 3.1 compares Nāwahī programming with typical US early, total foreign language immersion, 90:10 TWI, and an indigenous immersion program model derived from

Table 3.1 Percentage of immersion (minority) language use in different program models

Grades	Nāwahī	One-way	90:10 Two-way	Sheltered model*
K–1	100%	100%	90%	100%
2–3	100%	80%	80%	100% (Gr. 2); 50% (Gr. 3)
4–6	100%[†]	50%	50%	50%
7–12	100%[†]	20%	20%	*

* The Rough Rock Navajo immersion/sheltered program was derived from a developmental bilingual education model. In Grades 7–12 '... students, teachers and community resource people work together on in-class and field-based studies intended to integrate academic content with oral language and literacy experiences in Navajo' (McCarty, 2002: 185).
[†] Nāwahī teaches English language arts beginning in Grade 5, but uses Hawaiian, rather than English, as the medium of instruction.

developmental bilingual education (Fortune & Tedick, 2003, 2008; Genesee, 2008; Lindholm-Leary, 2001; McCarty, 2002).

Nāwahī's focus is on an emerging population of L1 speakers of Hawaiian and those who wish to join with them, with gradual movement to an enrollment of a majority of L1 speakers as in Francophone French-medium education in Canada. The infant/toddler program was opened in 2006 specifically to support an upsurge in families deciding to have one or both parents use only Hawaiian with their children from birth. The number of L1 speakers of Hawaiian has increased considerably at Nāwahī in recent years due to these new L1 Hawaiian-speaking families (Table 3.2).

Nāwahī's conscious use of L1 speakers to build L2 proficiency among other students has parallels with TWI (Lindholm-Leary, 2001, Chapter 5; see also de Jong & Bearse, Chapter 6, Dorner, Chapter 12 and Zehrbach, Chapter 4). Nāwahī differs from TWI, however, in its expectation that L2 speakers of Hawaiian matriculating from the program identify as completely with the minority language as L1 speakers and later pass it onto their own children as L1. This is indeed happening, as among the young parents of L1 speakers of Hawaiian are some of the earliest Nāwahī graduates.

Nāwahī's school culture includes the opening and closing of the school day with a gathering of the school community with chants, songs and speeches based in Hawaiian tradition. All students learn Hawaiian dance and arts. Hawaiian traditions expressed through Hawaiian are used in school student discipline and in faculty meetings, and also in interaction with parents and in larger community-inclusive events. Behind the school are traditional Hawaiian gardens, animal husbandry

Table 3.2 Enrollment profile of Nāwahī Students, Fall 2009

Program/Grades	Total enrollment	First language speakers*
Infant/Toddler	11	11 (100%)
Pre-Kindergarten	40	17 (42.5%)
K–3	87	26 (29.9%)
4–5	41	10 (24.4%)
6–8	31	13 (41.9%)[†]
9–12	51	10 (19.6%)
Total	261	87 (33.3%)

* One or both parents have spoken only Hawaiian with the child from birth. Others, not included here, have parents who use some Hawaiian with them, or who began its use with the child later.
[†] The anomaly in the middle-school population is due to a 2007 decision of the other immersion charter school in Hilo to add Grade 7 rather than send those students to Nāwahī as in the past. This resulted in Nāwahī's Grade 7 enrolling a higher percentage of L1 speakers, primarily children of parents who pioneered the opening of the Nāwahī elementary charter in 2000.

facilities and cooking areas providing resources incorporated into school celebrations and life passage events as well as being used for science and other academic areas.

The cultural base of Nāwahī also includes strong identification with academics. During the 19th century, Native Hawaiians had a very high literacy rate at the same time many were living a partially subsistence level based in earlier traditions (Wilson & Kamanā, 2006). Nāwahī specifically focuses on this aspect of earlier Hawaiian identity by requiring all students to pursue a college preparatory curriculum while also participating in traditions emanating from a subsistence lifestyle.

In 1997, the Hawai'i State Legislature mandated establishment of a state Hawaiian language college in the University of Hawai'i at Hilo that would provide both undergraduate and graduate education through Hawaiian. It further mandated that Nāwahī have the status of the initial laboratory school site for this immersion college. It is this status as a laboratory school of Ka Haka 'Ula O Ke'elikōlani College (henceforth the College) that draws the different components together with administrative leadership from the College. The College and 'Aha Pūnana Leo see Nāwahī as a demonstration site for programs taught through Hawaiian and other indigenous languages, and use the site to train teachers, test materials and establish new initiatives. A consortium of the 'Aha Pūnana Leo and the College also serves as a resource for teachers, administrators, curriculum developers and other staff through a range of postsecondary undergraduate and graduate programs, taught through Hawaiian (Wilson & Kawai'ae'a, 2007). In July 2010, the World Indigenous Nations Higher Education Consortium (WINHEC) accorded Ka Haka 'Ula O Ke'elikōlani the world's first indigenous P-20 (preschool to graduate programming) accreditation based on the strength of the program at Nāwahī and its close integration into the overall Hawaiian-medium programming of the College.

The Nāwahī model: Academic outcomes

Broadly, Native American immersion, including Hawaiian immersion at Nāwahī and elsewhere, follows the general pattern of immersion programs worldwide in producing students with IL proficiency in addition to academic and majority language outcomes equal to or surpassing those of peers in nonimmersion programs (e.g. Arviso & Holm, 2001; Cummins, 2001a; Genesee, 2008; Hoare, Chapter 11; Kipp, 2000; Lindholm-Leary, Chapter 5; Wilson & Kamanā, 2001). What must be remembered in the case of indigenous immersion programs is that their student bodies come from at-risk communities where both ethnicity and socioeconomic status are associated with low achievement (Takayama, 2008). In the case of Nāwahī, enrollment is highly Native Hawaiian (96.9% in fall of 2009) with many having a low socioeconomic profile (68% free and reduced lunch in the fall of 2009). This achievement pattern has also been reported in some TWI programs serving students with a similar profile (e.g. Zehrbach, Chapter 4).

Comparative data come primarily from standardized testing. Hawaiian immersion was implemented initially with an exemption from standardized testing until Grade 6, the grade after English was introduced. In the 1990s, data revealed that Hawaiian immersion students at tested grades outperformed Native Hawaiian students enrolled in English-medium classes, through to the secondary level (Wilson & Kamanā, 2001). Other measures of academic achievement are high-school graduation and college attendance. From its first graduating class in 1999 until the latest graduation in 2009, Nāwahī has had a 100% high-school graduation rate and 80% college attendance rate.

In response to the federal *No Child Left Behind* (NCLB) legislation (for details, see Zehrbach, Chapter 4), the state of Hawai'i has developed testing through Hawaiian through to Grade 4. In 2009, using such Hawaiian-medium assessments, Nāwahī's K–8 charter component-passed state NCLB testing with the topmost rating, that is 'Met Adequate Yearly

Progress – In Good Standing, Unconditional,' one of only eight schools (out of 55) receiving that ranking in the county. There were challenges to developing NCLB testing in Hawaiian for lower elementary grades, and federal obstructions to extending Hawaiian-medium NCLB testing through to Grade 12 remains an issue at Nāwahī.[6]

The Nāwahī model: Indigenous language outcomes

Nāwahī students have performed well in the state Hawaiian-medium reading test in early elementary, with 100% judged proficient in 2009, yet, the Nāwahī school community is skeptical of these tests and continues to use more rigorous internal examinations to inform instruction.[7] More recently, the College has been developing oral proficiency measures and piloted them at six sites in 2009. Preliminary results indicate oral proficiency being especially strong at Nāwahī; yet again, this does not mean that the goal of developing Hawaiian to the point of being the 'primary' language has been reached. Testing of proficiency, oral or written, in other Native American immersion programs is not common, but one example appears in Chapter 10. Peter, Sly and Hirata-Edds describe in detail how the Cherokee Nation has made the development and administration of Cherokee language assessments central to its immersion programming.

Anecdotally, Nāwahī has generally succeeded in making Hawaiian the normal peer-group language in lower elementary and to a certain extent in upper elementary. As in English-medium schools in Hawai'i, intermediate- and high-school students at Nāwahī use Hawai'i Creole English and American slang as an informal adolescent peer-group code (Wilson & Kamanā, 2009). In college and to a certain extent in the upper grades of high school, Nāwahī students move back toward the use of Hawaiian with each other (Wilson & Kamanā, 2009). Experience outside Nāwahī, where speaking Hawaiian is seen as a unique skill and identity marker, is a factor in increasing peer-group use of Hawaiian.

The Nāwahī model: Cultural identity

Cultural identity in Hawai'i is complicated by the fact that the majority of children, especially those who have Native Hawaiian ancestors, are multiracial. The Kumu Honua Mauli Ola philosophy used at Nāwahī focuses on strengthening the Hawaiian *mauli* or 'life essense', which includes besides language use, other factors relevant to identity as a member of a community descended at its core from Native Hawaiians ('Aha Pūnana Leo & Ka Haka 'Ula O Ke'elikōlani, 2009). In 1999, Hilo

High School, which administers high-school students at Nāwahī, did a self-study. The study found that 51% of Hilo High students were of Native Hawaiian ancestry. While approximately half of all students of Native Hawaiian ancestry at Hilo High School did not choose Native Hawaiian as their ancestry or primary ethnic identity, its students registered at Nāwahī overwhelmingly chose Native Hawaiian ethnicity, including, notably, a few students who had no Hawaiian ancestry (Wilson & Kamanā, 2001).

The high identification of multiracial Nāwahī students with Native Hawaiian ethnicity might be compared with the identity among high-school students educated in two-way Spanish/English immersion. De Jong and Bearse (Chapter 6) found that both students of Latino and Anglo backgrounds generally identified as bilingual, but only Latino students identified as bicultural. Furthermore, Latino students 'grounded their bicultural identity in their home environment where they spoke Spanish and lived both cultures' (de Jong & Bearse, Chapter 6: 110). Nāwahī is distinctive in its use of school programming to develop IL cultural identity among all students.

Future Possibilities for Nāwahī

Moving to official minority-language education

The goal of fostering a distinctive self-reproducing community of L1 speakers links Nāwahī's program to the Official Minority-Language-Medium Education found in countries with multiple official languages. A model for such a system in Hawai'i might be the educational system of Finland, where both Finnish and Swedish are official languages even though Swedish L1 speakers number far fewer than Finnish L1 speakers (Björklund & Mård-Miettinen, Chapter 2). As Björklund and Mård-Miettinen explain, despite their small population (approximately 289,000, comparable to Hawai'i's Native Hawaiian population), the approximately 5.5% of Finland's citizens who are Swedish L1 speakers have a full public education system from preschool through graduate school available to them in Swedish. Finnish speakers have the option of attending Finnish schools or Swedish immersion programs, where they learn the minority official language that is part of their country's heritage (much like the Anglophones who learn French through immersion in Canada).

The legal groundwork has also been laid to move to Official Minority-Language-Medium Education as an additional educational choice in Hawai'i. In 2004, the state legislature passed Act 133 permitting the

Hawai'i State Department of Education to work cooperatively with the College to establish a statewide Hawaiian-medium education agency targeting Hawaiian-speaking students and administered through Hawaiian.

Strengthening English by strengthening Hawaiian

Although Nāwahī students have higher academic outcomes on average than their Native Hawaiian peers enrolled in English-medium schools, Nāwahī seeks even higher English outcomes through transformation to an Official Minority-Language-Medium school. Indeed, we imagine the possibility of transforming linguistic minority status from being an academic disadvantage to an academic advantage.

Importantly for Hawaiian language revitalization purposes, current Nāwahī use of Hawaiian in English class for informal teacher–student classroom communication and directions is a strategy to strengthen Hawaiian and frame it as the language to be used at all times in actual communication with other Hawaiian speakers. The use of Hawaiian to teach English is also designed to reduce the threat of English to Hawaiian identity and the resistance that Native Hawaiian students can have toward using standard English (Cummins, 2001b; Ogbu, 2003). The movement of Nāwahī students beyond Native Hawaiian norms toward Hawai'i general population norms in English literacy by late high school is consistent with Ogbu's (2003) theory of the academic benefits of strong attention to minority student identity.

The use of Hawaiian as the communicative language in Nāwahī English classes also places greater focus on 'performance' aspects of English, that is use of formal standard English, rather than the students' informal register – typically Hawai'i Creole English. Narrowing the English target to formal production provides a mental association of the English spoken and written by Nāwahī students as academically focused. Movement to normalized peer-group use of Hawaiian by all students will increase Hawaiian proficiency at Nāwahī, and we believe, ultimately, will further improve English outcomes.

Consistent with Cummins's threshold hypothesis is a correlation between high Hawaiian performance in the lower grades with high English performance in the upper grades, even when high performance in Hawaiian in the lower grades is accompanied by low English performance at that time. Further development of Hawaiian-medium education expertise and teaching materials might result in student achievement at the end of high school moving toward the norms produced by the highly academic, multilingualism-oriented Scandinavian school systems. In

University of Hawai'i at Hilo English course placement examinations, foreign students educated in Scandinavian schools typically outperform Hawaiian students educated in English-medium high schools (Wilson & Kamanā, 2006).

Multilingualism beginning in elementary school

An ideal for Nāwahī would be to have its students highly fluent in several languages with Hawaiian primary. If the goal of re-establishing Hawaiian as the community's L1 can be reached, perhaps partial immersion in another language might be introduced without impacting negatively on Hawaiian proficiencies. Nāwahī has already made some movement toward this goal through its 'Heritage Language Program' for all students as a means to honor non-Native Hawaiian ancestors. The teaching of heritage languages also allows for honoring all students in the school along the lines discussed by Dagenais (2008) and Swain and Lapkin (2005).

In 2008–2009, all Nāwahī students in Grades 7 and 8 studied Latin for 90 minutes per week to honor ancestors from Portugal, Puerto Rico and the Hispanicized Phillipines. All students of Grades 1–6 studied Japanese for 90 minutes per week, while students of Grades 7–12 studied Chinese.

Metalinguistic and cultural comparison skills for older students

Ideally, intermediate and high school immersion students advance their academic abilities through reflection on the distinctiveness of the languages that they speak and of the cultures of those languages. While some metalinguistic and cultural diversity reflection can simply result from immersion students' experience of using two or more languages and exposure to differences in cultures, a higher level of awareness might be reached through teacher-directed activities provided to older, more cognitively prepared students. A challenge, however, is an assumption of many immersion students that, unlike standard high school Hawaiian language course students, they do not need to study Hawaiian grammar. Nāwahī's experimental Latin program provides a way to sidestep this assumption.

Latin instruction is from a perspective based in Hawaiian language, culture and history with a contrastive analysis, grammar-translation approach. This instruction also includes comparison with English language, culture and history from the time of the early Anglo-Saxon tribes. Metalinguistic skills developed from contrastive analysis with Latin provide Nāwahī students with tools to consciously improve overall vocabulary development and language performance, be it in Hawaiian, English or other languages.

Insights and Possibilities for Improved Immersion Outcomes

The development of Nāwahī for language revitalization purposes in a multiracial, indigenous population with academic challenges has required that we carefully reanalyze immersion goals and the means for reaching them. Insights gained at Nāwahī might prove useful to other indigenous immersion programs and to immersion education as a whole.

Insights for indigenous language immersion programs

The main insights from Nāwahī for indigenous language immersion are as follows.

(1) Success in developing high-level proficiency and skill in an indigenous language is directly proportionate to its level of use and supportive framing in the school.

(2) Programs that use the indigenous language and its heritage to an exceptional level, including full immersion through Grade 12, produce the same (or better) results in the nationally dominant language (e.g. English in the United States) and academics as standard English-medium programs (and partial immersion programs) for indigenous students.

(3) The existence of a community nonstandard dialect of the nationally dominant language does not preclude using indigenous immersion to reach goals of improved academic performance and improved proficiency in the standard dialect of the dominant language.

(4) Successful indigenous language revitalization can develop from high L2 proficiency when there is an environment encouraging and supporting young adult L2 speakers to establish indigenous language-speaking peer groups and homes.

(5) A stable source of skilled indigenous language-speaking (L1 or L2) teachers who are highly motivated to use the indigenous language with their own children and peer groups is central to a school-based indigenous language revitalization effort.

(6) The long-term process of generational change that characterizes language revitalization greatly benefits from highly language-revitalization-focused institutional support from stable indigenous-language-medium-operated entities with considerable administrative autonomy from the dominant-language-medium mainstream, for example the

nonprofit 'Aha Pūnana Leo, Inc., the internally self-governing, Ka Haka 'Ula O Ke'elikōlani College of Hawaiian Language at the University of Hawai'i at Hilo and charter schools.

In Table 3.3, we summarize the deconstruction of four goals of successful immersion schooling within the context of the development of

Table 3.3 Achieving common immersion goals: Comparison of standard US foreign language (FL) immersion and Nāwahī

Immersion goal	*US FL immersion approach*	*Nāwahī approach*
IL Proficiency	'Auxiliary' mastery sought in academic registers through minimally intense use	'Primary' mastery sought in all registers through highly intense use
Nationally Dominant Language	Maintenance of 'primary' mastery of all registers of English through in-school and out-of-school experiences and instruction	Development of 'auxiliary' mastery of academic registers equal to primary mastery by majority students through out-of-school experiences and English language arts and L3 instruction; maintenance of local dialect (Hawai'i Creole English) through ethnic community and contrastive analysis
Academic Achievement	Equal to, or greater than, majority group peers, through IL and L1 medium instruction	First, equal to, or greater than, indigenous group peers. Later, equal to, or greater than, majority group peers. Both through IL medium instruction
Cultural Competence (IL Culture)	Minimal, through some experiences/ instruction outside standard curriculum	Strong, through pervasive school structure and curriculum
Intercultural understanding	Minimal, mostly on an empathetic level, through cultural and linguistic experiences that remain relatively unexplored in curriculum	Fairly strong, both on empathetic and conscious levels, through pervasive use of IL language and culture

programming at Nāwahī and show how those goals are typically attained in US one-way (foreign language) immersion and at Nāwahī.

Insights for other immersion programs

Most immersion programs in the United States do not seek to effect a change in the primary language and culture of the home and community as Nāwahī does. However, like Nāwahī, they seek to produce high proficiency in the IL and strong intercultural competence. It is in the area of producing high IL proficiency and skills in the heritage of that language where many immersion programs might be further strengthened.

Nāwahī demonstrates that programming that is highly focused on the IL and its heritage can produce exceptional IL results, without negatively affecting academic outcomes or English proficiency. Thus, Nāwahī is an extreme example in support of research in favor of increased percentages of IL use in immersion programs at all grade levels.

Nāwahī also provides some ideas on how to strengthen IL and culture outcomes through structuring the immersion environment and through direct instruction in grammar, vocabulary and culture. In particular, teaching additional languages (L3, L4, etc.) through the medium of the IL (L2 for majority language students, L1 for minority language students) may serve as a means to strengthen both L1 and L2 grammar, vocabulary and culture skills for all students.

Finally, Nāwahī provides further evidence of the benefits of immersion both for minority and majority groups. The 20th century was a period of great losses for the Native Hawaiians, resulting in fears that the Native Hawaiian people themselves would disappear. Hawaiian immersion began as a highly focused family-based effort to assure the continuation of an indigenous people grounded in their traditional language. Today in this 21st century, Hawaiian language immersion is part of a larger effort where Native Hawaiians, supported by the rest of the population of the islands, are pursuing a better future for their children based in a strong indigenous identity. A most exciting development after completing a full generation of Hawaiian immersion at Nāwahī are second-language parents, graduates of Nāwahī, who are now raising their children as L1 speakers of Hawaiian.

Notes

1. Ni'ihau is the smallest inhabited Hawaiian island and entirely the property of Ni'ihau Ranch. Its isolation and a Ranch policy restricting visitors have played major roles in maintaining Hawaiian on Ni'ihau. Today there are approximately

70 people living permanently on Ni'ihau (Ni'ihau Cultural Heritage Foundation, 2009).

2. The United Nations Declaration on the Rights of Indigenous Peoples, adopted September 13, 2007, outlines a broad range of political, legal, economic, religious, educational and other rights for indigenous peoples. Cultural distinctiveness is a major area of concern with a specific focus on use of indigenous languages in education in Article 14.

3. The list of languages provided here is based on personal contact, either directly or through a second party who has direct ties to the site. Information on programs provided later in the chapter is also from such personal contact.

4. Hawai'i Creole English developed among children in Hawai'i during the period when Hawaiian was heavily suppressed in the schools. It is considered to be a distinct language by linguists, and can be incomprehensible to speakers of standard American English in its most basilectal forms.

5. To our knowledge, the only US indigenous programs outside of Hawai'i that presently go up to Grade 7 or 8 are Tséhootsooí Diné Bi'ólta' for Navajo in Arizona, Akwesasne Freedom School for Mohawk in New York, and Cuts Wood School for Blackfeet in Montana.

6. The NCLB legislation [Sec. 1111 (b)(3)(C)(x) of Title I http://www2.ed.gov/policy/elsec/leg/esea02/index.html] restricts use of languages other than English for testing to lower elementary schooling in all jurisdictions but Puerto Rico, and thus is in direct conflict with Sec. 105 of the Native American Languages Act of 1990 (http://www.nabe.org/files/NALanguagesActs.pdf).

7. In 2000, the 'Aha Pūnana Leo began working with American Indian education expert, William Demmert (Tlingit/Lakota), to develop alternative valid and reliable assessments through Hawaiian. The focus was not only to demonstrate academic progress, but to provide data useful in improving academic outcomes. The project then expanded to include other Native American language immersion schools and educational experts nationwide (Demmert & Towner, 2003).

References

'Aha Pūnana Leo (2008) *Nā Kula Pūnana Leo 2008–2009 (Data on Enrollments)*. Hilo, HI: Author.

'Aha Pūnana Leo and Ka Haka 'Ula O Ke'elikōlani (2009) *Kumu Honua Mauli Ola (A Hawaiian Educational Philosophy)*. Hilo, HI: Authors.

Arnold, R. (2001) To help assure the survival and continuing vitality of Native American languages. In L. Hinton and K. Hale (eds) *The Green Book of Language Revitalization in Practice* (pp. 45–48). San Diego, CA: Academic Press.

Arviso, M. and Holm, W. (2001) Tséhootsooídi Ólta'gi Diné Bizaad Bíhoo'aah: A Navajo immersion program at Fort Defiance, Arizona. In L. Hinton and K. Hale (eds) *The Green Book of Language Revitalization in Practice* (pp. 203–215). San Diego, CA: Academic Press.

Baker, C. and Jones, S.P. (1998) *Encyclopedia of Bilingualism and Bilingual Education*. Clevedon: Multilingual Matters.

Cummins, J. (2001a) The entry and exit fallacy. In C. Baker and N. Hornberger (eds) *An Introductory Reader to the Writings of Jim Cummins* (pp. 110–138). Clevedon: Multilingual Matters.

Cummins, J. (2001b) Research findings from French immersion programs. In C. Baker and N. Hornberger (eds) *An Introductory Reader to the Writings of Jim Cummins* (pp. 96–109). Clevedon: Multilingual Matters.

Dagenais, D. (2008) Developing a critical awareness of language diversity in immersion. In T.W. Fortune and D.J. Tedick (eds) *Pathways to Multilingualism: Evolving Perspectives on Immersion Education* (pp. 201–220). Clevedon: Multilingual Matters.

Demmert, W.G., Jr and Towner, J.C. (2003) A review of the research literature on the influence of culturally based education on the academic performance of Native American students – On WWW at http://educationnorthwest.org/webfm_send/196. Accessed 24.2.10.

Fishman, J. (1991) *Reversing Language Shift*. Clevedon: Multilingual Matters.

Fortune, T. and Tedick, D. (2003) What parents want to know about foreign language immersion programs. On WWW at http://www.cal.org/resources/digest/0304fortune.html. Accessed 24.2.10.

Fortune, T.W. and Tedick, D.J. (2008) One-way, two-way and indigenous immersion: A call for cross-fertilization. In T.W. Fortune and D.J. Tedick (eds) *Pathways to Multilingualism: Evolving Perspectives on Immersion Education* (pp. 3–21). Clevedon: Multilingual Matters.

Genesee, F. (2008) Dual language in the global village. In T.W. Fortune and D.J. Tedick (eds) *Pathways to Multilingualism: Evolving Perspectives on Immersion Education* (pp. 22–45). Clevedon: Multilingual Matters.

Grenoble, L. and Whaley, L. (2006) *Saving Languages: An Introduction to Language Revitalization*. Cambridge: Cambridge University Press.

Hale Kuamo'o (2008) *Nā Kula Kaiapuni Hawai'i 2008–2009 [Hawaiian Immersion Schools 2008–2009]*. Hilo, HI: Ka Haka 'Ula O Ke'elikōlani.

Hermes, M. (2006) Treaties that dominate and literacy that empowers? I wish it was all in Ojibwemowin. *Anthropology and Education Quarterly* 37, 393–398.

Hinton, L. (2001a) Language revitalization: An overview. In L. Hinton and K. Hale (eds) *The Green Book of Language Revitalization in Practice* (pp. 3–18). San Diego, CA: Academic Press.

Hinton, L. (2001b) Federal language policy and indigenous languages in the United States. In L. Hinton and K. Hale (eds) *The Green Book of Language Revitalization in Practice* (pp. 39–44). San Diego, CA: Academic Press.

Hornberger, N.H. and King, K.A. (1999) Authenticity and unification in Quechua language planning. In S. May (ed.) *Indigenous Community-Based Education* (pp. 160–180). Clevedon: Multilingual Matters.

Kawai'ae'a, K., Housman, A., Alencastre, M., Ka'awa, K., Māka'imoku, K. and Lauano, K. (2007) Pū'ā i ka 'Ōlelo, Ola ka 'Ohana: Three generations of Hawaiian language revitalization. *Hūlili: Multidisciplinary Research on Hawaiian Well-Being* 4, 183–237.

Kipp, D. (2000) *Encouragement, Guidance, Insights, and Lessons Learned for Native Language Activists Developing Their Own Tribal Language Programs*. Browning, MT: Piegan Institute.

Leap, W. (1982) The study of American Indian English: Status and direction of inquiry. In H.G. Bartelt, S. Penfield-Jasper and B.L. Hoffer (eds) *Essays in Native American English* (pp. 1–22). San Antonio, TX: Trinity University Press.

Lenker, A. and Rhodes, N. (2007) Foreign language immersion program features and trends over 35 years. On WWW at http://www.cal.org/resources/digest/flimmersion.html. Accessed 24.2.10.

Lindholm-Leary, K. (2001) *Dual Language Education*. Clevedon: Multilingual Matters.

McCarty, T.L. (2002) *A Place to be Navajo: Rough Rock and the Struggle for Self-Determination in Indigenous Schooling*. Mahwah, NJ: Lawrence Erlbaum Associates.

McCarty, T.L. and Watahomigie, L.J. (1999) Indigenous community-based language education in the USA. In S. May (ed.) *Indigenous Community-Based Education* (pp. 79–94). Clevedon: Multilingual Matters.

Meek, B. and Messing, J. (2007) Framing indigenous languages as secondary to matrix languages. *Anthropology & Education Quarterly* 38, 99–118.

Morgan, G. (2001) Welsh: A European case of language maintenance. In L. Hinton and K. Hale (eds) *The Green Book of Language Revitalization in Practice* (pp. 147–176). San Diego, CA: Academic Press.

Ni'ihau Cultural Heritage Foundation (2009) On WWW at http://www.niihauheritage.org/. Accessed 24.2.10.

Ogbu, J. (2003) *Black American Students in an Affluent Suburb: A Study of Academic Disengagement*. Mahwah, NJ: Lawrence Erlbaum Associates.

Pease-Pretty On Top, J. (2003) Native American language immersion: Innovative native education for children and families. On WWW at http://www.aihec.org/resources/documents/NativeLangugageImmersion.pdf. Accessed 24.2.10.

Peter, L. (2007) Our Beloved Cherokee: A naturalistic study of Cherokee preschool language immersion. *Anthropology & Education Quarterly* 38, 323–342.

Silva, K., Alencastre, M., Kawai'ae'a, K. and Housman, A. (2008) Generating a sustainable legacy: Teaching founded upon the Kumu Honua Mauli Ola. In M.K.P.A. Nee-Benham and K. Maenette (eds) *Indigenous Educational Models for Contemporary Practice – In Our Mother's Voice* (Vol. 2) (pp. 29–40). New York: Routledge Taylor & Francis.

Swain, M. and Johnson, R.K. (1997) Immersion education: A category within bilingual education. In R.K. Johnson and M. Swain (eds) *Immersion Education: International Perspectives* (pp. 1–18). Cambridge: Cambridge University Press.

Swain, M. and Lapkin, S. (2005) The evolving sociopolitical context of immersion education in Canada: Some implications for program development. *International Journal of Applied Linguistics* 15, 169–186.

Takayama, B. (2008) Academic achievement across school types in Hawai'i: Outcomes for Hawaiian and non-Hawaiian students in conventional public schools; Western-focused charters, and Hawaiian language and culture-based schools. *Hūlili: Multidisciplinary Research on Hawaiian Well-Being* 5, 245–283.

Tarone, E. and Swain, M. (1995) A sociolinguistic perspective on second language use in immersion classrooms. *The Modern Language Journal* 79, 166–178.

Todal, J. (1999) Minorities with a minority: Language and the school in the Sámi Areas of Norway. In S. May (ed.) *Indigenous Community-Based Education* (pp. 124–136). Clevedon: Multilingual Matters.

US Census Bureau (1990) Table 3.1. Detailed Language Spoken at Home and Ability to Speak English for Persons 5 Years and Over. On WWW at http://www.census.gov/population/socdemo/language/table5.txt. Accessed 24.2.10.

US Census Bureau (2000a) The Native Hawaiian and other Pacific Islander population. On WWW at http://www.census.gov/prod/2001pubs/c2kbr01–14.pdf. Accessed 24.2.10.

US Census Bureau (2000b) Detailed language spoken at home for the population 5 years and over. On WWW at http://www.census.gov/population/www/socdemo/lang_use.html. Accessed 24.2.10.

Wilson, W. (1999) The sociopolitical context of establishing Hawaiian-medium education. In S. May (ed.) *Indigenous Community-Based Education* (pp. 95–108). Clevedon: Multilingual Matters.

Wilson, W. (2008) Language fluency, accuracy, and revernacularization in different models of immersion. *Nieanews* (Newsletter of the National Indian Education Association) 39, 40–43.

Wilson, W. and Kamanā, K. (2001) Mai Loko Mai O Ka 'I'ini: Proceeding from a dream. The 'Aha Pūnana Leo connection in Hawaiian language revitalization. In L. Hinton and K. Hale (eds) *The Green Book of Language Revitalization in Practice* (pp. 147–176). San Diego, CA: Academic Press.

Wilson, W. and Kamanā, K. (2006) For the interest of the Hawaiians themselves: Reclaiming the benefits of Hawaiian-medium education. *Hūlili: Multidisciplinary Research on Hawaiian Well-Being* 3, 153–181.

Wilson, W. and Kamanā, K. (2009) Commentary from Hawaiian language activists William H. Wilson and Kauanoe Kamanā. Indigenous youth and bilingualism. *Journal of Language, Identity, and Education* 8, 369–375.

Wilson, W. and Kawai'ae'a, K. (2007) I Kumu; I Lālā: 'Let there be sources; let there be branches': Teacher education in the College of Hawaiian Language. *Journal of American Indian Education* 46, 37–53.

Chapter 4

Two-Way Immersion Charter Schools: An Analysis of Program Characteristics and Student Body Compositions

G. ZEHRBACH

Introduction

Since the passage of the US legislation known as the No Child Left Behind (NCLB) Act of 2001,[1] states, public school districts and local schools have been searching with fervor for ways to boost achievement for all learners, including English language learners (ELLs), or students not proficient in English (Klein, 2007). ELLs have traditionally not fared well within US public schools. One approach to better meet the needs of ELLs has been through the charter school movement.

Charter schools are found in 40 states and the District of Columbia, and they enroll over a million students across the United States (Center for Education Reform, 2008; US Charter Schools, nd). They are public schools without religious affiliation that are freed from the various statutory requirements that traditional public schools must follow. In exchange for this increased amount of regulatory freedom, charter schools must meet various measures of accountability that are stipulated in a legal charter contract (Green & Mead, 2004). Charter schools are designed to (1) increase academic achievement, (2) create educational options for parents and (3) spark innovation within the public school system. These schools must have sponsors or authorizers (often a state department of education or school district), and they are accountable to that sponsor by demonstrating positive academic results and adhering to their charter contract.

One example of a type of charter school that seeks to serve ELLs and language majority learners is the two-way immersion charter school (TWICS). Two-way immersion (TWI) is one of the immersion program models showcased in this volume, and its specific characteristics are summarized in the introductory chapter by Tedick, Christian and Fortune. The charter movement has also contributed to the growing number of one-way (foreign language) and indigenous immersion programs in the United States. For example, Wilson and Kamanā (Chapter 3) describe a Hawaiian immersion program that includes a K-8 charter school. A growing number of TWI schools are charters. Howard and Sugarman (2001) reported that 11 TWI charter schools existed in 2001. However, in 2007, a search of the Center for Applied Linguistics' (CAL) TWI program directory revealed that there were 20.[2] Details about this particular set of TWI schools are relatively unknown due to a scarcity of research. In the study described in this chapter I attempt to shed light on a number of aspects of TWICS. I also explore some of the unique possibilities that the flexibility of charter status affords to TWI programs.

History and Theory of US Charter Schools

The theory behind charter schools dates back to the mid-20th century (Dougherty & Sostre, 1992; Witte, 1990). In the 1950s, well-known economist Milton Friedman (1955) proposed the idea of giving educational choice to parents with vouchers. Under Friedman's plan, the government would distribute vouchers worth a certain sum of money to all US parents, who could choose to use them to send their children to any school (public or private). The main idea behind his proposal was that the principles of a market-based economy could be successfully applied to the educational sector. Friedman's vision remained rather dormant until the mid-1980s (Dougherty & Sostre, 1992) when ideas about 'school choice' saw new life. Unlikely coalitions of people such as liberal policy analysts, urban Blacks, Catholic school administrators, White parents and state governors were vocalizing their support for a school system that included an element of 'choice' (Dougherty & Sostre, 1992). It was during this time that two analysts from the Brookings Institution, one of the oldest think tanks in the United States, authored an attack on the way in which US public schools were governed and operated (Chubb & Moe, 1990). Chubb and Moe argued that educational reforms would never produce the change needed to improve America's schools and that the educational sector needed a true transformation vis-à-vis the implementation of market-based principles such as 'choice' and 'decentralization'. The concept of charter schools was thus a compromise based on a system of choice within the public school sector, and it became palatable to conservatives and liberals alike (Dougherty & Sostre, 1992). It incorporated the conservative principle of choice, while limiting its existence to the public school sector only, which appealed to liberals. It was then that the charter school movement began, and the number of schools has been increasing ever since.

Although charter schools continue to increase in number, they are not without controversy. One contentious area within the charter school debate is whether these schools are educating students like those found in traditional public schools. In other words, do charter schools enroll comparable percentages of students with background characteristics (i.e. poverty, students of color) that traditionally correlate with lower academic achievement? Some accuse charter schools of engaging in a process called 'creaming' (as in 'cream of the crop') or 'skimming from the top' (Wells, 1998; West, 2006). They believe that because charter schools are schools of choice, they get to select only those students who are most likely to succeed (i.e. 'the cream') or are less expensive to educate (Lacireno-Paquet *et al.*, 2002). This viewpoint, however, is not shared by all. For example, a study done on charter schools in Washington DC concluded that they did not seem to be enrolling students who were easier to educate (Lacireno-Paquet *et al.*, 2002).[3] Manno *et al.* (1999) conducted a study of over 100 charter schools and did not find any evidence to support the notion of 'creaming'. In fact, they found that many charter schools were purposefully serving students who have traditionally not fared well in traditional public schools. Various statistical reports also lend credence to the notion that charter schools do indeed serve 'high-need' student populations (RPP International, 2000; US Department of Education, 2007b).

In addition to a growing body of research on charter schools, there are also countless studies about, recommendations for and profiles of TWI programs in the United States (e.g. Christian, 1996; Christian *et al.*, 1997; Lindholm, 1990; Lindholm-Leary, 2001; Lindholm-Leary & Howard, 2008, among many others). Three recent examples are showcased in this volume: Lindholm-Leary provides an analysis of student outcomes in Chinese TWI, de Jong and Bearse present a study on TWI students at the high school level, and Dorner offers a policy analysis regarding TWI implementation. There is an unmistakable gap in the research, however, regarding the *intersection* of TWI and charter schools. In all the research on TWI and/or charter schools, only two profiles of TWICS can be found (US Department of Education, 2007b). Thus, for those involved with TWICS, there is very little available to inform them about how to operate. As a result, TWICS planning groups have no guidance about what to include in charter contracts. Additionally, current TWICS stakeholders have no way of understanding how their own program differs from other TWICS across the country. To illustrate this point, an examination of the admissions processes at TWICS reveals that while some schools, through dual lottery systems, are able to insure through their charter documents that they will have balanced linguistic populations (i.e. 50% Spanish-dominant and 50% English-dominant learners upon enrollment, or a minimum of one-third of each group as recommended in the literature (cf. Christian, 1996; Lindholm, 1990), other schools cannot.

Study Approach and Design

The research questions guiding this study were:

(1) Where are TWICS located?
(2) What key factors characterize TWICS?
(3) What are the student compositions and how do they compare with those of neighboring schools and the state?

Deemed suitable for this study given the research questions, the positioned-subjects approach (Conrad *et al.*, 2001), sees each stakeholder as occupying a position from which important information can be learned. This approach also views each unit of analysis as being greatly linked to its context. This means that each TWICS in this study is encompassed by an environment unique to its surroundings, from which insights were gained. Finally, this approach assumes that as the researcher, I also occupy a position from which I interpret and make meaning of the world based on my own 'experiences and perspectives' (Conrad *et al.*, 2001: 204). This study required the use of qualitative methods, as well as some descriptive statistics. Bogdan and Biklen (2003) describe qualitative research as: (a) naturalistic, (b) descriptive, (c) concerned with process, (d) inductive *and* (e) concerned with meaning. All five characteristics appropriately describe this study. Actual TWICS were studied and 'rich' descriptions were created. Because a purpose of this study was to 'map the universe' with respect to TWICS, many efforts were put forth to locate all these schools. I conducted an exhaustive search through the use of database inquiries (e.g. CAL's directory), my personal knowledge and information requests that I repeatedly sent to charter school and bilingual department officials at state education agencies. After locating the schools and completing location and enrollment analyses, I collected and examined the charter contracts for as many TWICS as possible. This effort was met with numerous obstacles. First, some districts were unwilling to share the documents. Second, fees for obtaining some charter contracts became cost prohibitive. Third, it often took significant effort to pinpoint a particular agency or person that had access to the charter contract. Thus, in some circumstances

I had to cease from trying to obtain them. Document analysis was the primary method used to uncover the data for the study. Whitt (2001) argues that document analysis is an effective yet underutilized form of data collection. For this study, both public and private records were sought; however, the bulk of documents were public. This was due to the ease of access and affordability as well as my commitment to a nonintrusive nature of inquiry. The key public record documents that were intensely scrutinized were school and district websites as well as charter contracts.

Results

My search for TWICS currently operating in the United States yielded a total of 45 programs. They are found in all regions of the country, including the three states that have legislation prohibiting bilingual education.[4] Thousands of children are enrolled in these schools along with hundreds of teachers, administrators and support staff members. Data were collected for nearly all of the TWICS found. The results are presented in three main parts: (a) location characteristics, (b) charter and operational characteristics and (c) student characteristics.

Where are TWICS located?

Table 4.1 reveals that TWICS operate in 16 states and the District of Columbia (DC). These states are not clustered together nor do they share similar bilingual education legislation. California has the largest share, with one-third of all TWICS. Texas has 15.5%. The other 14 states and DC account for the remainder. The western and southwestern regions of the United States contain 30 TWICS, or 67%. The northeast has 15%, and the midwest is slightly lower at 9%, followed by the southeast at 8.5%.

The vast majority of TWICS are located in major urban areas. More than half, or 57%, are found within cities having more than 250,000 people. An additional 16% of the schools are found in less populous cities. Suburban locales account for 17% of the total, while 11% are located in nonurban areas.

Similar to the trends for charter schools in general (US Department of Education, 2007a), the majority of TWICS are located in urban settings and are found in the west and southwest. Since the Howard and Sugarman (2001) report, the number of new TWICS has risen dramatically. Thirty-four TWICS have opened over the past eight years, representing a 309% increase, compared to a 42% increase in TWI programs overall (charter, noncharter, magnet) during the same time period, according to CAL's TWI

Table 4.1 Summary of location, charter and operational characteristics

Characteristic	No. of schools	% of total
Location (state) (n = 45)		
California	15	33.0
Texas	7	15.5
New Mexico	3	6.7
New York	3	6.7
Other states	17	37.7
Location (region) (n = 45)		
West	17	37.7
Southwest	13	28.8
Midwest	4	8.9
Northeast	7	15.6
Southeast	4	8.9
Setting (n = 45)		
Urban	32	71.1
Suburban	8	17.8
Rural/town	5	11.1
Authorizers (n = 45)		
District	30	67.0
State	13	29.0
University	2	4.0
Program model (n = 42)		
Whole school program	34	81.0
Strand within school	8	19.0
Years as charter (n = 43)		
1999 or before	11	25.6
2000 or after	32	74.4

(*Continued*)

Table 4.1 (*Continued*)

Characteristic	No. of schools	% of total
Start-ups vs. conversions (n = 43)		
Start-ups	33	76.7
Conversions	10	23.3
Target language (n = 45)		
Spanish and English	45	100.0
Spanish, English + 3rd/4th	3	6.7
Grades served (n = 45)		
PK3 or PK4	10	22.2
Middle school Grades (6–8)	20	44.4
K-3, K-4, K-5 or K-6	25	55.6
Type of model (n = 45)		
Balanced (50:50)	23	51.1
Anti-Bil Ed States	6	35.3
Non-Anti-Bil Ed States	17	60.7
K-3/K-6	17	73.9
K-8	6	26.1
Pre-NCLB	8	50
Post-NCLB	15	53.6
Minority lang. dominant (90:10)	22	48.9
Anti-Bil Ed States	11	64.7
Non-Anti-Bil Ed States	11	39.3
K-3/K-6	8	34.8
K-8	14	63.6
Pre-NCLB	8	50
Post-NCLB	13	46.4

directory, accessed in 2008, and Howard and Sugarman (2001). Numerous states have TWICS, and states other than those located in the southwest and west are seeing increasing numbers of TWICS. This is evidenced by the fact that 76% of the TWICS located in areas other than the southwest and west have opened in the last six years. That said, the state with the largest number of TWICS by far is California. This is not surprising given the large Spanish-speaking population. In addition, the establishment of TWI programs (be they charter or not) has been one way for the state to sidestep the antibilingual education legislation.

What key factors characterize TWICS?

All TWICS are Spanish/English programs and are typically authorized by public school districts (Table 4.1). In total, school districts authorized TWICS in 11 of the 16 states and established two-thirds of the overall number across the United States. State authorizers sponsored 28%, and universities authorized two TWICS, or 4%. In a select number of states, multiple authorizers are present.

Although the vast majority of TWICS are start-ups (i.e. newly established schools), close to one-fifth, or 23%, are conversion charters, schools that used to be traditional public schools but have 'converted' to charter status. Of these, 60% are located in California with the other four being located in Texas, Georgia and New York. Of those that converted in California, five of the six did so between 1998 and 2000, right after the antibilingual education legislation was passed. All but one of these schools was authorized by a local school district. As for the start-ups, there were multiple authorizers involved, and the schools were established as far back as 1995 and as recently as the fall of 2008.

Consistent with the study's population parameters, all TWICS studied are elementary schools. While some TWICS continue to serve children after 5th or 6th Grade, others start their programming in pre-kindergarten (pre-K-3 or 4 years old). In fact, slightly less than one-quarter, or 22%, of the total number of TWICS serve children in pre-kindergarten, including three schools that start at pre-K-3. As for those schools that extend beyond 5th or 6th Grades, 44% of TWICS are either currently serving or plan to serve children through the 8th Grade.

There is no universal model of TWI. Table 4.1 shows that while 51%, of the schools implement a 50:50 model, the other half uses a model with more time dedicated to the minority language, Spanish. The majority of schools with minority-language-dominant models follow the 90:10 design. Additionally, 64% of 90:10 schools serve students in the middle grades, while this percentage falls to 26% for 50:50 schools. Programs operating in states with antibilingual legislation use a minority-language-dominant model in 65% of the cases, while those in other states use a minority-language-dominant model in 39% of the cases.

During the pre-NCLB years, there were eight schools utilizing a 50:50 model and eight others employing a minority-language-dominant model

(70:30 or higher). Since the passage of NCLB, 15 schools have opted for the 50:50 model and 13 for 90:10.

The types of TWI models being implemented at TWICS are interesting for a number of reasons. First, it is somewhat surprising that no pattern is found with respect to the type of model used and the location of the schools. One might predict that models with the least amount of time allocated for the minority language (50:50) would be the favored model in states that have laws banning bilingual education. This is certainly not the case, as programs in California, one of the antibilingual states, are more likely to the use minority-language-dominant models.

Second, it does not appear that NCLB testing requirements have forced TWICS to use models with more instructional time in English. Although it is true that many schools in the post-NCLB years are electing the 50:50 model, it is also true that a similar number of TWICS have opted for a minority-language-dominant model. This is encouraging because research has consistently shown that 'more instructional time in English does not lead to an improvement in English language proficiency or achievement in reading/language arts and mathematics as measured in English' (Lindholm-Leary, 2007: 9). In other words, neither ELLs nor language majority students benefit from enrollment in 50:50 programs as opposed to 90:10 programs insofar as their English language and academic achievement are concerned. However, less instructional time in the minority language *does* have an impact on the proficiency level attained in that language (Lindholm-Leary, 2007).

The third note of interest regarding the TWICS models is that there is no detectable pattern between the number of grade levels served and type of model. One might think that TWICS without middle grades would be more likely to employ minority-language-dominant models since they have less instructional time overall in the target language. However, the findings here do not support such an assertion. Indeed, the majority of schools that utilize the 90:10 model continue into the middle level grades. Furthermore, three-quarters of the schools with a 50:50 design end their programming at or before grade 6.

Most of the TWICS (81%) are whole school programs. The remaining 19% are strands within larger charter schools. When TWI programming is not a whole school option, it is usually offered alongside other options such as English-only programming with enrichment courses in Spanish. This result reveals that unlike most TWI programs (Howard & Sugarman, 2001) the majority of TWICS provide bilingual programming as a whole school offering, rather than as a strand within a school. A considerable number of TWICS are in an expansion mode as well. Of the 45 schools, 14, or 31% are currently growing or planning to grow. These schools are either increasing the grade levels that they serve at the top end (i.e. adding 6–8th Grades) and/or they are planning to include pre-kindergarten programming.

What are the student compositions in TWICS?

Table 4.2 summarizes student enrollment figures. TWICS were serving just over 12,000 students in their 45 schools across the country when this study was done. When factoring in TWICS that opened in the fall of 2009, the number of students has surpassed 14,000. The average student enrollment of a TWICS is 275 students. The difference between the lowest and highest enrollment is large, ranging from 66 students in one school in New Mexico compared to 980 students in a California school.

Consistent with prior research on charter schools (RPP International, 2000; US Department of Education, 2004) is the fact that TWICS enroll smaller student populations. With an average total school enrollment of 275 (or 315 when accounting for 2009–2010 growth), the student populations are about twice as large as average charter school enrollments (RPP International, 2000), but they have about 170 fewer students on average than regular public schools (US Department of Education, 2008).

In addition to having the two largest TWICS, California has four schools with enrollments over 400 students. This translates into California serving almost one-half, or 46.9%, of the total student enrollment in TWICS. Texas serves 15% of the total.[5] Consistent with the distribution of schools, 73% of the total enrollment is found in the western and southwestern United States. The northeastern part of the country has 12% while their neighbors to the south have 7.5%. The midwestern states follow with almost 7%. These percentages remain similar even when factoring in future growth.

Data were collected for almost all the schools in the study with respect to race and ethnicity ($n = 39$ or 87% of the schools reporting). In nearly all cases, data were retrieved from state databases for the most recent year available that was typically 2006–2007 or 2007–2008. The overall race and ethnicity breakdown for the 39 schools in the study reveals that Hispanic (Latino) students comprise 70% of the current student body at TWICS. White students form the second largest group as they account for just under 12% of the total population. African-American (black) students are next with 5.6%, while Asian students represent less than 1%. Two subgroup populations frequently talked about are ELLs and children with special needs. With respect to the former, the overall mean is 45.5% and the median is 42.7%. The middle 50% (inter-quartile mean) of TWICS

Table 4.2 Summary of student enrollment

45 Schools	Enrollment	Plan to serve and avg. school size	Title I	% Poverty	% White	% Hispanic	% Black	% Asian	% ELL	% Special education
Totals	12,363	14,179	36	n/a	n/a	n/a	n/a	n/a	n/a	n/a
Average	275	315	81.8	68.8	12.6	75.3	8.4	1.0	47.0	7.3
Wt. average	n/a	n/a	n/a	63.9	11.1	71.4	5.5	0.8	45.5	4.5
Median	229	281	n/a	75.6	8.0	78.7	1.4	0.4	42.7	8.0
Range low	66	66	n/a	6.0	0.0	15.9	0.0	0.0	0.0	1.2
Range high	980	980	n/a	100	64.0	100	55	6.8	97.6	12.8
Upper limit/Q 1	148	221	n/a	54.9	1.0	60.0	0.5	0.0	31.4	4.2
Upper limit/Q 2	229	281	n/a	75.6	8.0	78.7	1.4	0.4	42.7	8.0
Upper limit/Q 3	343	375	n/a	84.9	16.9	95.2	9.2	1.1	65.7	10.0
Interquart. range	195	154	n/a	0	15.9	35.2	8.8	1.1	34.4	5.8
Interquart. mean	237	285	n/a	70.5	7.2	76.2	2.2	0.6	48.1	7.6
Wt. average Q 1	304	367	n/a	42.0	0.2	45.3	0.2	0.0	43.4	5.5
Wt. average Q 2	339	369	n/a	64.7	2.3	71.3	0.9	0.3	47.9	4.3
Wt. average Q 3	231	253	n/a	81.8	11	85.4	4.0	0.8	33.6	5.4
Wt. average Q 4	236	262	n/a	93.6	30.4	97.9	27.9	2.6	65.2	4.1

enroll almost a balance of ELLs and non-ELLs at 48.1%. The exact accuracy for ELL numbers is somewhat limited, however, as states differ on their procedures for identifying ELLs (Mahoney & MacSwan, 2005).

As for students with special needs (*n* = 24), 4.5% of the TWICS population is identified as having a learning disability. The median school value is 8% and the middle 50% are enrolling approximately 7.6% of their schools with children in special education.

The percentage of students living in poverty is a value frequently cited in the United States as a way to identify potential challenges posed by a particular student population. The reason for this is that researchers have found that high poverty levels are often negatively associated with certain variables such as student achievement (e.g. Battistich *et al.*, 1995), school climate (Battistich *et al.*, 1995), challenging home environments (Rothstein, 2004), minority density, larger schools and less qualified teachers (Ingersoll, 2004; Orfield & Lee, 2005). The most common way to speak about poverty in US schools is to report the percentage of students that qualify for 'free and reduced lunch', a government-funded program.

Data regarding poverty were collected from 42 of the 45 schools, or 93%. I would have preferred to disaggregate the data according to language minority and majority speakers; however, disaggregation was unfeasible due to the small number of schools reporting data in this way.[6] Table 4.2 shows that 64% of the overall student population enrolled at TWICS comes from poor households.

Those who are involved in education know that the makeup of schools can change dramatically as poverty levels increase or decrease. In order to look at differences among schools with differing rates of poverty, the TWICS in this study were ranked from the highest to the lowest and then were broken down accordingly into quartiles. Within each quartile, a new snapshot was taken which identified percentages of students with respect to race and ethnicity, ELL and special needs status. Table 4.3 contains the snapshot data broken down by the four quartiles.

With regard to the breakdown of the quartiles, one can see that as the percentage of poverty increases, so too does the percentage of minority students and the overall numbers of ELLs. Furthermore, within the third and fourth quartiles, there are virtually no white students. These data are consistent with other studies revealing a strong correlation between high poverty schools and large numbers of minority children (e.g. Orfield & Lee, 2005).

Moreover, no variation surfaces with regard to the type of TWI model used within each quartile. It was predicted that schools with lower levels of poverty would be more inclined to use minority language-dominant

Table 4.3 Demographics by poverty quartile

	Current enrollment	Future enrollment	% of schools Title I	Avg. % poverty	% White	% Hispanic	% Black	% Asian	% ELL	% Special education	No. of conversion TWICS	No. of 50:50 schools -	No. of 70:30, 80:20, 90:10 schools
Poverty Q 1	304	367	54.5	42.0	23.9	66.7	3.2	1.0	43.4	5.5	2	6	5
Poverty Q 2	339	369	70.0	64.7	14.4	73.9	3.5	1.1	47.9	4.3	2	5	5
Poverty Q 3	231	253	100.0	80.1	3.3	76.3	16.1	0.4	33.6	5.4	2	4	5
Poverty Q 4	236	262	100.0	93.6	0.8	88.4	4.4	0.6	65.2	4.1	2	6	6

models (90:10), while higher-poverty schools would be more likely to use 50:50 models. Higher-poverty schools, especially those with many ELLs, may feel pressure to use models with more instructional time in English despite research evidence to the contrary. The data confirm that this is not the case.

How do TWICS students compare to students in surrounding schools and the state?

In order to see whether charter schools are enrolling easier or harder to educate student bodies, the demographic information for surrounding schools and districts is also presented. Data for race and ethnicity, poverty, ELL and special education were collected for the majority of the surrounding schools and states involved in the study. Table 4.4 presents a comparison to show the percentage of cases when the TWICS have a greater percentage of particular subgroups when compared with nearby schools and to the state average.

Table 4.4 shows that in almost all of the cases, TWICS enroll greater percentages of Hispanic students than do the average public schools in the states with TWICS. In the majority of these situations, the TWICS are enrolling Hispanic students on a percentage basis of 20 points or more when compared with other public schools at the state level. At the local level, four out of every five TWICS, or 80%, enroll greater percentages of Hispanics than do their neighborhood counterparts. Furthermore, in 51% of these cases, the difference between the enrollments of the TWICS and the local average is equal to or greater than 20 percentage points.

Table 4.4 Comparison of TWICS demographics with those of states/districts

TWICS	*>than state (%)*	*>20% +*	*>than district (%)*	*>20% +*
Hispanic	95	62	80	51
Black	19	5	17	0
Asian	0	0	0	0
White	8	0	20	0
Poverty	80	55	64	26
ELL	88	62	77	46
Special education	5	0	10	0

When compared with their corresponding state averages, 28 TWICS, or 80% of the total, have higher levels of poverty (Table 4.4). More than half of the TWICS, or 64%, maintain higher levels of poverty in comparison to their neighborhood counterparts. With respect to ELLs, close to 90% of TWICS enroll more ELLs when compared with state averages. This same trend is true at the local level as 77% of TWICS have higher percentages of children who are not proficient in English. While the majority of TWICS have ELL populations that are 20% points or greater than the average state public school, a little less than half, or 46%, of the existing TWICS report ELL populations that are 20 percentage points or higher than other schools in their respective areas. This pattern of greater percentages for the TWICS is not upheld with regard to the number of students needing special education services. State and local averages are greater than those at TWICS in 95% and 90% of the cases, respectively.

The findings related to the demographic portraits of TWICS are notable. The TWICS are enrolling disproportionately high numbers of Hispanic children. Indeed, Latino students easily comprise the largest segment of the total student population, and the average school can expect to enroll the overwhelming majority of its student body with Hispanic pupils. Although there are some exceptions, the vast majority of the schools are sparsely populated with students from the other subgroups. This is perhaps not a surprise because TWI programs target language minority learners to have a balanced student population. In addition, it is well known that TWI programs are popular heritage language programs for Latino children being raised in English-speaking homes (Christian, 2008).

The trend regarding enrollment is similar for TWICS and children living in poverty. Although there is a high degree of variation from the low to the high, it is clear that the majority of these schools possess very high percentages of economically disadvantaged students. In fact, only seven schools, or 15% of the total, have poverty rates lower than 50%. This means that for 85% of the TWICS, at least one out of every two students is living in poverty. Even more astounding is the fact that 42% of the schools have a poverty rate of 80% or more.

Such enrollment patterns do not support prior claims that charters serve a select, or elitist, clientele (Wells, 1998; West, 2006). The majority of TWICS are enrolling more students with background characteristics (ELL, minority and poverty status) that have historically been associated with lower achievement. These data substantiate the findings of large national studies claiming that charter schools serve a largely minority and poor clientele (RPP International, 2000; US Department of Education, 2004; US Department of Education, 2007b). However, because the enrollment numbers are so disproportionately tilted toward poor Hispanic youth, the data here also lend some credence to the findings of a number of researchers who argue that charter schools are isolating students, both racially and socioeconomically (Frankenberg & Lee, 2003; Ni, 2007).

The fact that TWICS are enrolling such high numbers of Hispanic students as well as possessing disproportionately high shares of economically disadvantaged children may be a potential red flag. There are two reasons for this. The first is that TWICS strive to provide a multicultural experience for their students. Indeed, it cannot be forgotten that one of the goals of TWI is for the students to develop cross-cultural competencies (Lindholm-Leary, 2001). de Jong and Bearse (Chapter 6) examine that very issue. The following statement articulates the need for a diverse student body: '[p]romotion of an appreciation for the diversity found within their [TWI] schools is a defining characteristic of two-way immersion programs' (Howard & Sugarman, 2007: 100). Although it can be said that there is much diversity within any particular subgroup, it can also be said that a rich cross-section of several racial and ethnic subgroups can be valuable as well.

One caveat in this analysis of student composition is that TWICS are not enrolling comparable percentages of students qualifying for special education. The fact that they enroll fewer special needs students is consistent with other studies that have found similarly low percentages in charters (RPP International, 2000). This finding gives partial credence to those claiming that charter schools may be less likely to enroll students who are more expensive to educate (Lacireno-Paquet *et al.*, 2002).

Programmatic Possibilities for TWICS and other Immersion Programs

Because charter schools are free to implement their own vision and are not bound by district mandates, TWICS afford us a window into the many possibilities for innovative program practices, including multilingual, curricular and admissions innovation.

Multilingual innovation

Some TWICS are incorporating more than two languages into their curricular offerings. Although all TWICS use Spanish as their target language, a few stipulate in their charter contracts the option of incorporating a third or fourth language. For instance, Balere Language Academy (Florida) incorporates French into its educational design and suggests that Portuguese may be included in the future. The World Language Academy (Georgia) utilizes Mandarin Chinese in its curriculum. According to its contract:

> A primary emphasis of the school, however, will be the study of world languages. Initially, these languages will be Spanish and Mandarin Chinese; however, the school will be in partnership with North Georgia College and State University as a demonstration school, and other languages, including Arabic, may follow.[7]

In addition, the charter contract for the Worthington Area Language Academy (WALA, Minnesota) says that it will use Lao and a fourth language, to be chosen by the parents of the school. The WALA charter contract states:

> WALA will make a strong effort to market to various communities in the area and hopes to achieve a population of approximately with 30% of the students with English as their primary language, approximately 30% of the students with Spanish as their primary language, approximately 30% would be bilingual, and approximately 10% of the students would have a third language (most likely Lao) as their primary language.[8]

Such multilingual approaches are also found in the Hawaiian immersion program (with K-8 charter) described by Wilson and Kamanā (Chapter 3) and in the Swedish immersion programs in Finland (Björklund & Mård-Miettinen, Chapter 2).

Curricular innovation

Several TWICS embed other curricular highlights in their immersion programming. For example, the main focus of Namaste (a school in Chicago that offers a TWI strand) is not bilingualism, but healthy living. The founders established the school so that children can learn to live well by eating healthily and exercising regularly. They are also committed to a 'Peaceful People' curriculum, similar to WALA. Designated as an official 'PeaceBuilders®' (a violence prevention youth program) site, WALA's curricular focus is on peace-making. The Latin American Montessori Bilingual (LAMB) TWICS integrates the curriculum with the Montessori approach. Several other schools promote curricular offerings such as an emphasis on technology use or the arts.

Yet another example of curricular innovation can be found at the Chula Vista Learning Community Charter (CVLCC) School in California, where 61% of the learners are ELL and over 50% qualify for free and reduced lunch. The students at this whole school TWICS actively take part in

'MicroSociety®' (www.microsociety.org), a program designed to teach students how to create functioning small communities and learn the realities of a free-market economy. Students from all grade levels form groups that design businesses and implement them throughout the school year. Some businesses have a 'green' focus by building and maintaining school gardens while others target student demand by making fruit smoothies. Parents speak enthusiastically about the program and affirm that it is critical to the school's overall success. MicroSociety, other curricular innovations and high expectations for all learners in their standards-based approach have contributed to recent academic successes at CVLCC (Christyn Pope, personal communication, 2 February 2010). In 2005, student achievement was not living up to expectations; only 27.8% of all students reached or exceeded standards in English language arts and only 39% in math. For ELLs, the percentages were 21% and 37%, respectively. Just four years later, in 2009, 67.3% of all students scored as proficient or advanced in English language arts and 86.7% in math. ELLs also showed improvement with 57% achieving or exceeding standards in English language arts and 81.6% in math. These results have made CVLCC #1 in math and #3 overall in the Chula Vista public school district (Christyn Pope, personal communication, 2 February 2010).

Admissions innovation

The enrollment figures presented earlier should not discourage people from attempting to implement Spanish (or other languages) and English TWI in areas with high concentrations of students from non-Latino or non-White racial and ethnic backgrounds. It is not uncommon for immersion programs in the United States (both one-way and two-way) to have difficulty attracting diverse student groups, especially African-Americans and third-language learners. To address this challenge, some TWICS utilize innovative recruitment and program marketing strategies. Although they were definitely in the minority, a few TWICS have above average African-American enrollment. For example, Unidos (Georgia) and Eugenio Maria de Hostos Charter School (EMHCS) in Rochester, New York both had African-American student enrollments greater than 50% at the time of this study, and others (e.g. Balere Language Academy, LAMB) enrolled between one-fifth to one-half African Americans. Each year EMHCS has improved student achievement, with the most recent test scores showing that of students in Grades 3–6, 81% and 99% scored at or above proficiency level in English language arts and math, respectively. Ninety-eight percent of 4th graders scored at or above proficiency in science, and 97% of 5th graders scored at or above proficiency in social studies (http://www.emhcs.org/prod/demographics.asp). Although these schools are few in number, they serve as proof that immersion can be an attractive option for African-Americans and other students of color. Most impressive are the achievement data reported by EMHCS (as one example), indicating the potential that TWI has for helping to lower the 'achievement gap' between students of color and White students that is so prevalent in US schools.

TWICS have a very promising future and present a host of possibilities for charter and noncharter immersion programs to consider. They offer children the chance to develop bilingualism and biliteracy, and some provide opportunities for third-/fourth-language learning and exposure to meaningful, relevant curricular options such as those described above. Freedom from common school district mandates indeed fosters innovation.

Notes

1. The US NCLB Act is federal legislation that requires school districts to achieve high academic standards and to comply with NCLB requirements in order to receive federal funding. The basic goal of the legislation – higher achievement and standards for ALL learners – is without dispute among educators. However, the 'test and punish' approach built into the legislation continues to receive criticism. Under the current Obama administration, the legislation is up for reauthorization by US Congress. For more information on NCLB, visit http://www.ed.gov/nclb/landing.jhtml. Accessed 25.2.10.
2. The Center for Applied Linguistics manages a Directory of TWI programs that can be accessed at http://www.cal.org/jsp/TWI/SchoolSearch.jsp. Accessed 25.2.10.
3. It is important to note that these authors, however, did find significant differences in the student populations of charter schools that were run by educational management organizations.
4. Bilingual education has a tumultuous history in the United States for a variety of political and historical reasons. Three states – California, Arizona and Massachusetts – have banned traditional bilingual programs, and TWI programs have been established in response. A chart documenting the growth of TWI in the United States since 1962 shows a tremendous increase in these programs during the late 1990s and 2000s (http://www.cal.org/twi/directory/twigrow.htm. Accessed 26.4.10). This growth is explained in large part by the antibilingual education legislation, which started in California in 1998 (Crawford, 2003).
5. These numbers for California and Texas do not change when factoring in for future growth.
6. A previous study (Howard & Sugarman, 2001) showed that on average, more language minority speakers come from impoverished backgrounds than do language majority speakers.
7. This quote is from the 2008 charter contract of the World Language Academy in Flowerly Branch, GA. It is an internal, unpublished (albeit public) document that I was given access to for this research.
8. This quote is from the 2004 charter contract of the Worthington Area Language Academy in Bigelow, MN. It is an internal, unpublished (albeit public) document that I was given access to for this research.

References

Battistich, V., Solomon, D., Kim, D., Watson, M. and Schaps, E. (1995) Schools as communities, poverty levels of student populations, and students' attitudes, motives, and performance: A multilevel analysis. *American Educational Research Journal* 32, 627–658.

Bogdan, R. and Biklen, S.K. (2003) *Qualitative Research for Education: An Introduction to Theory and Methods* (4th edn). Boston: Allyn and Bacon.

Center for Education Reform (2008) Quick facts about charter schools. On WWW at http://www.edreform.com/Issues/Charter_Connection/. Accessed 24.2.10.

Christian, D. (1996) Two-way immersion education: Students learning through two languages. *The Modern Language Journal* 80, 66–76.

Christian, D. (2008) School-based programs for heritage language learners: Two-way immersion. In D. Brinton, O. Kagan and S. Bauckus (eds) *Heritage Language Education: A New Field Emerging* (pp. 257–268). New York: Routledge.

Christian, D., Montone, C.L., Lindholm, K.J. and Carranza, I. (1997) *Profiles in Two-Way Immersion Education*. Washington, DC: Center for Applied Linguistics.

Chubb, J.E. and Moe, T.M. (1990) *Politics, Markets, and America's Schools*. Washington, DC: Brookings Institution.

Conrad, C.F., Haworth, J.G. and Millar, S.B. (2001) A positioned subject approach to inquiry. In C.F. Conrad, J.G. Haworth and L.R. Lattuca (eds) *Qualitative Research In Higher Education – Expanding Perspectives* (2nd edn) (pp. 203–216). Boston: Pearson.

Crawford, J. (2003) Hard sell: Why is bilingual education so unpopular with the American public? On WWW at http://www.languagepolicy.net/articles.html. Accessed 15.1.10.

Dougherty, K.J. and Sostre, L. (1992) Minerva and the market: The sources of the movement for school choice. *Educational Policy* 6, 160.

Frankenberg, E. and Lee, C. (2003) Charter schools and race: A lost opportunity for integrated education On WWW at http://epaa.asu.edu/ojs/article/view/260. Accessed 25.2.10.

Friedman, M. (1955) The role of government in education. In R.A. Solo (ed.) *Economics and the Public Interest* (pp. 123–144). New Brunswick, NJ: Rutgers University Press. On WWW at http://www.friedmanfoundation.org/friedman/friedmans/writings/1955.jsp. Accessed 8.3.10.

Green, P.C. and Mead, J.F. (2004) *Charter Schools and The Law: Establishing New Legal Relationships*. Norwood, MA: Christopher-Gordon.

Howard, E.R. and Sugarman, J. (2001) *Two-Way Immersion Programs: Features and Statistics*. Berkeley, CA: Center for Research on Education Diversity & Excellence.

Howard, E.R. and Sugarman, J. (2007) *Realizing the Vision of Two-Way Immersion: Fostering Effective Programs and Classrooms*. Washington, DC: Center for Applied Linguistics.

Ingersoll, R.M. (2004) *Why Do High-Poverty Schools Have Difficulty Staffing Their Classrooms with Qualified Teachers?* Washington, DC: Center for American Progress and the Institute for America's Future.

Klein, A. (2007) Governors enter fray over NCLB (cover story). *Education Week* 26, 1–28.

Lacireno-Paquet, N., Holyoke, T.T. and Moser, M. (2002) Creaming versus cropping: Charter school enrollment practices in response to market incentives. *Educational Evaluation & Policy Analysis* 24, 145–158.

Lindholm, K. (1990) Bilingual immersion education: Criteria for program development. In A. Padilla, H. Fairchild and C. Valadez (eds) *Bilingual Education: Issues
and Strategies* (pp. 91–105). Newbury Park, CA: Sage.

Lindholm-Leary, K. (2001) *Dual Language Education*. Clevedon: Multilingual Matters.

Lindholm-Leary, K. (2007) Top ten research findings on minority language
learners in two-way immersion programs. *ACIE Newsletter* 10, 9, 12.

Lindholm-Leary, K. and Howard, E.R. (2008) Language development and aca-
demic achievement in two-way immersion programs. In T.W. Fortune and
D.J. Tedick (eds) *Pathways to Multilingualism: Evolving Perspectives On Immersion
Education* (pp. 177–200). Clevedon: Multilingual Matters.

Mahoney, K.S. and MacSwan, J. (2005) Reexamining identification and reclassifica-
tion of English language learners: A critical discussion of select state practices.
Bilingual Research Journal 29, 31–42.

Manno, B.V., Vanourek, G. and Finn, C.E. (1999) Charter schools: Serving disadvantaged youth. *Education and Urban Society* 31, 429–445.

Ni, Y. (2007) *Are Charter Schools More Racially Segregated Than Traditional Public
Schools?* (Policy Rep. No. 30). East Lansing: Education Policy Center, Michigan
State University.

Orfield, G. and Lee, C. (2005) *Why Segregation Matters: Poverty and Educational
Inequality*. Cambridge: The Civil Rights Project at Harvard.

Rothstein, R. (2004) *Class and Schools: Using Social, Economic, and Educational Reform
to Close the Black–White Achievement Gap*. New York: Teachers College Columbia
University Economic Policy Institute.

RPP International (2000) *The State of Charter Schools, 2000. National Study of Charter
Schools, Fourth-Year Report*. Emeryville, CA: Author.

US Department of Education (2004) *Evaluation of the Public Charter Schools Program
Final Report*. Washington, DC: Office of the Undersecretary.

US Department of Education (2007a) *The Condition of Education 2007* (NCES 2007-
064). Washington, DC: National Center for Education Statistics. On WWW at
http://nces.ed.gov/pubs2007/2007064.pdf. Accessed 8.3.10.

US Department of Education (2007b) *K–8 Charter Schools: Closing the Achievement Gap*.
Washington, DC: Office of Innovation and Improvement. On WWW at http://
www2.ed.gov/admins/comm/choice/charterk-8/report.pdf. Accessed 8.3.10.

US Department of Education (2008) *The Condition of Education 2008*. Washington,
DC: National Center for Educational Statistics. On WWW at http://nces.ed.
gov/pubs2008/2008031.pdf. Accessed 9.3.10.

US Charter Schools (nd) On WWW at http://www.uscharterschools.org/pub/
uscs_docs/index.htm. Accessed 25.2.10.

Wells, A.S. (1998) *Beyond the Rhetoric of Charter School Reform: A Study of 10 California
School Districts*. Los Angeles: UCLA Graduate School of Education and
Information Studies.

West, A. (2006) 'Skimming the cream'? Admissions to charter schools in the United
States and to autonomous schools in England. *Educational Policy* 20, 615–639.

Whitt, E.J. (2001) Document analysis. In C.F. Conrad, J.G. Haworth and L.R. Lattuca
(eds) *Qualitative Research in Higher Education: Expanding Perspectives* (2nd edn)
(pp. 447–454). Boston: Pearson Custom Publishing.

Witte, J.F. (1990) Choice and control: An analytical overview. In W.H. Clune and
J.F. Witte (eds) *Choice and Control in American Education* (pp. 11–46). New York:
Falmer.

Part 2

Program Outcomes and Implications for Practice

Chapter 5

Student Outcomes in Chinese Two-Way Immersion Programs: Language Proficiency, Academic Achievement and Student Attitudes

K. LINDHOLM-LEARY

Introduction

The past five years have witnessed a surge in the interest and popularity of Chinese language programs in the United States (Asia Society and The College Board, 2008). A number of factors have converged to fuel this increase. One major stimulus is the rising economic and political power of China, which has led many businesses, educators and parents to request programs that can provide students with much higher levels of proficiency in Chinese (Asia Society and the College Board, 2008). Also, Chinese is the most widely spoken first language in the world (Asia Society, n.d.). Because of its expanding influence in the world, many K–12 school systems are recognizing the need to include Chinese in their language course offerings. At the federal level, funding has been provided by the US Department of Education in grants (e.g. Foreign Language Assistance Program, StarTalk and the Flagship programs) whose purpose is to establish foreign language programs that promote high levels of proficiency in US defense department-defined critical languages such as Chinese (US Department of Education, 2008). However, this interest also coincides with other factors, such as the active participation of various nongovernment organizations (e.g. American Council on the Teaching of Foreign Languages-ACTFL, Asia Society) and universities interested in furthering opportunities to promote Chinese language and culture in the United States. In addition, the Chinese government supports the teaching of Chinese, in part through the Confucius Institutes, which are located around the world, but headquartered in Beijing. Hoare (Chapter 11) addresses a related issue of immersion in a Chinese/English context, but looks at English immersion in Hong Kong and a program in Xi'an, China.

Chinese community issues

Demographic factors are also fueling the increasing interest in Chinese educational program options. According to US census reports and future estimates, the Asian population is expected to grow 213%, from 11.9 million in 2004 to 34.4 million in 2050 (US Census Bureau, 2004). Chinese Americans comprise about 1.2% of the US population, about one-fourth of all Asian Americans in the United States (Shinagawa & Kim, 2008). Close to one-third of the Chinese in the United States are US born, with about half of American-born Chinese living in either California or New York, and the remaining in 13 other states. The Chinese-American community consists of about half first-generation and half second- or later-generation individuals (Shinagawa & Kim, 2008).

Shinagawa and Kim (2008) describe the educational background of the Chinese population as following a bimodal distribution. They found that among Chinese Americans 25 and older, about 52% hold a college degree, which is twice the rate in the general population. On the other hand, at the lower end of the education continuum, slightly more Chinese Americans have less than a high school diploma (19%) than in the general population (16%).

Since the intermarriage rate is fairly high among Chinese Americans, it is not surprising that about one-tenth of Chinese Americans are multiethnic or multiracial. However, within this group, about 60% are a mix of Chinese and another Asian group, while 40% are Chinese and White non-Hispanic.

Added to the increasing Chinese population through immigration and reproduction is the continuing adoption of Chinese babies – mostly girls – into American homes, with approximately 67,842 adoptions since 1985 (Statistical Information on Adoptions from China, 2008); some adoptive parents request programs in Chinese to help their adopted children connect with their heritage language and culture.

The majority of Chinese Americans are bilingual, with 83.5% reporting that they speak a language in addition to English at home (Cantonese, Mandarin, Taiwanese or another language). Among immigrant Chinese individuals, about a third report that they are fluent in speaking English (Shinagawa & Kim, 2008).

Given the high rate of bilingualism in the Chinese-American community, it is not surprising that Chinese parents and communities request

Chinese programs for their children (Chang, 2003a). In studies of parental attitudes toward Chinese or Chinese-English bilingual education, Chinese parents – both native Chinese speaking (NCS) and native English speaking (ENS) – strongly support Chinese language or bilingual programs and want their children to be able to communicate within the Chinese-speaking community (Lao, 2004; Liao & Larke, 2008; Wu, 2005). Tse (2001) studied adult Chinese bilinguals and found that becoming biliterate required access to Chinese heritage language and literacy environments.

Several studies have documented the widespread cultural assimilation and language shift that occurs in second-generation and 1.5-generation Chinese children (e.g. Leung, 1997; Rosenthal & Feldman, 1990; Wong Fillmore, 1991; Zhang, 2005). While these children generally speak Chinese, they prefer English and feel considerable pressure to assimilate, both culturally and linguistically (Leung, 1997; Zhang, 2005). This pattern is parallel to that observed in Latino communities in the United States (see de Jong & Bearse, Chapter 6 and Dorner, Chapter 12, for additional reference to this phenomenon). Given this acculturation pressure in first versus later-generation Chinese-American children and adolescents, a study of two-way immersion (TWI) program students should differentiate between outcomes of NCS and ENS students, using primary language use as a proxy for acculturation (Deng & Walker, 2007). This is especially important in light of previous research on Spanish/English two-way programs that has shown important differences and similarities in comparing native Spanish-speaking versus English-speaking Hispanic students (e.g. de Jong & Bearse, Chapter 6).

Chinese language issues

Chinese is classified as part of the Sino-Tibetan language group, which includes about a billion or so speakers from Southeast Asia, South Asia and East Asia. In the United States, many people refer to the Chinese language as if it were one language, like English. However, there is actually no Chinese language per se; rather, we can think of Chinese as a language family (like the Romance language family) (Mair, 1991). Standard Mandarin is based on the Beijing dialect, and is the official language of the People's Republic of China, the Republic of China and is one of four official languages of Singapore. Other major Chinese languages include Standard Cantonese (one of the official languages of Hong Kong) and Hokkien (which is spoken in Taiwan, where it is called Taiwanese, and in Southeast Asia). While these spoken languages are mutually unintelligible, there is a common writing system, which is Mandarin. 'Along with the spread of literacy in China has been the extension of the use of Mandarin as the national spoken language, and the adoption of a standard spelling system called Pinyin, which uses the Roman alphabet to spell the pronunciation of Chinese characters' (Asia Society, n.d.).

While recognizing the fact that Chinese is not a language but a family of languages, Chinese is the term that will be used in this chapter. One reason is that the two schools discussed here differed in their Chinese-speaking populations so that one school taught Mandarin and another taught Cantonese. Because one school requested that they not be identified in any publications, that request is respected, leading to my use of the more general term Chinese.

Chinese language programs

Ten years ago, the National Council of Associations of Chinese Language Schools estimated that 82,675 students were enrolled in 634 Chinese language programs (including Saturday schools and after-school programs) across the country (Lao, 2004). The Center for Applied Linguistics' current National K–12 Foreign Language Survey of programs in the United States from 1987 to 2008 indicates that Chinese programs continue to increase and are offered at more schools than 10 years ago (Rhodes & Pufahl, 2009). Although there is no comprehensive study of schools offering Chinese, there may be about 779 Chinese programs, with about 57% of these programs in public schools and 43% in private schools, reflecting a growth of 200% from 2004 to 2006 (Asia Society and the College Board, 2008). While most students participate more in traditional Chinese programs (FLES or secondary foreign language), 15 immersion programs (Mandarin and/or Cantonese) – seven of which are TWI – are currently offered in the United States.

Clearly, there is a need for programs in Chinese, and research certainly demonstrates an increase in programs in Chinese at all levels, from elementary to middle school to high school to university. However, there appears to be more interest than current capability in offering these programs, largely due to a lack of national coordination efforts, an insufficiency of instructional materials and a shortage of credentialed teachers proficient in Chinese, among other factors (Asia Society and the College Board, 2008).

What is absent from the literature on Chinese language programs is research on language proficiency and achievement outcomes. Thus, in this chapter I will begin to fill this gap with an examination of students in Grades 4–7 who have participated since kindergarten or first grade in

Chinese TWI programs. More specifically, I report on students' oral language and reading and writing proficiencies in Chinese, academic achievement in English, and their language and cross-cultural attitudes.

Chinese TWI Programs

TWI programs in the United States typically bring together native Spanish-speaking and ENS students for academic instruction that occurs through both languages. While Spanish/English TWI programs are far more common than other language combinations, there is increasing interest in Chinese/English (mostly Mandarin/English) TWI programs. Regardless of the languages of the TWI program, the goals include bilingualism and biliteracy, academic achievement at or above grade level and cross-cultural competence for all students.

The definition of TWI programs encompasses four critical features: (a) instruction through two languages, where the non-English language (Chinese) is used for a significant portion (from 50% to 90%) of the students' instructional day, at least throughout elementary school; (b) periods of instruction during which only one language is used (i.e. no translation or language mixing); (c) approximately equal numbers of NCS and ENS students; and (d) students are integrated for most or all instruction (Lindholm-Leary, 2001). As Chang (2003b) has noted, characteristics of effective instruction noted for Spanish TWI programs (e.g. Howard *et al.*, 2007) are the same characteristics of high-quality instruction in Chinese TWI programs.

Most Chinese immersion programs use Mandarin, though there are a few Cantonese programs. Also, some programs follow the 80:20 TWI model and some follow the 50:50 TWI model. In the 80:20 TWI model, at the kindergarten and first grades, 80% of the instructional day is devoted to content instruction in Chinese, with the remaining 20% of instruction provided in English. Most content instruction occurs in Chinese, and English time is used to develop oral language proficiency and literacy skills. Reading instruction begins in Chinese and English for all students. In the second grade, students receive 70% of their instruction through Chinese and 30% through English; in the third grade, 60% is in Chinese and 40% is in English. By fourth and fifth grades, the students' instructional time is balanced between English and Chinese, and students continue to receive formal language arts instruction through both languages. In the 50:50 TWI model, students receive half of their instruction in Chinese and the other half in English throughout all of the elementary years.

As for the programs described here, Program 1 is 80:20 and Program 2 is 70:30. In both programs, students continue to study Chinese at middle school, with one or two periods of instruction devoted to Chinese. Both middle schools have a zero period (before school) Chinese language arts class and one school also has a content course taught through Chinese. As reiterated by Tedick, Christian and Fortune (Chapter 1), the program with only one course taught in Chinese does not qualify as an immersion continuation program.

Along with traditional Chinese characters, Mandarin phonetics (*zhu yin*) are taught, since they can be conceptually transferred to English phonetics. The pin yin (English character) Chinese phonetic system is taught in grades 4 and 5 (computer input for Chinese characters is in pin yin). Simplified Chinese characters are also taught in Grades 4–5. Research conducted by Chang and her colleagues (Chang, 2003a; Hung *et al.*, 1994) has shown that readers in both the Chinese and English writing systems use similar processes to construct meaning from print, though word identification clearly differs because of variations in the alphabetic writing system between English and Chinese (Hung & Tzeng, 1981).

In most states, Chinese TWI programs in public schools use the same district and state English curriculum standards as the English programs at their school sites. These Chinese programs have also developed many instructional materials, and they have purchased educational materials through online suppliers and through visits to Taiwan, Hong Kong and Mainland China.

At the sites included in our sample, the teachers are all native Chinese speakers and most received their education in a Chinese-speaking country. Thus, most teachers tend to be more traditional in their instructional approaches (Asia Society, n.d.).

Community descriptions

The two Chinese programs are located in two school districts in California. Each has been in existence for at least 10 years and has students in TWI who continue to study in Chinese at middle- and high-school levels. Because the demographics of the two communities differ, each will be described separately.

Program 1 is located in a very ethnically and socioeconomically diverse city, which includes pockets of various ethnic groups, including a substantial population of Asian (over 30%) and Chinese-background individuals.[1] About one-third of the population is foreign born and almost half speaks a language other than English at home. Median family income (over $80K) is well above the state average of $60K, and close to half of the adults above 25 years of age has a BA degree. About two-thirds of the elementary school's population includes Asian students, over 10% are English language learners (ELLs), and almost one-quarter are participating in the free-reduced price lunch program, which serves as a low-income indicator in the United States.

Program 2 is situated in a suburban community; its population includes about half Asian Americans – who are mostly Chinese – and half individuals who are foreign born. Median family income is high (over $130K), and close to three quarters of adults hold a BA degree or higher. Over three quarters of the elementary school population is Asian, with a small percentage of ELLs (over 10%) and a small percentage of students on free or reduced price lunch (around 5%).

At both sites, the TWI program is an articulated K–6 program that has a strand within one elementary school. Students can continue studying Chinese at the middle and high schools, where AP courses are offered.

The demographics of the Program 2 community are consistent with the stereotype of Chinese Americans (high parental education and income) while those of Program 1 are more consistent with the bimodal distribution of education as reported by Shinagawa and Kim (2008).

Student participants

A total of 320 students in Grades 4–8 from the two programs were included in this study. Table 5.1 provides information about these students according to some salient background characteristics. As Table 5.1 indicates, the great majority of participants in both programs were Chinese ethnic background (75% in Program 1 and 83% in Program 2), followed by students of other Asian backgrounds, and then about 10% in each program of non-Asian background students (e.g. Euro-American). While a greater majority of Program 1 students were native English speakers (60%), a slight majority of Program 2 students were native Chinese speakers (55%). By intersecting these categories of ethnicity and language, we can distinguish between ethnic Chinese native speakers (Chinese native speakers, CNS) and ethnic Chinese English speakers, or heritage language students (Chinese-English speakers, CES). Then we can also include other ethnic background students who speak English (English native speakers, ENS), though they might also speak another language at home.[2] As Table 5.1 indicates, there were more CNS students in Program 2 (54%) than

Table 5.1 Student characteristics in two Chinese TWI programs

	Program 1	*Program 2*
Number of students (number)	153	167
Grades 4–5 (Elementary school)	153[6]	103
Grades 6–8 (Middle school)	153	64
Ethnicity (%)		
Chinese background	75	83
Other Asian background	15	8
Non-Asian background	10	10
Language background (%):		
Chinese	39	55
English	60	45
Other	1	
Ethnicity and language background (%)		
CNS – Chinese native speaker	35	54
CES – Chinese English speaker	28	28
ENS – Other ethnic English speaker	37	18
Entered school as ELL (% of all students)		
Current ELL	5	1
English proficient	32	23
SES: Percent on free/reduced price lunch	26	NA
Educational background of mother (%)		
Up to high-school graduation	34	6
Some college	21	9
College degree	45	85
Special education	2	0

Program 1 (35%), but the same percent of CES (28%) in each program. There were twice as many ENS students in Program 1 (37%) compared to Program 2 (18%).

Despite the high number of CNS, especially in Program 2, there were very few students currently classified as ELLs (1–5%). Further, it appears that most of the CNS students in Program 1 entered school as ELLs though most of them were recategorized by the state assessment as English Proficient. In contrast, while there were 54% of CNS students in Program 2, only half of those entered school as ELL (23% English Proficient + 1% Current ELL), and almost every one of them had been reclassified as Fluent English by the time of this study.

Table 5.1 also shows the educational background of the mother as reported by the students. Clearly, most of the mothers in Program 2 had at least a college degree (85%) while half of the mothers in Program 1 had earned a college degree and one-third of Program 1 parents had a high school diploma or less. Thus, twice as many mothers in Program 2 had a college degree compared to mothers in Program 1. Also, 26% of Program 1 students were low SES, as defined by participation in the free/reduced price lunch program. This information was not available for Program 2 students. Finally, we see that 0–2% of students were identified for special education.

Student Outcomes

Research on TWI programs has consistently shown that TWI does meet its goals of bilingualism and biliteracy, academic achievement, and cross-cultural competence. However, most of this research has been conducted with Spanish programs and little research examines other language combinations (for reviews of research, see Bickle *et al.*, 2004; Lindholm-Leary, 2001; Lindholm-Leary & Howard, 2008). Most of this research has concentrated on academic achievement, with a few studies of oral language and literacy development, cross-cultural attitudes and behaviors (e.g. de Jong & Bearse, Chapter 6), teacher attitudes and knowledge, and parental attitudes and involvement.

Oral language development

Most research on oral language development in TWI programs has focused on Spanish TWI programs. This research has largely used rubrics to assess student proficiency in Spanish. Results from this body of research indicate that TWI native Spanish speakers and native English speakers develop intermediate to high levels of oral proficiency in Spanish. Not surprisingly, native speakers tend to develop higher levels of Spanish than English speakers (e.g. Lindholm-Leary & Howard, 2008). Lindholm-Leary (2003; Lindholm-Leary & Ferrante, 2005) compared TWI middle school and high school Hispanic Spanish native speakers to Hispanic native

English speakers and Euro-American English speakers, and found some interesting differences: Hispanic students, whether they were native Spanish or English speaking, were more comfortable in speaking Spanish, used Spanish more often, and rated themselves higher in Spanish fluency and grammar than Euro-English speakers. Otherwise, major differences in oral proficiency were related to whether the students were native Spanish or native English speakers. Based on this research, we would expect that native Chinese speakers would demonstrate higher levels of Chinese proficiency than native English speakers, but it is not clear whether we would expect differences between CES and ENS students.

In this research with Chinese TWI programs, each program developed a different measure of Chinese language proficiency:

- **Program 1:** the district developed a language proficiency rubric that could be used with a variety of different languages in their district. The teachers used the rubric to rate the students from 1 (beginning) to 6 (advanced) across the domains of listening, speaking, reading and writing.
- **Program 2:** district and school staff developed a test that students completed to assess speaking and listening, character recognition, reading and writing. This test was not normed and thus the metric provided was the percent of items answered correctly.

Figures 5.1 and 5.2 present the ratings given by the teachers to the Chinese- (CNS) and English-speaking (CES and ENS) students in

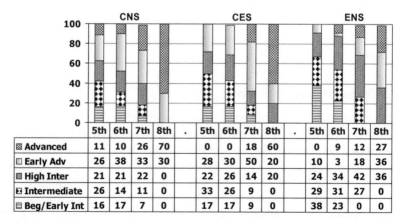

	CNS					CES					ENS			
	5th	6th	7th	8th	.	5th	6th	7th	8th	.	5th	6th	7th	8th
▨ Advanced	11	10	26	70		0	0	18	60		0	9	12	27
▢ Early Adv	26	38	33	30		28	30	50	20		10	3	18	36
▨ High Inter	21	21	22	0		22	26	14	20		24	34	42	36
▨ Intermediate	26	14	11	0		33	26	9	0		29	31	27	0
▤ Beg/Early Int	16	17	7	0		17	17	9	0		38	23	0	0

Figure 5.1 Listening/Speaking Development measured in Chinese (Rubric = 1, Beginning to 6, Advanced) – Program 1

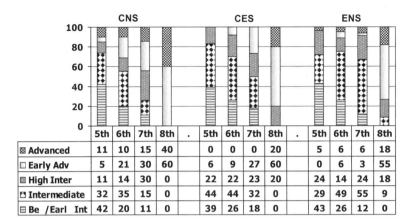

	CNS					CES					ENS			
	5th	6th	7th	8th	.	5th	6th	7th	8th	.	5th	6th	7th	8th
▨ Advanced	11	10	15	40		0	0	0	20		5	6	6	18
☐ Early Adv	5	21	30	60		6	9	27	60		0	6	3	55
▤ High Inter	11	14	30	0		22	22	23	20		24	14	24	18
▣ Intermediate	32	35	15	0		44	44	32	0		29	49	55	9
▤ Be /Earl Int	42	20	11	0		39	26	18	0		43	26	12	0

Figure 5.2 Reading Development measured in Chinese (Rubric = 1, Beginning to 6, Advanced) – Program 1

listening/speaking (Figure 5.1) and in reading (Figure 5.2) in Program 1. As these figures show, over time, from Grade 5 to Grade 8, we see fewer students in the lowest two categories (Beginning, Early Intermediate) and more in the Intermediate categories and then the Advanced categories. By eighth grade, all CNS were Early Advanced or Advanced in both listening/speaking and reading/writing (100%). Most CES (80%) and the majority of ENS (63–73%) eighth graders were also rated as Early Advanced or Advanced (80%) in listening/speaking and reading. While the trend was that CNS had the highest level of proficiency followed by CES and then ENS, this trend was not statistically validated. However, at Grades 6 and 7 for oral proficiency and at Grade 7 for reading, there were significant ethnic/language differences.

In Figure 5.3, we see the median percent correct achieved by students in Grades 4–7 in listening/speaking and reading/writing for Program 2. As Figure 5.3 indicates, students had fairly high median scores in both listening/speaking and reading/writing (at/above 81% correct) though the scores were lower for fourth graders (64–70%) and fifth-grade English speakers (72%).

Students' ratings of their Chinese proficiency

Students also rated their development of Chinese language and bilingual skills in a survey. In one set of items on the survey, students indicated their extent of agreement on a four-point Likert scale (from strongly agree

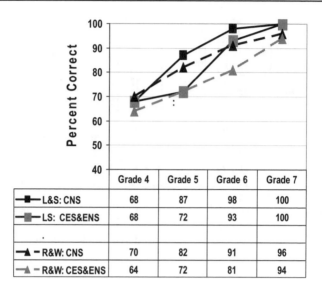

	Grade 4	Grade 5	Grade 6	Grade 7
■ L&S: CNS	68	87	98	100
■ LS: CES&ENS	68	72	93	100
▲ R&W: CNS	70	82	91	96
▲ R&W: CES&ENS	64	72	81	94

Figure 5.3 Listening/Speaking and Reading/Writing Development measured in Chinese (Median Percent Correct) – Program 2

to strongly disagree) about whether they have a variety of Chinese skills. Overall, students believed they possess various skills in Chinese, with the following percentages of students who agreed or strongly agreed: have conversations with their peers (83%), provide and obtain information (86%), express feelings and emotions (70%), express opinions about various topics (81%), understand and interpret written and spoken Chinese on a variety of topics (80%), and present information, concepts and ideas to an audience on a variety of topics (73%). Clearly the lowest level of agreement is on expressing feelings, an area of language development that is typically lacking in most immersion programs (Potowski, 2004; Tarone & Swain, 1995).[3] Broner and Tedick (Chapter 9) also report that children typically used English for socializing and Spanish for academic tasks. However, the Chinese TWI students also scored lower on being able to present information and ideas on a variety of topics, indicating that some students were not fully confident with the range of contexts or topics about which they can present information.

Students were also given rubrics to self-rate their Chinese listening comprehension, fluency and vocabulary on a scale from 1 to 5. Like most rubrics, there were descriptions of each numerical score for each language component. Results showed that there are some statistically significant differences between the means of the Chinese native speakers (CNS),

Chinese heritage/English speakers (CES) and English native speakers (ENS). Overall, findings indicated that:

(1) *Chinese listening comprehension:* (1 = understand simple questions/ statements, to 5 = understand everything at normal speed) – CNS students scored significantly higher than CES and ENS students; two-thirds of CNS, one-half of CES and one-third of ENS students rated themselves at a level 4 or 5 on the five-point scale for listening comprehension.

(2) *Chinese fluency:* (rating of 1 = participate in simple conversations on familiar topics at slower-than-normal speed, to 5 = native-like fluency); half of CNS and a quarter of English speakers (CES and ENS) rated their fluency as a 4 or 5, while close to half of English speakers rated their fluency at a level of 1 or 2.

(3) *Chinese vocabulary:* (1 = enough vocabulary to make simple statements/ask simple questions, to 5 = extensive native-like vocabulary); only 38% of CNS, 14–18% of CES and ENS gave themselves a 4 or 5. However, half of English speakers (CES and ENS) rated themselves a 1–2 while 28% of Chinese speakers did so.

When students were asked whether they believe they are 'very', 'somewhat' or 'not very' bilingual, 58% reported 'somewhat' and 39% responded 'very'. Not surprisingly, CNS students had significantly higher scores (were more likely to respond 'very') than CES and ENS students. Thus, it appears that students believe they have a range of skills in Chinese and that they are at least somewhat bilingual.

When students were asked to respond, from strongly agree to strongly disagree whether they read and write well in Chinese for their grade level, 70% agreed, though only 15% strongly agreed. Students also perceived that they can translate from Chinese to English or from English to Chinese (78%; 22% in strong agreement), though 79% indicated that they would like to learn to translate better.

Overall, these results show that both native Chinese speakers and native English speakers develop listening/speaking and reading/writing skills in Chinese as measured by the programs' assessments. These results are consistent with research in Spanish TWI programs. In self ratings, many Chinese native speakers rate their proficiency at higher levels than native English speakers, again a similar finding as in Spanish TWI programs. De Jong and Bearse (Chapter 6) report parallel results based on high-school students' (Latino and Anglo) ratings of their literacy skills in Spanish. In both Spanish and Chinese programs, there are about 10% of native speakers and English speakers who rate their

Chinese/Spanish skills at a fairly low level. Overall, in terms of language proficiency, results in Chinese TWI programs are consistent with those in Spanish TWI programs, showing that both TWI programs are able to help students develop bilingual skills at intermediate to high levels, which enable students to feel comfortable using these skills in a variety of contexts.

Academic achievement

Considerable research has examined the academic achievement of students in TWI programs (for reviews, see Bickle *et al.*, 2004; Lindholm-Leary, 2001; Lindholm-Leary & Borsato, 2006; Lindholm-Leary & Genesee, 2010; Lindholm-Leary & Howard, 2008). This research consistently demonstrates that students in TWI programs achieve at or above the performance of their peers who are not in TWI programs. These results hold whether we examine native English or native Spanish or Korean speakers. Lindholm-Leary (2001) reported that in three Korean 70:30 TWI programs, second- through fourth-grade native English-speaking students at one site scored well above grade level though students at another TWI site achieved below grade level. Native Korean-speaking third- and fourth-grade students achieved at or above grade level. Similarly, Bae (2007) and Chiappe *et al.* (2007) examined the English reading and writing progress of native English- and Korean-speaking first- and second-grade students in Korean TWI programs. They reported that both native English-speaking and native Korean-speaking children showed reading and writing development in English that was comparable or superior to their English-speaking peers in English mainstream programs.

There were two measures of achievement used in the programs in this study; both of these assessments were required by the State of California:

- **California Achievement Test (CAT6)** is a norm-referenced standardized test to assess academic achievement in English in the areas of reading and math.
- **California Standards Test (CST)** is a criterion-referenced achievement test developed by the State of California to assess students' level of achievement in English language arts and the content areas (e.g. math). This test categorizes students into five classifications: Far Below Basic, Below Basic, Basic, Proficient (at grade level) and Advanced (well above grade level).

On the CAT6, at all Grades 4–7, the Chinese TWI students achieved above grade level (defined as the 50th percentile) and slightly higher than the state average for students (whose parents had a college degree or higher) in both reading and math. By Grade 7, achievement was well above average to very high in both programs – and in both reading and math.

In addition, in comparing the math achievement of TWI students in Grade 6 to non-TWI English mainstream students at the same school, there was no difference (percentiles = 74 for TWI vs. 72 for English mainstream). What these results show is that Chinese TWI students achieve at or above grade-level norms and at least comparable to or higher than their same school and state peers in English while also continuing to develop proficiency skills in Chinese.

Although the goal as defined by the federal *No Child Left Behind* legislation (see Zehrbach, Chapter 4, for details) is for all students to score at Proficient or Advanced, the reality is that this goal is not reached at the state level in California with any subgroup of students. If we look at the state's average achievement for fourth- through eighth-grade students who have parents with a college education, between 62% and 73% of these students achieve at Proficient or Advanced, and about a third score as Advanced in English Language Arts. Comparing the state average to Program 1 students' average indicates that achievement in the Chinese TWI program is fairly comparable to the state average in English Language Arts (72–77% Proficient or Advanced), despite the fact that only half of these students have parents with a college degree and a third have parents who have a high school diploma or less. Program 2 students achieve at very high levels, with almost all students (89–100%) achieving at least Proficient and most (65–77%) reaching Advanced; their achievement is much higher than that of both Program 1 students and the state average in reading/language arts. Results in math paralleled findings in English language arts, though achievement was higher in math than language arts.

Collectively, these data indicate that students in Chinese TWI programs achieve at or above grade level and similar to or well above their peers who are not in TWI programs. Such results are consistent with previous research on Spanish TWI and Korean TWI programs (e.g. Bae, 2007; Chiappe *et al.*, 2007; Lindholm-Leary, 2001; Lindholm-Leary & Howard, 2008), which demonstrates that TWI students meet the goal of academic achievement at or above grade level while learning content through two languages. These data also provide further impetus for parents who might be concerned that students will not be able to learn content through a language as difficult as Chinese and be able to compete with their English-speaking monolingual peers.

Students' attitudes: Culture and cultural competence

At both program sites, curriculum was enhanced to incorporate culture, as consistent with the ACTFL Standards for Foreign Language Learning[4] (National Standards in Foreign Language Education Project, 2009). In Program 2, teachers carefully planned how they could incorporate these standards into their daily routines. In terms of addressing culture, teachers included activities such as Chinese New Year, Lantern Festival activities, making a travel brochure, cooking Chinese food and comparing and contrasting Chinese culture with other cultures as appropriate at different grade levels.

Students' attitudes toward and knowledge about culture were assessed on a student survey completed by 143 students. Students were asked to rate the following statement, 'I would say that I have __ knowledge of Chinese culture.' Their response options were 'little', 'some' and 'considerable'. About half of students responded that they have 'considerable', and close to half 'some', knowledge of culture. Similarly, when asked whether they understand some aspects of Chinese culture (literature, art, music), 91% of students agreed with that statement, though only a quarter of them strongly agreed. More specifically, when asked whether they enjoy Chinese music and/or art and literature, 66% of students agreed they did. There were no statistically significant differences in any of these items according to their ethnic/language group (CNS vs. CES vs. ENS).

About half of students (58%) agreed that they participate in cultural activities outside of school, and Chinese native speakers were no more likely to agree than English speakers, nor Chinese more than other ethnic groups.

Another important consideration in TWI programs is that students are provided with competencies and confidence to engage in cross-cultural interactions. Students were asked to respond to the statement, 'Interacting in situations/groups with mostly (Chinese or Chinese Americans; White/Euro-Americans; Other, select a group), I would say that I feel ...,' where the response options were Uncomfortable, Fairly Comfortable and Very Comfortable. Thus, the first question asked students to indicate their comfort with Chinese or Chinese Americans. For this ethnic group, 97% of TWI students reported feeling at least fairly comfortable (41% very comfortable). When rating other ethnic groups (e.g. White/Euro-Americans), most students (88–91%) were at least comfortable. These results suggest that the great majority of students report comfort in interacting with groups that are similar to and those that are different from them. De Jong and Bearse (Chapter 6) report similar results, though their survey prompts were more generic (i.e. referring to 'friends from different racial and ethnic backgrounds').

Finally, most students are glad they are in the Chinese program (81%), though only 68% of students say they enjoy studying through two languages. Interestingly, de Jong and Bearse (Chapter 6) found that 89% of Latinos and 97% of Anglos in TWI indicated that they enjoy learning Spanish and English. Such differences may be due to how the survey prompts are phrased. Nonetheless, the students in this study perceive advantages such as having a greater appreciation for other languages (88%) and understanding Chinese people better through learning Chinese (90%). About two-thirds of students report that when they have difficulty understanding something that is presented in one language (e.g. Chinese), they will use the second program language (i.e. English) to help them understand better (64%). This reliance on integrating their languages (i.e. using their multilingual competence), is also evident in Swedish immersion students in Finland (Björklund & Mård-Miettinen, Chapter 2).

Student background differences

Research with Spanish/English TWI programs suggests that student outcomes are positive and that the programs meet the language and achievement needs of most student participants regardless of certain student characteristics (e.g. Genesee *et al.*, 2006; Lindholm-Leary & Genesee, 2010; Lindholm-Leary & Howard, 2008). This research has consistently shown that students of different ethnicities, language backgrounds, socioeconomic levels and even those in special education develop proficiencies and reading and content area (e.g. mathematics) skills in the two languages of the TWI program. Thus, by the upper grade levels (late elementary or middle school), these students are able to score at least as well as their non-TWI same background peers. There is no research that supports the belief held by some educators that certain student characteristics should limit participation in TWI programs. See Fortune chapter (Chapter 13), which provides more discussion on students with special education needs who are in immersion programs.

In this study of Chinese TWI students, the only additional background factor that was examined was Socio-Economic Status, defined according to free/reduced price lunch program eligibility. When TWI students on free lunch were compared with their non-TWI peers at the same school who were also on free lunch, there was no significant difference between TWI students and their non-TWI peers ($M = 60.4$ vs. $M = 54$) on the norm-referenced CAT6 test. However, using scaled scores on the CST language arts test, TWI students scored significantly higher than non-TWI peers ($M = 375$, SD = 40.8 vs. $M = 354.5$, SD = 48.6, $t = 2.0$, $p < 0.05$). There were no significant differences between TWI and non-TWI students in the assessment of math achievement using either the CAT6 or CST.

Conclusions, Challenges and Possibilities

In this chapter, I have examined the oral language proficiency, literacy development, math achievement and attitudes of students in Chinese TWI programs at late elementary and middle school levels to determine the progress and attitudes of students in these programs. The findings have demonstrated that overall CNS, CES and ENS students: (a) make remarkable progress in both languages, (b) score at or above grade level in English, (c) perform at comparable or often superior levels compared to non-TWI peers and (d) report an interest in and knowledge about Chinese culture.

Several important conclusions can be drawn from this focus on Chinese TWI programs. First, there is much consistency between the findings reported here and those described for Korean and Spanish TWI programs. First, and most importantly, students in each of these programs are able to develop bilingual proficiency and literacy skills in both languages, and they are able to achieve in English at levels that meet or exceed their non-TWI peers. These Chinese program data join the Spanish program outcomes in demonstrating a native speaker effect, such that native speakers generally perform higher than second-language speakers in terms of both oral and written language proficiency (Lindholm-Leary, 2001; Lindholm-Leary & Howard, 2008). Second, Chinese programs are just as effective for native English speakers as Spanish programs in that these programs are capable of promoting literacy and content area skills in English; thus, parents of English-speaking children do not need to worry that Chinese will be too hard and will disrupt their children's language development and academic achievement. Rather, English speakers in Chinese and Spanish programs often outscore their English-speaking peers in English mainstream classes. Third, even low-SES children achieve as well or higher than their peers in English mainstream classes, showing that the Chinese programs do not work only for children from more advantaged family backgrounds. Again, these results are consistent with previous research in Spanish TWI programs showing that TWI programs are effective for students from different socioeconomic backgrounds (Genesee *et al.*, 2006). These results show the tremendous possibilities of TWI for promoting language proficiency and achievement in different populations of students in programs with different language combinations. While it is exciting to see the consistency of this research, far more studies are needed in TWI programs to better understand progress and relationships across the two languages, especially for languages that are very different from one another.

Another important finding is that sometimes but not consistently, the heritage language students (Chinese English speakers, Hispanic English speakers) have higher levels of self-rated proficiency in the heritage language or more positive attitudes than nonheritage English speakers (Lindholm-Leary, 2003; Lindholm-Leary & Ferrante, 2005). Even if the heritage language students do not show measurably higher language proficiency at this point, certainly they have an advantage that they possess the skills to maintain their language and culture if they desire to do so in the future. Both Li (2005) and Tse (2001) showed that Chinese heritage language students needed access to some sort of heritage language instruction in order to preserve their ability to use the language later on. Considerably more research needs to be done with this population to better understand the language and cultural needs and pressures of these students (Leung, 1997; Rosenthal & Feldman, 1990; Zhang, 2005). For now, this research joins other scholarship on heritage speakers, such as that of Peter *et al.*, Chapter 10, Ó Duibhir, Chapter 8, and Wilson and Kamanā, Chapter 3, in showing the possibilities provided by two-way, one-way and indigenous language immersion programs in promoting heritage language development in students.

The proficiencies and educational backgrounds of teachers are challenges in Chinese and other Asian language programs due largely to the shortage of teachers with appropriate credentials and language proficiencies for teaching in these programs (Asia Society, n.d.; Asia Society & The College Board, 2008). Considerably more research and policy attention is needed to address these challenges. Postsecondary programs that combine immersion teacher preparation with continued language development, such as that mentioned by Wilson and Kamanā (Chapter 3), are clearly needed to address the shortage of qualified immersion teachers with Chinese proficiency.

Another challenge addressed in this study concerns assessment. As mentioned previously, the two districts had developed their own assessment instruments for examining language proficiency and literacy in Chinese, with most based on teacher and student perceptions. While these instruments were helpful in understanding student development in Chinese, further work is needed in developing reliable and valid instruments in Chinese and other languages as well. More recently, newer measures of language proficiency in Chinese have been developed (e.g. STAMP, NOELLA).[5] However, these measures were developed for students in traditional foreign language programs, and more research is needed to determine their applicability for students, especially native speakers, in immersion programs. In this study, we noted that most students say they can translate between Chinese and English but would like to learn how to translate better. This area opens up an important avenue of possibilities. More information is needed about translation and how to effectively teach students to translate, especially since research shows that translation benefits student language proficiency (McQuillan & Tse, 1995).

In conclusion, the research presented in this chapter demonstrates that students in Chinese TWI programs develop bilingual, biliterate and multicultural competencies in addition to achieving at or above grade level in content areas. Considerably more research is needed to better understand program factors, student and family characteristics, teacher background and proficiencies, and other contextual factors that influence these patterns of proficiency and achievement.

Notes

1. Community demographic information is obtained from US Census Bureau American FactFinder 2005–2007. Figures are rounded to provide some anonymity.
2. There were insufficient students to further differentiate bilingual from English-Only students in this group.
3. Broner and Tedick (Chapter 9), Tarone and Swain (1995) and Potowski (2004) found that immersion students often possess a limited vernacular in the target language to explain everyday topics such as, feelings, likes and dislikes, greetings and so on.
4. First published in 1996, the ACTFL standards describe content standards that specify what students should know and be able to do with the language they are learning. Although these standards are more commonly used in one-way foreign language immersion programs, they can serve as a valuable resource for TWI and indigenous immersion programs. The executive summary of the standards can be accessed at: http://www.actfl.org/i4a/pages/index.cfm?pageid=3324. Accessed 28.4.10.
5. For more information on assessment in second language learning students and programs, see the Center for Applied Linguistics Resource Guide on Second Language Proficiency Assessment, http://www.cal.org/resources/archive/rgos/assessment.html; Center for Advanced Research on Language Acquisition (CARLA) Virtual Assessment Center, http://www.carla.umn.edu/assessment/VAC/research/theory.html. Accessed 28.4.10.
6. The 153 students in Grades 6–8 were the same students in Grades 4–5. Longitudinal data provides information on student outcomes at this grade level.

References

Asia Society (n.d.) Chinese language: Myths and facts. On WWW at http://www. asiasociety.org/education-learning/world-languages/chinese-language-initiatives/chinese-language. Accessed 28.4.10.

Asia Society and The College Board (2008) Chinese in 2008: An expanding field. On WWW at http://www.asiasociety.org/files/Chinesein2008.pdf. Accessed 28.4.10.

Bae, J. (2007) Development of English skills need not suffer as a result of immersion: Grades 1 and 2 writing assessment in a Korean/English two-way immersion program. *Language Learning* 57, 299–332.

Bickle, K., Hakuta, K. and Billings, E.S. (2004) Trends in two-way immersion research. In J.A. Banks and C.A.M. Banks (eds) *Handbook of Research on Multicultural Education* (2nd edn) (pp. 589–604). New York: Macmillan.

Chang, J.M. (2003a) Language and literacy of Chinese American communities. In B. Perez (ed.) *Sociocultural Contexts of Language and Literacy* (pp. 163–187). Mahwah, NJ: Lawrence Erlbaum.

Chang, J.M. (2003b) Strategies for effective two-way immersion programs: A Chinese American perspective. *NABE News* 26, 28–31.

Chiappe, P., Glaeser, B. and Ferko, D. (2007) Speech perception, vocabulary, and the development of reading skills in English among Korean- and English-speaking children. *Journal of Educational Psychology* 99, 154–166.

Deng, J. and Walker, G.J. (2007) Chinese acculturation measurement. *Canadian Ethnic Studies Journal* 39, 181–217.

Genesee, F., Lindholm-Leary, K.J., Saunders, W. and Christian, D. (2006) *Educating English Language Learners: A Synthesis of Empirical Evidence.* New York: Cambridge University Press.

Howard, E.R., Sugarman, J., Christian, D., Lindholm-Leary, K.J. and Rogers, D. (2007) *Guiding Principles for Dual Language Education* (2nd edn). Washington, DC: Center for Applied Linguistics.

Hung, D.L. and Tzeng, O.J. (1981) Orthographic variations and visual information processing. *Psychological Bulletin* 90, 377–414.

Hung, D.L., Tzeng, O.J., Lee, E.L. and Chang, J.M. (1994) Orthography, reading disability, and cerebral organization. In W.C. Watt (ed.) *Writing Systems and Cognition* (pp. 11–35). Amsterdam: Kluwer Academic Publishers.

Lao, C. (2004) Parents' attitudes toward Chinese-English bilingual education and Chinese-language use. *Bilingual Research Journal* 28, 99–117.

Leung, E.K. (1997) Acculturation gap and relationship between first and second generation Chinese Americans. Paper presented at Annual Meeting of the Mid-South Educational Research Association, Memphis, TN, November 13.

Li, M. (2005) The role of parents in Chinese heritage-language schools. *Bilingual Research Journal* 29, 197–207.

Liao, L. and Larke, P. (2008) The voices of thirteen Chinese and Taiwanese parents sharing views about their children attending Chinese heritage schools. *US-China Education Review* 5, 1–8.

Lindholm-Leary, K.J. (2001) *Dual Language Education.* Clevedon: Multilingual Matters.

Lindholm-Leary, K.J. (2003) Dual language achievement, proficiency, and attitudes among current high school graduates of two-way programs. *NABE Journal* 26, 20–25.

Lindholm-Leary, K.J. and Borsato, G. (2006) Academic achievement. In F. Genesee, K. Lindholm-Leary, W. Saunders and D. Christian (eds) *Educating English Language Learners* (pp. 176–222). New York: Cambridge University Press.

Lindholm-Leary, K.J. and Ferrante, A. (2005) Follow-up study of middle school two-way students: Language proficiency, achievement and attitudes. In R. Hoosain and F. Salili (eds) *Language in Multicultural Education* (pp. 157–179). Greenwich, CT: Information Age.

Lindholm-Leary, K. and Genesee, F. (2010) Alternative educational programs for English language learners. In California Department of Education (eds) *Improving Education for English Learners: Research-Based Approaches* (pp. 323–382). Sacramento: CDE Press.

Lindholm-Leary, K.J. and Howard, E. (2008) Language and academic achievement in two-way immersion programs. In T. Fortune and D. Tedick (eds) *Pathways to Bilingualism: Evolving Perspectives on Immersion Education* (pp. 177–200). Clevedon: Multilingual Matters.

Mair, V.H. (1991) What is a Chinese 'Dialect/Topolect'? Reflections on some key Sino-English linguistic terms. On WWW at http://sino-platonic.org/complete/spp029_chinese_dialect.pdf. Accessed 28.4.10.

McQuillan, J. and Tse, L. (1995) Child language brokering in linguistic minority communities: Effects on cultural interaction, cognition, and literacy. *Language and Education* 9, 195–215.

National Standards in Foreign Language Project (2009) *Standards for Foreign Language Learning: Preparing for the 21st Century* (3rd edn). Alexandria, VA: American Council on the Teaching of Foreign Languages (ACTFL).

Potowski, K. (2004) Student Spanish use and investment in a dual immersion classroom: Implications for second language acquisition and heritage language maintenance. *Modern Language Journal* 88, 75–101.

Rhodes, N.C. and Pufahl, I. (2009) *Foreign Language Teaching in U.S. Schools: Results of a National Survey*. Washington, DC: Center for Applied Linguistics.

Rosenthal, D.A. and Feldman, S.S. (1990) The acculturation of Chinese immigrants: Perceived effects on family functioning of length of residence in two cultural contexts. *Journal of Genetic Psychology* 151, 495–514.

Shinagawa, L.H. and Kim, D.Y. (2008) *A Portrait of Chinese Americans*. UCSB: Linguistic Minority Research Institute.

Statistical Information on Adoptions from China (2008) On WWW at http://www.fwcc.org/statistics.html. Accessed 28.4.10.

Tarone, E. and Swain, M. (1995) A sociolinguistic perspective on second language use in immersion classrooms. *Modern Language Journal* 79, 166–178.

Tse, L. (2001) Resisting and reversing language shift: Heritage-language resilience among U.S. native biliterates. *Harvard Educational Review* 71, 676–708.

US Census Bureau (2004) Asian alone population in the United States: (Based on Census 2000). On WWW at http://www.census.gov/population/www/socdemo/race/ppl-184.html. Accessed 28.4.10.

US Department of Education (2008) Enhancing foreign language proficiency in the United States: Preliminary results of The National Security Language Initiative. On WWW at http://www.ed.gov/about/inits/ed/competitiveness/nsli/about.html. Accessed 28.4.10.

Wong Fillmore, L. (1991) When learning a second language means losing the first. *Early Childhood Research Quarterly* 6, 323–346.

Wu, C. (2005) Attitude and behavior toward bilingualism for Chinese parents and children. In J. Cohen, K.T. McAlister, K. Rolstad and J. MacSwan (eds) *ISB4: Proceedings of the 4th International Symposium on Bilingualism* (pp. 2385–2394). Somerville, MA: Cascadilla Press.

Zhang, D. (2005) Home language maintenance and acculturation among second-generation Chinese children. Dissertation thesis, University of Pennsylvania.

Chapter 6

The Same Outcomes for All? High-School Students Reflect on Their Two-Way Immersion Program Experiences

E.J. DE JONG and C.I. BEARSE

Introduction

Two-way immersion (TWI) programs have become a successful model for bilingual development for majority and minority language speakers in the United States. As mentioned in the introductory chapter by Tedick, Christian and Fortune, TWI programs ideally enroll equal numbers of native speakers of both languages of instruction in the program. Like the other immersion program models showcased in this volume, TWI programs are an example of additive, enrichment-oriented bilingual education programs that aim to develop high levels of bilingualism and positive cross-cultural attitudes while maintaining high standards for academic achievement for all students through an integrated approach (cf., Dorner, Chapter 12; Lindholm-Leary, 2005; Chapter 5; Zehrbach, Chapter 4).

Most of the research on TWI has focused on the language, academic and sociocultural outcomes of elementary programs, especially at the Grade K–3 level (for overviews, see Howard *et al.*, 2003; Krashen, 2004). The outcomes for elementary programs appear consistently positive and in favor of students attending a TWI program when compared to similar students in other programs (Lindholm-Leary, 2001; Chapter 5). In contrast, only a handful of studies have focused on students in secondary TWI programs. The purpose of this chapter is to report on a study that was concerned with the experiences of high school students who had attended TWI in elementary and secondary school and were still attending a specialized class in high school. We begin with a brief overview of developments and research in secondary TWI in the United States. We then present findings from a study with 48 high school TWI students and conclude with a discussion of possible future directions for improving the design and implementation of secondary TWI programs.

Secondary TWI Programs: Trends and Outcomes

The development of secondary TWI programs is challenging due to the complexity of secondary school organization and the absence of vertical articulation of a TWI program across school levels. Finding qualified teachers, developing appropriate curricula and addressing differences in student proficiency levels and motivation are additional factors that affect secondary TWI program design and implementation (Cruz, 2000; Montone & Loeb, 2000). In addition, many elementary TWI programs have not yet matured into K–5/6 programs to then be able to feed into a middle school or the program ends at Grade 5/6 because a middle school continuation program is not available. Not surprisingly, then, secondary-level TWI programs are much smaller in number than elementary programs. As of December 2009, the Center for Applied Linguistics TWI Directory listed 70 middle school and 15 high school programs,[1] most of them located in the Southwest.

Few data exist to guide secondary TWI program implementation. Longitudinal studies that have considered the achievement of secondary TWI students suggest a mixed outcome pattern, varying between no differences between TWI and non-TWI student performance and a positive effect of TWI participation on some but not all indicators. For instance, TWI 7th-grade students consistently outperformed peers attending the same school on the California's state-mandated achievement test in English (Lindholm-Leary, 2005). Middle school Anglo and Latino students in the Amigos program in Cambridge, Massachusetts did as well as or outperformed their control groups on the California Achievement Tests in English reading and math (Cazabon *et al.*, 1998). In contrast, Cobb *et al.* (2006) found no significant differences at the middle school level between TWI and non-TWI students in terms of English reading or math. Kohne (2006) looked at high school TWI students who had attended an elementary TWI program and found that they selected a significantly higher number of advanced placement classes in high school and that TWI-Hispanic students had more positive attitudes toward school and higher self-esteem than non-TWI-Hispanic students. Students in a similar study by Lindholm-Leary and Borsato (2001, 2005) also reported that being in TWI played an important role in staying in school.

While secondary-level studies address English achievement, there are scant findings about minority language and literacy development. Only a few studies report on performance in Spanish at the secondary level (Cazabon *et al.*, 1998; Lindholm-Leary, 2001). Students in 90:10 TWI programs perform at grade level in Spanish reading, language and math in middle school (Lindholm-Leary, 2001). In the 50:50 Amigos program, on the other hand, Spanish achievement declined in middle school, resulting in below grade-level scores in Spanish reading (Cazabon *et al.*, 1998). As a proxy for Spanish language development, Kohne (2006) looked at advanced foreign language classes (defined as level III or IV) and found that 91% of Caucasian and 61% of Hispanic TWI students enrolled in these classes as opposed to 42% of Caucasian and 48% Hispanic non-TWI students. Lindholm-Leary (Chapter 5) reports on positive academic and socioaffective outcomes for Chinese language and literacy development in upper elementary (Grades 4–5) and middle school (Grades 6–8) TWI students.

In addition to these program evaluation studies, a few studies have documented the experiences of TWI secondary teachers and their classrooms practices (Freeman, 2000; Hsieh, 2007) and parent or student attitudes and experiences (Hsieh, 2007; Lindholm-Leary & Borsato, 2005; McCollum, 1999). Interviews with administrators and teachers stress the challenge of scheduling, balancing the two languages and professional development for teachers (Cruz, 2000; Freeman, 2000; Montone & Loeb, 2000). McCollum's work (1999) is a notable exception to the dearth of qualitative studies in secondary TWI classrooms (see also Cruz, 2000; Hsieh, 2007 for observational data). Observing in a middle-school TWI program, she found that the Spanish teacher's explicit disapproval of the students' nonstandard Spanish language use and group work undermined the students' motivation and opportunity to use Spanish. English held more social and cultural currency for the students, even for relative newcomers to the United States. As a result, the students' identity and language investment shifted to English acquisition rather than Spanish maintenance and bilingualism.

In order to implement quality secondary TWI programs there is a need to better understand how the three program goals – academic achievement, bilingualism/biliteracy and the development of cross-cultural competence – can be realized at this level. The purpose of this study was to begin to address this gap by focusing on students' experiences. Specifically, we sought to explore the following research questions in a secondary TWI program in one district:

(1) Do high school TWI students still attending a TWI program consider themselves bilingual and bicultural?

(2) Why is remaining in the TWI program important?
(3) In what ways does the TWI program design support the desired out-
     comes (as perceived by the high school TWI students)?

Research Design

In this qualitative study we explored how TWI high-school students
perceived their middle and/or high school TWI program experiences. The
study took place in a medium-sized, linguistically and culturally diverse
school district in the Northeast of the United States. The site was selected
because of the existence of a longstanding TWI program that is articulated
from kindergarten through the 12th grade.

The TWI program began with kindergarten and first grade in 1990 as a
strand within an English-medium school. The program has typically
enrolled 50% (Anglo) native English speakers and 50% (Latino) Spanish-
dominant and generally limited English-proficient students. Elementary
TWI students received literacy development in their native language in
K–2; as of third grade 50% of instruction is in English and 50% is in Spanish.
The 6–8 TWI program is a strand located in a separate English-medium
middle school. At this level, TWI students take Language Arts and Social
Studies in Spanish; all other subjects are in English and taken with non-
TWI students. Students can continue their Spanish language development
at the comprehensive high school (Grades 9–12) in specialized Spanish
Language and Literature classes for three years, though, strictly speaking,
this is no longer considered immersion.[2] In the 12th grade, they enroll in
an Advanced Placement (AP) Spanish language class in their final year
and take the AP Spanish language exam. All other classes are standard
curriculum classes where the TWI students are fully integrated with non-
TWI students.

Data collection and analysis

Data were collected over a period of almost one year (June–March) at
three intervals. Data sources consisted of individual student survey
responses and focus groups involving three or four students. The survey
asked students to indicate which language they spoke most at home and
with friends, and which language they spoke, read, wrote and liked best
(Spanish, English or both). The second part of the survey consisted of
statements about attitudes toward school and bilingualism. Students were
asked to indicate their agreement or disagreement with each statement
on a 4-point scale (4 = strongly agree; 1 = strongly disagree). Whenever

feasible, focus groups consisted of students having the same ethnicity. Students were asked to describe their experiences at the elementary, middle and the high school level in general, though many talked about the TWI classes in particular. They were also asked to identify what made a particular school level difficult or easy and what teachers could do to help them learn better. Finally, each student was asked to reflect on whether they considered themselves bilingual and bicultural. Focus groups were audiotaped and transcribed for coding.

This high school study is part of a larger study where both middle and high school students were surveyed and interviewed. For the high school sample (Grades 9–12), all students in designated TWI classes and the Advanced Placement Course were surveyed ($n = 48$); 33 students participated in six focus groups lasting on average 35 minutes. Of those students surveyed, 40% were Latino and 60% Anglo; 27% were male and 73% female. To analyze the interview and short answers on the survey, we followed the standard coding technique of categorizing and sorting data (Lofland & Lofland, 1995), using the NVIVO qualitative research tool. From the patterns that emerged from the data, theories were generated collaboratively between the two researchers and triangulated with the data (Glaser & Strauss, 1967). Descriptive statistics and comparisons between groups and grades were conducted for the Likert-scale items of the survey.

Findings

We first focus on whether students in this high-school TWI program sample saw themselves as bilingual and bicultural (Research question 1). Then, we address the question of student-defined outcomes (Research question 2) and themes related to program structure and design (Research question 3).

Bilingualism and biculturalism

Two major goals of TWI programs are that their students become bilingual and bicultural. During the focus groups, students were asked whether they thought they were bilingual. All TWI students indicated that they felt they were. In the case of Anglo students, the reasoning was often that they had been in the program since kindergarten and had been speaking Spanish since the beginning.

> I'd say that everyone that started the bilingual program since kindergarten is bilingual because if you compare their Spanish with the

Spanish of the other kids who started in like middle school, it's a lot better and there's like no comparison between the two. So I would say everyone is bilingual. (Grade 10 Anglo male)

For the Latino students, being bilingual was linked to speaking Spanish at home in addition to being in the program. As one female Latina 10th grader stated, 'I can speak both languages, even though I speak Spanish because that's what I usually speak at home.'

The individual student survey extended the question of bilingualism to include biliteracy. The survey asked students to agree or disagree with the statement 'I am a strong reader/writer in English/Spanish' and to indicate which language they felt was their strongest in speaking, reading and writing. Anglo students indicated they felt stronger in English than Spanish on all items. The Latino students indicated they felt both languages were their strong languages but agreed more strongly with 'I am a strong reader in English (Spanish)' than with the statement 'I am a strong writer in English (Spanish)' (Table 6.1).

In terms of (bi)culturalism, Anglo students felt more culturally aware yet not bicultural, whereas Latino students identified themselves consistently as bicultural (see also Bearse & de Jong, 2008). Several Anglo students referenced projects they had done in middle school about different countries (country studies, readings) as illustrations of their increased cultural knowledge. They also referenced increased sensitivity and comfort level with students from diverse backgrounds, particularly when comparing themselves with friends who had not attended the program.

Table 6.1 TWI high-school students' perception of their literacy skills in English and Spanish

Statement	Latino students				Anglo students			
	SA	A	D	SD	SA	A	D	SD
I am a strong writer in Spanish.	32%	42%	26%	0%	10%	45%	45%	0%
I am a strong reader in Spanish.	68%	32%	0%	0%	17%	45%	34%	3%
I am a strong writer in English.	26%	63%	5%	5%	61%	36%	4%	0%
I am a strong reader in English.	58%	37%	5%	0%	69%	31%	0%	0

SA = Strongly agree; A = agree; SD = strongly disagree; D = disagree.

Table 6.2 Students' attitudes toward diversity and bilingualism

Statement	Latino				Anglo			
	SA	A	D	SD	SA	A	D	SD
I like meeting and listening to people who speak another language.	63%	26%	11%	0%	59%	38%	3%	0%
I have many friends from different racial and ethnic backgrounds.	84%	11%	0%	5%	45%	45%	10%	0%
It is important to know another language to learn about other people.	68%	26%	0%	5%	59%	38%	3%	0%
Knowing two languages makes you smarter than only knowing one language.	37%	21%	32%	11%	38%	57%	7%	3%
Knowing two languages will help you get better grades.	37%	32%	16%	16%	31%	38%	28%	3%
Knowing two languages helps you get a good job when you grow up.	79%	16%	0%	5%	69%	31%	0%	0%
I like learning Spanish and English.	68%	21%	11%	0%	69%	28%	3%	0%
I want to continue learning Spanish and English, like I do now.	84%	5%	5%	5%	76%	21%	3%	0%

SA = Strongly agree; A = agree; SD = strongly disagree; D = disagree.

Table 6.2 shows that most Anglo students indicate having diverse friends and enjoy speaking with people who speak other languages.

The Latino students grounded their bicultural identity in their home environment where they spoke Spanish and lived both cultures. Even though most of them were second or third generation, they still felt a close affinity with their Latino cultural group because of their family relationships. As one 9th-grade Latina student explained, 'I say I'm bicultural 'cause at home I, like, it's our native culture. But then, again, when we're at school and when we're out you know, we live in America, so I'm American, too.' Most Latino students indicate having diverse friends (95% agreed or strongly agreed) and enjoy meeting other people (Table 6.2).

Whereas students were unanimously positive about the program, their perceptions of attaining bilingualism and biculturalism and the importance of learning Spanish differed. Both Anglo and Latino students saw themselves as bilingual but only the Latinos also viewed themselves bicultural. Although Anglo students thought they were more culturally sensitive and knowledgeable than their non-TWI Anglo peers, they did not identify as bicultural. According to students, the program appears to meets its goal of bilingualism for all but the goal of biculturalism is perceived differently for Latinos and Anglos.

Reasons for remaining in the program

Although all students in the sample were still enrolled in a TWI class, they are a select group of those students who remained in the program. The almost 50 high school students (9–12) represent four cohorts of elementary program students. Considering that each cohort entering kindergarten, on average, consists of about 50 students (25 Anglo and 25 Latino), the remaining students represent about one-quarter of the original cohorts. Anecdotally, it is known that about 20% of the elementary students leave the program, primarily due to families moving out of the district. Between middle and high school, attrition is partially due to students going to private high school or, particularly in the case of the Latino students, electing to attend the vocational high school. Additional reasons mentioned by teachers and students were the selection of a different language and need of more communication and follow-up as students move from middle to high school.

The second research question focused on students' views of the value of bilingualism and why they remained in the program. The survey questioned them about their attitudes toward the value of bilingualism. As responses indicate (Table 6.2), students clearly agreed that they like learning two languages and they see bilingualism as important for improved job opportunities and for learning about other people. Students are less convinced that bilingualism results in better grades, however.

In the focus groups, both groups of students reiterated some of these arguments but also added some different emphases. Anglo students stressed having a competitive edge in the job market and the value of program attendance for college application. They also discussed being able to use Spanish when traveling.

> I think it's really helpful knowing Spanish, being fluent in it. Like a couple years ago I went to Mexico and I was speaking with like the

natives and stuff. That's pretty cool. I like that, and also it's really helpful in terms of getting into a good college, getting a job and stuff like that. (Grade 10 Anglo male)

Latino students also frequently mentioned employment opportunities. However, they stressed their ability to help those who may not be able to speak English

By talking the both languages, having them equal is a good advantage for the future. And if you want to get a good job it's good, because you'll understand more people ... and you would be able to understand them. (Grade 10 Latina)

In addition, the Latino students referenced that their parents felt it was important for them to stay in the program.

It was good because I got to be in both Spanish and English classes, which is what my parents wanted so I wouldn't lose my Spanish which was my first language ... because my grandparents speak Spanish so they don't want me to lose that and not be able ... it would be harder to communicate, so it helped me with keeping my original Spanish but learning English, too. (Grade 12 Latina)

Most students indicated that they would stay in the program even after the foreign language requirement had been met. Most argued that it would be a waste to stop after so many years of attending the program. A Grade 10 Anglo male student commented: 'Also, I think if you've invested so many years into something, like the bilingual program, I think it's a waste to stop after that ...'

Some of the Latino students commented how the program allowed them to see their friends, and this was an important incentive for staying in the program. For example, one 10th-grade Latina asserted: 'Well, I sort of didn't want to leave, one, because of my friends, 'cause I've been with them since kindergarten, so why would I want to like go out into – I'm sort of shy in that case. So like I didn't want to leave them ...' A few Latinos students thought about changing to another language after 10th grade because they felt they were already fluent in Spanish. 'My first language was Spanish, so obviously I already know Spanish and I'm good at that. But learning a different language, I guess, would be fun. It would be fun 'cause you could communicate with people in different ways' (Grade 9 Latina).

Most TWI high school students intended to remain in the program after 10th grade (after having fulfilled foreign language requirements) to ensure that their investment would pay off and to remain with friends. Anglo students' responses reflected an instrumental motivation (Gardner, 2001). Their answers also reflected cross-cultural dimensions as they thought it would be useful for traveling. While mentioning job opportunities as well, Latino students particularly stressed the importance of Spanish for maintaining social (family and community) relationships, or integrative motivational reasons. This finding paralleled the emphasis of Latino middle school students on family and identity in our previous work (Bearse & de Jong, 2008). When talking about work, Latino students recounted their bilingual abilities to be able to communicate with others and helping others who do not speak English. The ability to help others was also identified as a major reason for enrollment in a bilingual education program by Soto (2002).

Interestingly, these differential motivations seem to parallel parents' reasons for placing their child in a two-way program. Latino parents tend to stress the importance of Spanish language maintenance for the purpose of ethnic identity, connections with family and relatives, and instilling a sense of pride in the language and culture of their own ethnic group (e.g. Giacchino-Baker & Piller, 2006; Shannon & Milian, 2002). Anglo parents, while certainly mentioning the importance of exposure to cultural diversity, emphasize job opportunities and college entrance (see also Schmidt, 2007, who exclusively looked at Anglo parent attitudes).

This finding reflects important cultural differences between the two groups. The importance of family in Latino cultures has been documented in numerous studies (Louie, 2006; Quiroz, 2001; Suarez-Orozco & Suarez-Orozco, 1995; Zarate *et al.*, 2005). This cultural difference also helps to explain the centrality of maintaining proficiency in Spanish for minority language parents because such proficiency plays a key role in sustaining family relationships with immediate and extended family (many of whom are often still in the home country) as well as to help children negotiate the realities of cyclical migration (transnationalism) (Vega de Jesús & Sayer, 2006).

Program design and program outcomes

By the time they leave their elementary program, the TWI program increasingly becomes defined in terms of Spanish and Spanish classes. A dominant theme in the focus groups was a strong sense of loss of 'two-way' identity. As a 10th-grade Anglo male commented

> I felt like [the elementary program] had a better structure because it's more two-way. And then like each school you go to it kind of dies a

little bit … It's not really like two-way. I can't really think of it as that. And then at [the high school] then it's just like a Spanish class where you're advanced.

Another 10th grader commented, 'In middle school there's an actual legitimate bilingual program, and when you get to high school you just take a Spanish class, but they don't actually have the bilingual program. After 8th grade we had our graduation from the bilingual program.' By the time the TWI program arrives at the high school level, students don't really consider it to be TWI anymore. 'I don't really think it's a two-way program now with just one class. And most people don't even know it exists.'

The students identified areas that emerge as barriers to long-term program success for comprehensive Spanish language development and maintenance: diminished amount of instructional time in Spanish, the role of the content area for Spanish language development, and the focus of the Spanish language arts curriculum. These three themes are illustrated in more depth in the following sections.

Instructional time in Spanish. Students commented extensively on their diminishing oral proficiency as a result of the decreased time spent in Spanish. In high school, their lives predominantly consist of English for social and academic purposes. As one Anglo 10th-grade male student explained,

It almost feels like we've kind of reached a plateau. We're all like kind of stuck. I'm not really getting better because it's hard to like keep improving and not speak Spanish full time. Like you go like five of the seven days just for an hour. That's the only time I ever use Spanish.

The Latino students also expressed their concerns about the diminished time, although the impact on their proficiency appeared mediated by the fact that they continued speaking Spanish at home. Even though they spoke Spanish at home, they felt they were at risk of losing their language. 'And like we don't practice the language like Spanish, and we might like start losing it, 'cause most of our classes are in English. But I speak Spanish at home, too so …' (Grade 9 Latina student). Another Latina reflected on the decline on oral language use, 'Last year (9th grade) we didn't really do much speaking in Spanish because we spoke most of the time in English because he (the teacher) didn't really enforce it. So, that's how like our vocabulary went down and our speaking skills went down because of that.'

The current program is unable to maintain a structure that supports language status equalization. By design, English increasingly dominates in the program and marginalizes Spanish. After 5th grade, the amount of Spanish drops to 30% in middle school and then to 10% (one class) in high school. In fact, it must be stressed that at the high school level the program is, in fact, no longer a TWI program. Students were quite aware of this shift and framed it as a loss of a much-cherished 'two-way identity', which included the integration of Anglo and Latino students and a balanced use of the two languages. Students indicated that the reduction in Spanish instruction negatively affected their ability to maintain their (oral) fluency in Spanish.

Content learning in Spanish

A second, related, factor that affected the program's ability to scaffold (oral) language proficiency is that Spanish is no longer taught through the content areas. Interestingly, different responses to this aspect of the program emerged. The Anglo students were mixed in their response to the loss of content instruction in Spanish. On the one hand, they recognized they lost a specific type of opportunity to use Spanish for communicative purposes.

> It's helpful to use Spanish in context, like a different subject ... using it in conversations and learning different things about the world. I just think that's pretty important. That's what I got out of middle school in the History class in Spanish. (Grade 10 Anglo male)

On the other hand, other Anglos were concerned about learning content. 'Learning History in Spanish I thought affected me like negatively, because I understood it, but I didn't understand it as well as other kids who were taking it [in English]' (Grade 10 Anglo male).

The loss of the Spanish-medium social studies class gave the Latino students one less opportunity to 'be at home' and freely use their native language for communicative purposes. A 10th grader commented, 'Especially in the History class you kind of need to express your opinions more and just get more involved.' The difference between the two groups about the content classes also emerged on the survey. Nearly 80% of Latino respondents agreed or strongly agreed that another content class taught in Spanish should be added whereas nearly 70% of Anglo students disagreed or strongly disagreed with the statement.

Spanish language arts curriculum

As the program moves from elementary to secondary school, Spanish language arts becomes the main identifier for the program. Students remember their elementary program as being 50–50% in English and Spanish, switching languages each week and learning all subjects in both languages. As mentioned above, the middle school program has two classes taught in Spanish (Spanish language arts and social studies), and at the high school there is one Spanish language and literature class (9th through 11th grade). In 12th grade, the TWI students join advanced world language students in the Spanish Advanced Placement (AP) class. The change in program design is accompanied by a change in the nature of learning Spanish.

Whereas the elementary program was a more informal learning environment, with a focus on learning language through other content areas, in middle-school Spanish language arts becomes more about grammar, and the focus shifts to learning (about) Spanish. 'Sixth grade was just like BOOM. A lot of grammar in Spanish. A lot of grammar' (11th grade, Latina). Students often indirectly contrasted this with the Spanish used in content classes. 'History in Spanish, it made you use Spanish in like different subjects rather than just learning like grammar and stuff' (10th grade, Latina). Students also described the shift from middle to high school as one of less emphasis on productive skills in favor of reading Spanish literature

> I think the curriculum's pretty like very similar [from middle to high school] because you focus on grammar, all different aspects of grammar, and also reading. But the one difference is that we have less writing in high school than in the bilingual program from middle school and elementary school because I remember we used to have a lot of writing assignments. (Grade 10 Anglo male)

The high school Spanish AP class further exemplifies the trend toward grammar and a focus on form. Overall, the TWI seniors were not satisfied with their AP class because it focused so much on grammar. They felt that they were not getting the most out of the class since they were integrated with students who had only attended foreign language classes. One student stated it this way:

> I feel like their [non two-way students'] classes were so language based because they had to catch up grammatically and like learn all the rules, so language-wise they might actually be more advanced. They might know more the fine-points of grammar. And like some random subjunctive tenses that we never learned ... But literature-wise, they, you know, they read a passage and it takes us an hour and a half to figure out what's going on. It takes [them] like three or four days to figure out what's going on. So I feel like there should almost be that AP literature [is] offered, even for it's just open .... if it's open to anyone, but the two – I think the two-way kids would flourish in a class like that. (Grade 12 Anglo male)

For the native Spanish speakers the emphasis on being able to label their own native language in grammatical terminology was not always easy: 'We always speak Spanish and we know how to say it; we just don't know what it's called' (Grade 12 Latina). They also commented on the difference between their Spanish (primarily from Latin America) and that of the teacher who had studied and used Castilian Spanish. Sometimes, this resulted in differences in language use and expectations: 'And sometimes we'll be like, "Oh you know you can also say it this way," and she's [the teacher] kind of like, "You can?" and then we're like ... she knows, like, a certain Spanish' (Grade 12 Latina).

Over time, the Spanish language arts curriculum shifts from a focus on function or use (using the language to learn) to a focus on form (learning the structure of the language). The fact that the AP Spanish language class is the culminating course for the TWI students is the most explicit example of this trend. Students perceived the elementary program as a natural learning environment where they did not even realize they were 'learning' Spanish. In contrast, they predominantly described their secondary experiences in terms of studying the language itself, that is grammar.[3] In addition, they also engaged in reading and discussing literature from different countries. Not without reason, the students now refer to the class as a regular Spanish 'foreign language' class. They would rather have an advanced literature class than an AP class, which stresses knowledge of grammar rather than use. The shift toward more emphasis on grammar (and literary analysis), in combination with the fact that Spanish is no longer used for content (other than Spanish Language Arts) began in middle school and in high school, TWI Spanish has become, as several students explained, 'a normal Spanish' class and no longer a two-way class.

There is value in developing formal language skills through literature and explicit grammar instruction. If students intend to use Spanish for literacy-dependent jobs or advanced course work in Spanish, they will need to develop an academic discourse in Spanish, but this can also be developed through continued subject-matter courses taught in Spanish. We wonder, therefore, about the relationship between the focus of the Spanish language arts classes and the intended goals of the program. It appears that the value of Spanish for 'real life purposes' may be more difficult to maintain in this environment. Although students indicate they intend to use Spanish for daily communication and job opportunities, they have few opportunities to explore bilingual practices that are directly connected to the community or future jobs that rely on (advanced) bilingual skills. This disconnect may also inform some of the Latino students' plans possibly to take another language instead of Spanish because 'they already speak Spanish', perhaps not realizing the level of skill necessary to take advantage of their bilingualism.

Possibilities for Secondary TWI Programs

Our study raises a number of questions that are important to explore in the future, for example is it acceptable (perhaps more realistic) to have differential goals and outcomes for different target groups in TWI programs? If so, what are the implications for curriculum development? How do we define 'bilingualism', 'biliteracy' and 'biculturalism' or 'multicultural competence' for secondary students, and how do we align our instructional practices with these definitions? Many of the students in our study called for a functional approach: they want to use Spanish for real-life purposes. This reminds us to ensure that secondary TWI Spanish language arts classes not only remain aligned with rich language and literacy instruction but also demonstrate real-life reasons why bilingualism and biliteracy is important. Community-based inquiry projects where students interview community members and engage in problem-solving projects may be one way to encourage such a functional approach (Smith & Arnot-Hopffer, 1998).

Our Latino students also stressed the importance of acknowledging the importance of the relationship between language and identity, in addition to instrumental reasons for the value of bilingualism and biliteracy. This finding has important curricular implications for material and activity selection as it points to the need to create spaces for bilingual and bicultural identity development and exploration. Students could be engaged in reading identity literature from different parts of the Caribbean, Latin America and South America (e.g. 'In the Time of the Butterflies'), as well as the United States ('The House on Mango Street' or 'Parrot in the Oven'). They can be invited to write identity poems such as 'Who Am I?' or 'My Special Place?' Poetry can also be used to teach grammar: odes lend themselves well to exploring the imperative or subjunctive moods when using phrases such as 'If I were ...' In this way, students are learning grammar in a nonthreatening, context-embedded way to express themselves. Many of these poems can be expanded into writing memoirs, descriptive essays and self-portraits (Bearse, 2005). Finally, secondary TWI educators could explore curricular possibilities that focus on students' real-life circumstances and multilingual and multicultural experiences through the creation of student-generated dialogues, skits, debates or plays.

The intent of TWI programs is to equitably negotiate both agendas for all students, resulting in high levels of bilingualism and biliteracy, academic achievement and biculturalism for all. Countering the sociopolitical realities of the status difference between English and Spanish has been shown to be challenging at the elementary level (Amrein & Peña, 2000; Freeman, 1998) and appears to be even more difficult at the secondary level (Montone & Loeb, 2000). Based on the issues raised in our study, several possible pathways suggest themselves to address some of these challenges at the secondary level.

First and foremost, secondary TWI programs need a clear definition of what different configurations constitute a TWI program at this level. Whereas there are clear general model descriptions available for elementary level TWI programs, an equivalent widely agreed-upon delineation of secondary TWI programs does not yet exist, though Fortune and Tedick (2008) and others have suggested a minimum of two, year-long subject-matter courses in secondary continuation programs to qualify as immersion. Although the Spanish language and literature classes in Grades 9–11 had been specifically designed for TWI students, the drop in Spanish instructional time no longer qualified as TWI.

Second, there is a clear need to ensure sufficient instructional time in the minority language at the secondary level. The phenomenon of diminished use of and access to Spanish in secondary TWI programs is not unique to this particular context (Montone & Loeb, 2000), although examples of middle school programs that maintain a 50–50% distribution do exist. The latter distribution can be challenging due to scheduling, smaller numbers of TWI students, access to quality teachers at this level. TWI educators could look at some of the strong heritage language immersion programs in existence, such as Irish immersion (Ó Duibhir, Chapter 8) and Hawaiian immersion (Wilson & Kamanā, Chapter 3). In addition, collaboration with other bilingual programs designed for language minority learners may also help provide access to a wider range of content classes in the minority language.

If a 50–50 allocation of instructional time cannot be achieved during core academic subjects, secondary programs may need to explore possibilities for increasing Spanish instructional time through electives and after-school programs. For instance, schools and communities (workplaces) can collaborate to extend opportunities for minority language use beyond traditional course work. In Cambridge, Massachusetts, for example, the district is offering a medical interpreter course as an elective for bilingual students (Cazabon, 2008). Bilingual internships (or other work–study options) or service-learning projects are other possibilities for maintaining the relevance of Spanish learning and increasing students' oral proficiency and literacy skills.

Conclusion: Equal Outcomes for All?

The TWI high school students' voices give legitimacy to the dual agenda in TWI programs as cautioned by Valdés (1997), particularly when the student population is distinctly different in terms of ethnic and language background, as was the case in our study. Torres-Guzman asserts that '[e]ven with the best intentions of equalizing opportunity and learning for students of all backgrounds, the reality is that schools, more often than not, tend to mirror social and political injustices, leaving minority speakers on the periphery' (Torres-Guzman, 2005: 9). In our study, we saw an increased privileging of English as well as a narrowing of the curriculum in favor of form over function, culminating in the AP Spanish class. Our analysis shows the increasingly difficult task for secondary TWI programs to negotiate these realities and maintain the status equalization and learning opportunities necessary to support the traditional three TWI goals for *both* languages and *both* groups of students. Without a commitment to purposefully address language status issues, secondary TWI programs will be hard-pressed to continue to achieve language status equalization which, in turn, will undermine the bilingualism developed. If TWI programs intend to sustain their three goals for long-term K–12 sequences, bilingual and biliteracy development as well as issues of culture and identity need be given more equal space.

Notes

1. The Directory of Two-Way Bilingual Immersion Programs in the United States is updated periodically and can be accessed at http://www.cal.org/twi/directory/index.html (Accessed 23.2.11). It is important to note that the directory relies on programs to self-report. Thus, it is likely that there are more middle-/high-school TWI programs than those listed in the directory.
2. Fortune and Tedick (2008) among others stipulate that at the secondary level, at least two-year-long subject-matter courses must be offered in the immersion language for the continuation program to qualify as immersion.
3. Grammar instruction was not necessarily perceived negatively by students. Indeed some of the Anglo students were upset that they had not been told that they were making errors in elementary school.

References

Amrein, A. and Peña, R.A. (2000) Asymmetry in dual-language practice: Assessing imbalance in a program promoting equality. *Education Policy Analysis Archives* 8(8). On WWW at http://epaa.asu.edu/epaa/v8n8.html. Accessed 28.4.10.

Bearse, C.I. (2005) *The Sky in my Hands: Accelerating Academic English Through the Writing Process*. Cambridge, MA: Language Learning Innovations.

Bearse, C.I. and de Jong, E.J. (2008) Cultural and linguistic investment: Adolescents in a secondary two-way immersion program. *Equity & Excellence in Education. Special Topics Issues on Bilingualism* 41, 325–240.

Cazabon, M.T. (2008) Two-way students become medical interpreters. Paper presented at the 2-Way CABE Conference, Newport Beach, CA.

Cazabon, M.T., Nicoladis, E. and Lambert, W.E. (1998) *Becoming Bilingual in the Amigos Two Way Immersion Program.* Santa Cruz, CA: Center for Research on Education Diversity & Excellence.

Cobb, B., Vega, D. and Kronauge, C. (2006) Effects of an elementary dual language immersion school program on junior high school achievement. *Middle School Research Journal* 1, 27–47.

Cruz, G.I. (2000) Learning in two languages: A case study of a two-way bilingual education program at the middle school. Dissertation thesis, State University of New York, Albany.

Fortune, T.W. and Tedick, D.J. (2008) One-way, two-way and indigenous immersion: A call for cross-fertilization. In T.W. Fortune and D.J. Tedick (eds) *Pathways to Multilingualism: Evolving Perspectives on Immersion Education* (pp. 3–21). Clevedon: Multilingual Matters.

Freeman, R. (1998) *Bilingual Education and Social Change.* Clevedon: Multilingual Matters.

Freeman, R. (2000) Contextual challenges to dual-language education: A case study of a developing middle school program. *Anthropology & Education Quarterly* 31, 202–229.

Gardner, R.C. (2001) Integrative motivation and second language acquisition. In Z. Dörnyei and R. Schmidt (eds) *Motivation and Second Language Acquisition* (pp. 1–19). Honolulu, HI: The University of Hawaii Second Language Teaching & Curriculum Center.

Giacchino-Baker, R. and Piller, B. (2006) Parental motivation, attitudes, support, and commitment in a Southern Californian two-way immersion program. *Journal of Latinos and Education* 4, 5–28.

Glaser, B.D. and Strauss, A.K. (1967) *The Discovery of Grounded Theory.* Chicago, IL: Aldine.

Howard, E.R., Sugarman, J. and Christian, D. (2003) *Trends in Two-Way Immersion Education: A Review of the Research* (Rep. No. 63). Baltimore, MD: Center for Research on the Education of Students Placed At Risk (CRESPAR).

Hsieh, J.Y. (2007) The perceived effectiveness of dual language programs at the middle school level. Dissertation thesis, University of Southern California.

Kohne, L.E. (2006) Two-way language immersion students: How do they fare in middle and high school? Dissertation thesis, University of California Irvine and University of California Los Angeles.

Krashen, S.D. (2004) The acquisition of academic English by children in two-way programs: What does the research say? On WWW at http://www.sdkrashen.com/articles/the_2-way_issue/all.html. Accessed 28.4.10.

Lindholm-Leary, K. (2001) *Dual Language Education.* Clevedon: Multilingual Matters.

Lindholm-Leary, K.J. (2005) The rich promise of two-way immersion. *Educational Leadership* 62, 56–59.

Lindholm-Leary, K.J. and Borsato, G. (2001) *Impact of Two-Way Bilingual Programs on Students' Attitudes toward School and College.* Santa Cruz, CA: Center for Research on Education Diversity & Excellence.

Lindholm-Leary, K.J. and Borsato, G. (2005) Hispanic high schoolers and mathematics: Follow-up of students who had participated in two-way bilingual elementary programs. *Bilingual Research Journal* 29, 641–652.

Lofland, J. and Lofland, L.H. (1995) *Analyzing Social Settings: A Guide to Qualitative Observation and Analysis*. Boston: Wadsworth.

Louie, V. (2006) Growing up ethnic in transnational worlds: Identities among second-generation Chinese and Dominicans. *Identities: Global Studies in Culture and Power* 13, 363–394.

McCollum, P. (1999) Learning to value English: Cultural capital in a two-way bilingual program. *Bilingual Research Journal* 23, 113–134.

Montone, C. and Loeb, M. (2000) Implementing two-way immersion programs in secondary schools. On WWW at http://escholarship.org/uc/item/23d3c1bm. Accessed 28.4.10.

Quiroz, P.A. (2001) The silencing of Latino students 'voice': Puerto Rican and Mexican narratives in eighth grade and high school. *Anthropology & Education Quarterly* 32, 326–349.

Schmidt, J.S. (2007) Anglo parents' decision to enroll in a dual language program. Dissertation thesis, University of Iowa.

Shannon, S.M. and Milian, M. (2002) Parents choose dual language programs in Colorado: A survey. *Bilingual Research Journal* 26, 681–696.

Smith, P. and Arnot-Hopffer, E. (1998) Éxito bilingüe: Promoting Spanish literacy in a dual language immersion program. *Bilingual Research Journal* 22, 103–119.

Soto, L.D. (2002) Young bilingual children's perspectives of bilingualism and biliteracy: Altruistic possibilities. *Bilingual Research Journal* 26, 599–610.

Suarez-Orozco, C. and Suarez-Orozco, M. (1995) *Transformations: Immigration, Family Life, and Achievement Motivation among Latino Adolescents*. Stanford, CA: Stanford University Press.

Torres-Guzman, M. (2005) Self-designated dual-language programs: Is there a gap between labeling and implementation. *Bilingual Research Journal* 29, 1–15.

Valdés, G. (1997) Dual-language immersion programs: A cautionary note concerning the education of language-minority students. *Harvard Educational Review* 67, 391–428.

Vega de Jesús, R. and Sayers, D. (2006) Bilingual youth constructing and defending their identities across borders, a binational study of Puerto Rican circular migrant students. *Multicultural Education* 14, 16–19.

Zarate, M.E., Bhimji, F. and Reese, L. (2005) Ethnic identity and academic achievement among Latino(a) adolescents. *Journal of Latinos and Education* 5, 42, 95–114.

Chapter 7

French Immersion Studies at the University of Ottawa: Programme Evaluation and Pedagogical Challenges

S. BURGER, A. WEINBERG, C. HALL, P. MOVASSAT and A. HOPE

> *Universities need to place more value on French second-language learning and need to recognize the extra effort made by many students in becoming bilingual. We shouldn't have to make you choose between bilingualism and a high-level education. These two elements should go hand in hand.*
> Graham Fraser (2009),
> Canadian Commissioner of Official Languages

Introduction

In this chapter, we report on tertiary French immersion in Canada and focus in particular on the French Immersion Studies academic stream (FIS) at the bilingual University of Ottawa. We first describe the immersion context at post-secondary institutions in Canada and the research derived from this environment. Then we move to the University of Ottawa programme, its implementation and challenges, as well as the results of three programme evaluations (an institution-level 'macro' evaluation, and two course-level 'micro' evaluations). Finally, we identify certain factors that experience has shown to be essential to our implementation of the immersion model. We conclude with an exploration of future possibilities for post-secondary immersion.

Immersion Context in Canada

From its humble beginnings in the 1960s in a suburb of Montreal, Quebec (Lambert & Tucker, 1972), French immersion quickly spread across

Canada, and by 1982 more than 75,000 English-speaking students in elementary and junior high schools across the country were studying in immersion programmes. By 2006/2007, there were 314,680 K–12 immersion students in Canada and 9673 Grade 12 immersion graduates. This number has remained relatively stable since 1997 and represents 7.9% of the eligible public school student population, according to statistics from Canadian Parents for French.[1] The Canadian immersion model also inspired the development of immersion programmes around the globe, including, among many other examples worldwide, Swedish immersion in Finland (Björklund & Mård-Miettinen, Chapter 2), English immersion in Hong Kong (Hoare, Chapter 11), as well as indigenous language immersion (Wilson & Kamanā, Chapter 3). The success of immersion in Canada, in terms of achievement of near-native proficiency in reading and listening comprehension, and functional proficiency in oral and written communication with no detriment to academic achievement or English development, has been well documented (Genesee, 1987; Harley *et al.*, 1990; Lapkin *et al.*, 1983; Rebuffot, 1993).

While immersion was thriving in elementary and secondary schools, there was relatively little attention paid to maintaining and further developing language skills at the postsecondary level through an ongoing immersion experience. Given the very different environment at this level, there are many issues that need to be addressed, from programme structure, to instructional techniques, to appropriate goals and expectations. Some of these issues are considered in this chapter.

Post-secondary immersion in Canada

Canada has 95 post-secondary institutions, most of which are English medium. Of Quebec's 17 universities, 14 are French speaking, and there are also a few small French institutions in New Brunswick, Nova Scotia, Ontario, Manitoba and Alberta. The University of Ottawa is one of Canada's three bilingual universities (all in Ontario) that offer programmes in both French and English – Canada's two official languages. It is the oldest and largest bilingual university in North America. Ottawa lies on the border between Ontario (mostly Anglophone) and Quebec (mostly Francophone), and the University offers programmes in both official languages to approximately 25,146 Anglophone and 11,098 Francophone students (2009).[2]

When immersion graduates of Canadian high schools want to pursue their second language studies at the post-secondary level, their choices are limited. If the goal is for individuals to achieve superior levels of bilingualism for the workplace, a more advanced post-secondary programme is needed. According to a report of the Office of the Commissioner of Official Languages (2009: 8), 'immersion is very limited at the university level in Canada'.[3]

Three institutions have proposed new models of post-secondary immersion to meet this need, with the support of both provincial and federal governments – Simon Fraser University in British Columbia, Glendon College (the French campus of York University in Toronto), and the University of Ottawa. At Simon Fraser University, a new four-year Bachelor's degree programme in Public Administration and Community Services taught in French was created in 2004. This programme provides an opportunity for 15–20 students to continue their studies in French at the university level.[4] In 2008, the Ontario provincial government named Glendon College the Centre of Excellence for French Language and Bilingual Post-Secondary Education in southern Ontario and awarded the college a grant to provide better access to higher education in French for immersion graduates, and the programme is still under development (Mougeon, 2009).

With a grant from Heritage Canada in 2005, the bilingual University of Ottawa, our focus in this chapter, introduced its French Immersion Studies academic stream. FIS has an enrolment of approximately 250 new students per year from all over Canada in 60 different courses representing 50 disciplines. FIS is, therefore, a large-scale four-year academic stream that provides follow-up French studies for Anglophone graduates from a range of programmes, including immersion.

Immersion at the University of Ottawa

Since the 1980s, the University has been committed to promoting bilingualism. To advance this goal, 'sheltered courses' were initiated in the early 1980s to provide language support to students taking content courses in their second language (L2). This model was chosen because students would be exposed to authentic academic language with modified input to insure comprehensibility.

The model followed the high school immersion format in that students received subject matter instruction in their L2 in a class with fellow L2 speakers taught by the discipline professor. In contrast to the high school format, though, L2 exposure was short (3 hours per week), and a language professor attended the class and provided a short language lesson on the subject matter material within the regular class time. Students followed the prescribed curriculum, used the recommended textbook and wrote the same multiple choice examinations as students in the first language

(L1) sections. Special needs of L2 learners were taken into account by discipline professors who were willing to adjust their instruction and evaluation procedures. This format was continued for two more years. Due to cost, however, the format was altered in 1985.

From 1985 until 1995, the less expensive adjunct model (Brinton *et al.*, 2003), was adopted in five disciplines. In that model, L2 students joined regular three-hour content courses, with no adjustments made to accommodate their language needs. To address these needs, students took a complementary 90-minute adjunct language course with 10–15 students, taught by a language professor who attended all content lectures to align language instruction with the content. However, due to insufficient enrolment, the University was forced to drop the format. This left students with two options to improve their French: regular French as a second language (FSL) courses or discipline courses in French with no language support.

One of the four stated aims of the University's plan for the future, presented in its *Vision 2010: Academic Strategic Plan*, was 'to play a leadership role in promoting Canada's official languages' (University of Ottawa, 2005: 4). As a result, the University put resources into fostering bilingualism and L2 learning. The Official Languages and Bilingualism Institute (OLBI) was created, and the FIS programme, based on the adjunct model, was launched.

This FIS stream was designed to provide follow-up French studies for French immersion graduates, regular FSL graduates and students with a love for French who had enriched their pre-university studies with exchange programmes, extra courses, or work in bilingual environments. The goal is to encourage such students to pursue their post-secondary education partially or entirely in French either with or without linguistic help and enable them to receive an official French immersion designation on their university diploma.

The FIS academic stream requires that students obtain 36 credits in courses taught in French, while fulfilling the requirements of a regular degree programme. These credits can be earned through advanced FSL courses, French literature or culture courses in the French (L1) department, regular content courses taught in French or content courses taught in French with associated adjunct language courses.

Students are admitted to FIS based on their scores on the Immersion Admission Test, an online reading and listening comprehension exam. Students must meet the 'low-advanced'[5] level for admission; this same level allows them to enrol in the first-level adjunct courses. Once they arrive on campus, students also take a computerized speaking and writing test, the results of which are used to help students develop personalized study plans for language improvement. In order to graduate with the French Immersion designation, students are required to pass the university's Second Language Certification Test in all four skills.[6]

The University provides strong support for the FIS programme in the form of 375 scholarships, an Immersion Mentoring Centre, an Academic Writing Help Centre, an Immersion Club and, most important, the immersion and adjunct courses themselves. The student mentors help students develop individual immersion study plans, introduce them to resources available on and off campus and assist them in developing strategies for academic success. The Immersion Mentoring Centre provides a place to study with access to computers equipped with Antidote, a computerized self-help French editor,[7] as well as the opportunity to watch French movies and practice French in a casual atmosphere.

In many respects, the French immersion content courses with adjunct courses form the core of FIS. In 2006, the programme began with 25 content courses taught in French, and it has quickly expanded to approximately 60 courses in 50 disciplines in four faculties. The content courses are offered in many fields, principally in social sciences and arts. The adjunct courses are offered at three different levels. At Level 1, instruction focuses on receptive skills, reading and listening 'to develop the students' capacity for comprehension in the second language and therefore help them to better understand the content of the discipline course' (Weinberg & Burger, 2007: 13). University of Ottawa students have the right to write their assignments and exams in either official language, and many Level 1 students choose to write in English. Level 2 concentrates on productive skills, 'to develop the students' capacity for oral and written production in the second language and therefore help them to gain confidence to express their ideas in French' (Weinberg & Burger, 2007: 14). Students are encouraged to write their content papers in French, but many are still reluctant to do so, fearing that they will not be able to express their ideas clearly or they will be penalized for poor French. The third and most advanced level targets either speaking or writing more intensively. This newly introduced (fall 2008) level is not discussed in this chapter. First-level adjunct courses are capped at 20 students, and to ensure maximum opportunities for practice only 12 can enrol in Level 2 courses.

Research on Post-secondary Immersion

Research on post-secondary immersion in Canada has been mostly limited to the experiences of content-based language teaching at the University of Ottawa. Conducted in the 1980s, the first studies on both the sheltered and adjunct formats confirmed the success of both models in terms of receptive linguistic and motivational gains (Edwards *et al.,* 1984; Hauptman *et al.,* 1988; Ready & Wesche, 1992). Two small-scale studies (Burger, 1989; Burger & Chrétien, 2001) were able to show gains in productive skills. Ready and Wesche (1992) also looked at the different instructional techniques used by adjunct language professors to identify which activities students found most useful for learning subject matter and which were most valuable for language development. Burger *et al.* (1984) explored the role of the language professor and Wesche and Ready (1985) documented adjustments made by content professors to tailor the input to L2 learners.

Current research on the new FIS continues in the same vein with Bayliss (2009), finding that students believe the new immersion format yields content mastery as well as good gains in L2 proficiency. Other studies are in progress, including investigations of the effectiveness of online vocabulary activities, a comparison of vocabulary acquisition in content courses in history and law and long-term proficiency gains in speaking and writing. In this chapter, we report on three evaluation studies.

An institutional macro evaluation

A large-scale programme evaluation of FIS (Ryan *et al.,* 2008) was undertaken in its second year of operation at the request of the University's administration. Data collected for the study included archival information and an online survey of 196 of the 527 first- or second-year FIS students registered for the winter 2008 term. In addition, four groups were targeted for focus group interviews: FIS students, adjunct language professors, content course professors and programme administrators.

Archival data from the Registrar's office for 2007–2008 showed that FIS students had a higher entry grade average (84.3%) than the general University of Ottawa population (81.5%). Half the students were graduates of secondary school French immersion (51%), while 20% were graduates of Core French (regular FSL), and a quarter had taken extended French. Sixty-five percent indicated that French immersion was the main reason for choosing the University of Ottawa.

All 10 Canadian provinces were represented among FIS students. Many reported experience learning other languages and having had some opportunities to use French in their homes, communities and jobs. Almost half of the FIS students were enroled in the Faculty of Social Sciences (45%), while a quarter were in the Faculty of Arts. Other faculties were also represented (Health Sciences 15% and Management 11%).

Table 7.1 Evaluation of FIS students' speaking and writing levels, Fall 2007

Speaking (n = 221)			Writing (n = 180)		
Level	*Number*	*Percent*	*Level*	*Number*	*Percent*
1	34	15.4	1	78	32.9
2	82	37.1	2	83	35.0
3	80	36.2	3	54	22.8
4	25	11.3	4	22	9.3

The online Admissions Test characterized the ability levels of incoming FIS students' receptive skills in fall 2007. Of the 261 students tested, 91 (34.9%) had 'low advanced' proficiency and 94 (36%) 'advanced proficiency'. These two groups (approximately 70%) were assigned to first-level adjunct courses, while the remaining students 76 (29.1%) were assigned to the second-level, having tested as 'high advanced'.

Table 7.1 shows incoming FIS students' productive skills in fall 2007 as given by their results on tests of French speaking and writing. Fewer students completed the writing test than the speaking test due to technical difficulties. These tests were each marked on a four-point scale, with '4' representing native-speaker abilities and '1' indicating some difficulty in communicating.

Table 7.1 shows that these incoming students, while all at least 'low advanced' in reading and listening, often have quite low abilities in the productive skills and generally display stronger speaking than writing skills. These results concur with the findings of Harley *et al.* (1990), Rebuffot (1993) and Swain (1985) to the effect that elementary school early French immersion students reached near-native comprehension skills in some contexts, but showed weakness in oral and written production. For immersion graduates entering the programme, lower productive skills may be the result of not enough practice time in French in their previous studies. Swain (1988) observed that in Grade 6 classes on average two students talked per minute in the French portion of the day compared to about six students per minute in the English portion of the day and that only about 14% of the utterances were longer than a clause. The findings were similar for Grade 2 classes. Allen *et al.* (1990) further noted that teacher-initiated student talk tended to elicit minimal linguistically controlled responses. Broner and Tedick (Chapter 9) found parallel results for Grade 5 students, particularly during teacher-fronted, whole class instruction. Hoare (Chapter 11) reports a similar pattern in late English immersion in Hong

Kong. Allen *et al.* (1990) and others, thus, recommend greater opportunities for sustained talk through group work, student-initiated talk and more open-ended questions. The adjunct language classes are designed to provide that opportunity.

The evaluation results summarized above show that the preliminary answer to the first research question, 'Is the programme being delivered to the appropriate audience?' is yes. The students choosing FIS represent immersion graduates, and Core and Extended French graduates. They come from all 10 provinces, pursue studies in four faculties and demonstrate a commitment to improving their French by their course selections. The students enter with sufficient French language proficiency to participate in FIS with room for further language development. These are the kinds of students that the University of Ottawa sought to attract as specified in the Vision 2010 Strategic Plan.

A corollary to the first question is: why are some eligible students not choosing the programme? To answer this question, a questionnaire was distributed to all students eligible for FIS who did not choose the programme. The reasons given for not choosing immersion included: fear of getting low marks, concern that their French was not good enough to succeed in the programme, lack of awareness about the programme, the perception that they did not need it and scheduling problems.

The second question investigated in this programme evaluation was 'Is the programme being delivered as intended?' The evaluation considered several indicators such as course enrolment patterns as well as student and staff satisfaction with programme components. The FIS programme requires that students take about one-third of their coursework in French. Course enrolment patterns confirmed that FIS students are respecting this requirement. Based on information from the Registrar's office, FIS students choose to take on average approximately 37% of their courses in French while the general Anglophone population averages about 3%. Table 7.2 breaks down the numbers and types of courses in French in which FIS students were enrolled in 2007–2008. There were fewer second-year students because there were fewer admissions in the programme's first year.

By 2008, the 187 second-year students averaged 4.04 courses in French per year, and first-year students averaged 3.42, when the average undergraduate course load is 10 courses per year. More striking is the fact that second-year students are choosing to take more regular content courses taught in French (an average of 2.62 courses) than first-year students (1.05 courses). Furthermore, these second-year students are taking fewer immersion content courses and therefore fewer accompanying adjunct courses and slightly fewer FSL courses (average 0.35 versus 0.88). This suggests

Table 7.2 FIS Student Enrolment in Courses Given in French in 2007–2008

	1st Year students (n = 303)	2nd Year students (n = 187)
Regular content courses taught in French in various departments	319	490
Immersion content courses	267	65
Adjunct course for FIS students.	267	65
French language courses	182	135
Total	1035	755
Average # courses per student	3.42	4.04

that FIS students are increasingly able to pursue their studies in French without the support of adjunct courses as they proceed through their undergraduate studies.

Responses to the student survey confirmed their comfort with their level of French. Eighty-two percent of students responded positively to the question 'Have you improved your French language skills?' Seventy-six percent indicated they were able to take courses in their field in French. Thirty-nine percent responded that they had become acquainted with French-speaking students at the University. These results indicate that the programme seems to be working in the way it was intended.

As for the components of the programme, students indicated satisfaction with the scholarships, the orientation sessions, the Immersion Club, the Student Resource Center, the Writing Help Center, the conversation groups and the Immersion Mentoring Center, although some of these services were not widely used. Comments from students also illustrated their general satisfaction.

> Overall French immersion at the University of Ottawa is excellent – I loved my professors and I can already feel an improvement in my listening skills.

> I am immensely satisfied with my decision to enrol in FIS. I have seen incredible improvements in my French capacities.

Against this backdrop of overall satisfaction, students expressed several concerns with adjunct courses. Sixty-two percent of students reported being 'very satisfied' or 'satisfied' with the adjunct classes, a level of endorsement that university administrators would have preferred to see higher.

Specific comments made by students varied. Some felt that the language course was not tied closely enough to the content course. Some indicated that they needed more help with comprehension of the content material. In addition, students were sometimes confused about the division between receptive skills and productive skills courses.

Language professors in focus groups also expressed some frustration with the split between receptive and productive skills and did not agree with their separation at the two different course levels. These concerns echo those found in the first-year programme evaluation, completed in 2007 (Ryan *et al.*, 2008). Focus groups of language professors and administrators at that time also expressed a need for even more teacher development. An evaluation of an earlier version of immersion at the University of Ottawa also identified the exceptional challenges of adjunct courses (Burger *et al.*, 1984).

In summary, overall, the FIS programme was found to be targeting the appropriate students and delivering the programme as intended. Students, professors and administrators generally were satisfied with the programme and provided evidence that FIS was meeting expectations. Not surprisingly, however, among the specific recommendations made in the area of pedagogy were strengthening professional development and supervision of adjunct language instructors and encouraging standard assessment practices. Programme evaluators also recognized a need for greater publicity of the programme and of the university services offered to support FIS students.

Micro-evaluations: Student evaluation of adjunct language class activities

Two micro-evaluations of FIS focused on the adjunct courses themselves. The first was undertaken in 2006 (Weinberg *et al.*, 2008). A Likert-scale questionnaire was administered to students in the adjunct courses to examine their perceptions of the helpfulness of particular course activities. The questionnaire was based on one developed by Ready and Wesche (1992) to evaluate the university's earlier content-based institutional programme. The second micro-evaluation, conducted in 2008 (Weinberg & Burger, 2010), was a qualitative study concerning the language activities completed in four adjunct classes. It was based on focus group discussions with 22 students, who defined and discussed these activities.

Three main research questions were addressed in the two micro-evaluations: Were the language activities helpful to students in either learning the content course material or improving language skills? Did the perceptions towards their language activities differ between students registered in first-level and second-level adjunct classes? In the latter evaluation, one supplementary question was added: Were there differences in the perception of language activities depending on which content course the students were taking?

First micro-evaluation

The following information reflects a summary of responses from the 172 participants in the first study. The first part of the survey asked students to rate the quality of the adjunct course instruction in six areas: vocabulary, listening, reading, speaking, writing and grammar. The ratings ranged between 2.60 and 3.01 out of a possible score of 4, indicating a perception that the instruction was generally good. As shown in Table 7.3, the six areas were generally rated very similarly by the two groups of students.

However, the teaching of vocabulary was rated highest, with a mean rating of 3.01. As the first-level and second-level adjunct courses are designed to focus on different areas, Level 1 students rated the teaching of receptive skills a bit stronger than Level 2 students. Similarly, Level 2 students rated the teaching of productive skills a bit stronger than Level 1 students.

Students were also asked how helpful various activities were for learning content and language. All activities were rated as helpful for both purposes with minimal differences between levels; however, the extra individual attention provided to students, probably because of the small class size, won the highest rating both for content and language learning.

Table 7.3 Perceived quality of instruction in the language course

	Total N = 172	*Level 1 N = 136*	*Level 2 N = 36*
	Mean (SD)	*Mean (SD)*	*Mean (SD)*
Teaching of vocabulary	3.01 (0.87)	2.99 (0.89)	3.06 (0.85)
Teaching of listening	2.74 (0.99)	2.78 (0.98)	2.63 (1.04)
Teaching of reading	2.73 (0.90)	2.79 (0.92)	2.60 (0.81)
Teaching of speaking	2.74 (1.01)	2.72 (1.03)	2.86 (0.91)
Teaching of writing	2.60 (0.96)	2.59 (0.95)	2.69 (0.96)
Teaching of grammar	2.63 (0.95)	2.58 (0.95)	2.81 (0.97)

Scale: 1 = poor; 2 = fair; 3 = good; 4 = very good.

Second-language professors provided students with lecture notes and multimedia activities such as online links to sound files or supplementary readings related to the content course. Students found both of these helpful for their language improvement. Review of lectures and charts as well as discussion of supplementary readings received high ratings for helping with content learning. Reading exercises based on textbooks appeared to be more important for both language and content learning for Level 1 (receptive skills) students than for Level 2 (productive skills) students. This may be an indication that Level 1 students still need more help with reading comprehension.

Some students responded to open-ended questions asking them to name the activities that were the most helpful for learning language or content. From this, a different picture emerged. Students most often mentioned oral presentations and other speaking activities as being most helpful for language improvement. Students also strongly endorsed vocabulary teaching. Review of lectures was cited as helpful more often for content learning than language learning. Somewhat surprisingly, writing activities, which should have been perceived as helpful for synthesizing content and beneficial for improving written production, were not mentioned often as being useful for content learning and even less often for language learning.

Because each content course is unique, many variables must be factored into the context: the content itself, reading material required, lecture style of the content professor, type of student evaluation implemented in the content course, language level of immersion students, level of the content course (first or second year), immersion experience of the language professor and so on. A closer look at the first level psychology, political science and history groups highlighted these differences. Two of these groups indicated a high level of satisfaction with their immersion and adjunct courses while the history group expressed great dissatisfaction. Reasons given for the dissatisfaction included poor organization of both the content and adjunct courses, a perceived negative attitude of the content professor towards L2 students, a comparatively large language class (23 students), and the inability of the language professor to meet students' language needs. Overall, however, in these results representing 20 courses, students indicated general satisfaction with their content and adjunct courses. After the negative experience with the large class of 23 students, a limit of 20 students was mandated for adjunct classes. If this maximum is exceeded, the class is split into two sections.

Second micro-evaluation

The second micro-investigation, organized in April 2008, was a follow-up of the previous Weinberg *et al.* (2008) study. This research involved 22 immersion students registered in Level 1 and 2 adjunct classes linked to two different content courses, psychology and political science. These courses were selected because they represented two types of content delivery. Psychology courses were highly scaffolded with many tables and graphics and incorporated multiple choice exams that emphasized receptive skills. In contrast, political science was taught in a dense, wordy style with limited scaffolding; evaluation involved essay questions that emphasized productive skills.

Four focus groups were formed. Two groups represented Level 1 students, one comprised of psychology students ($n = 5$) and one of Political Science students ($n = 3$). Of the two groups representing Level 2, one had mostly psychology students ($n = 5$) along with three political science students, and the other primarily political science students ($n = 5$) along with one psychology student. These focus groups identified and discussed the language activities used in adjunct classes. They evaluated how useful each activity was for learning French and the content material. In addition, they said whether or not they enjoyed the activity. Students developed their own framework for defining and rating the language activities they participated in. The construct analysis approach (Bourassa *et al.*, 2007; Peters *et al.*, 2007; Philion, 2007) was used to elicit a description and rating of activities offered in their adjunct courses. By arriving at consensus, the focus groups rated each activity mentioned on three five-point Likert scales: hate/love, useless/useful for learning content and useless/useful for language learning. Six types of activities were described and rated by all four groups: listening comprehension activities, reading comprehension activities, vocabulary activities, the weekly log, summary writing and activities involving oral expression.

For the various activities, there were differences between how well students liked them and how useful they found them for learning content or language. For example, all groups rated oral expression activities highly on all scales and found that discussing content in the L2 was useful for improving both their content knowledge and linguistic skills. Reading comprehension activities were liked more by first-level students than second-level students. Students from all groups found reading activities useful for learning content, however. Listening comprehension activities received similar ratings to reading except that both political science groups found such activities quite useful for learning content and language. Political science lectures were seen as difficult to grasp, and readings tended to be scholarly articles proving difficult to comprehend and relate to lectures.

Surprisingly, second-level students liked summary writing less (2 on the hate/love scale) than first-level students, even though their adjunct class focused on writing, but most students found it useful for language learning. Only the first-level political science students reported liking the weekly log activity, which consisted of tasks such as building annotated vocabulary lists, reflecting on learning strategies and summarizing lectures. Other students did not see the purpose of the activity or understand why they had to reflect on their metacognitive awareness. Finally, all students found vocabulary activities useful for language learning. Most were neutral as to their usefulness for learning content and ambivalent about how they liked the activities.

Overall, first-level students tended to be slightly more positive about the adjunct course activities than second-level students, perhaps because they start off at a lower level and learn more, giving them a more positive view of their learning activities as they see improvement over the term. The second-level students, in contrast, are tasked with improving their writing and speaking skills. These are difficult to master and may be graded by their professors to a high standard, thus, possibly impacting student satisfaction with the activities.

Were there any trends in differences between the ways psychology students and political science students scored their various activities? The two political science groups tended to be slightly more positive and more similar in their scoring than the psychology groups – especially for listening and reading comprehension activities. As the programme expands, this research could be pursued on a larger scale with more students per focus group and more disciplines represented.

In sum, the language activities in the adjunct classes were perceived to be useful both for learning content and for improving language skills. At higher language proficiency levels, students tended to prefer productive activities over receptive ones. Speaking and oral presentation activities were those most appreciated by students, followed by vocabulary activities. Differences in reactions corresponded to students taking different content courses. Because each content course is unique, the objectives, evaluation, presentation, homework and activities in a given adjunct course may have been more suitable for certain content courses than others.

Possibilities for Improvement

In this final section we present some challenges, suggest possibilities for programme improvement and conclude with a consideration of the results of the evaluations summarized above.

Challenges

The FIS programme presents unique challenges to language professors and programme administrators, partly due to differences between K–12 and post-secondary contexts. In the typical high school immersion model, teachers teach language and content simultaneously. In the university adjunct model, a clearer distinction is made between content and language teaching. The content course and the adjunct course are separate courses with distinct curricula. They are taught by different professors with different areas of expertise. This separation of language and content leads to many constraints, some of which are beyond the control of programme planners.

One constraint is the selection of content professors; they are chosen by academic departments. For example, a particular content course may be deemed unsuitable for FIS students because it is poorly planned or poorly delivered by a professor who is not sensitive to the language needs of FIS students or who lacks the pedagogical skills that would make the content more comprehensible.

The accompanying adjunct courses pose similar challenges with respect to staffing. There is a heavy reliance on part-time teaching staff who do not have the security of being able to offer a particular course more than once, and a disproportionate number of new and inexperienced language instructors teach these courses. Also the selection of language instructors is subject to union seniority regulations, and the university may not be able to give the same adjunct course to the same instructor from one semester to the next. The methodology required for immersion teaching is different from that of regular French teaching, and experience makes a difference. The instructor must be flexible, able to address problems as they arise, and skilled in developing appropriate support materials. Each time an instructor offers a course, she/he will make improvements, develop new material and become more comfortable with the language of the discipline. Thus, continuity in teaching staff would noticeably improve course delivery.

This administrative distinction between content and language also has implications for pedagogy and assessment. The content course has its own assignments and exams, prepared and evaluated by the content professor. Evaluating the students' content mastery lies exclusively with the content professor. This means that teaching or testing skills such as recalling facts, synthesizing ideas from content lectures and texts, or reflecting critically on the merits of a theory all belong to the content professor. The language instructor cannot intrude into that domain. So, although students in an adjunct course learn language through the content material – indeed, that is the very rationale for the course – the language instructor must be careful not to teach or assess content.

The course progression structure of the FIS programme also creates pedagogical and assessment challenges for language instructors. The first-level adjunct courses focus on receptive skills only; in these courses, students can be assessed only on their proficiency in reading and listening. Thus, instructors must distinguish between productive and receptive skills in assessing students. French language instructors are accustomed to marking student work for grammar, spelling and writing ability. Directing them to ignore such concerns on receptive skills tests is especially challenging because it conflicts with their training and experience. In addition, while formal, standardized proficiency measures tend to separate the four language skills, classroom-based assessments tend to be more integrative in nature, making it challenging and artificial for instructors to keep the skills separate.

Possibilities for programme improvement

Given the instructional challenges of implementing immersion at the post-secondary level, professional development for participating instructors could improve programme quality. The FIS programme holds a one-day orientation session every year for adjunct instructors, in addition to workshops on special topics such as testing content and language separately or testing receptive versus productive skills. However, the language instructors do not consistently attend such sessions. An improvement would be a one-week pre-service, compulsory session required for instructors assigned to adjunct courses. The University might further demonstrate its commitment to the FIS programme by paying instructors to participate in such sessions (or creating some other incentive) and by working with the union to allow instructors the opportunity to teach the same adjunct courses on a consistent basis so that their skills will improve with experience.

Language instructors also have access to pedagogical advisers who observe their teaching and provide constructive feedback. Guides (Dansereau, 2010; Weinberg & Burger, 2007) are distributed to new instructors to familiarize them with the expectations and characteristics of the programme. Full-time professors have developed a collection of activity templates for adjunct language instruction (Dansereau & Buchanan, 2009), but because each course is unique, activity templates may not transfer easily between courses. In addition, an online repository of adjunct course syllabi and activity templates might be created so that instructors have an opportunity to use and revise previous instructors' plans and activities.

Other possibilities for programme improvement include, ideally, professional development for content professors who teach FIS courses. Hoare (this volume), Lindholm-Leary (Chapter 5) and many others argue for immersion-specific training to improve content teachers' effectiveness. In addition, content professors and adjunct course instructors would benefit from collaboration to plan for more coordinated instruction. Again, University administrators may be encouraged to provide incentives for such collaboration, such as a course release after teaching X number of FIS courses to compensate for the time it takes to plan for and deliver high-quality immersion instruction.

Given the challenges of immersion at the post-secondary level, cooperation among universities involved in immersion and other forms of content-based instruction could also hold promise for mutual benefit and programme improvement. At the University of Ottawa, research is in progress on different ways of measuring FIS students' language improvement. The Research Center of the OLBI, the Canadian Centre for Studies and Research on Bilingualism and Language Planning, has elaborated a research plan for FIS and possible pathways for improvement. They might share research plans and findings with other postsecondary immersion programmes, such as the programmes at Simon Fraser University and Glendon College in Canada and at the University of Hawaii at Hilo (Wilson & Kamanā, Chapter 3) or with programmes such as Foreign Language Across the Curriculum, popular in the United States, or content-and-language-integrated-learning (CLIL), increasingly popular in Europe and elsewhere in higher education.

Conclusion

Based on the evaluation studies presented in this chapter, university administrators feel that the immersion programme is a success and is attracting high-achieving secondary immersion (and other programme) graduates from across Canada. The rich bilingual environment of the University of Ottawa provides an excellent setting for students to continue to enhance their second language skills as they learn disciplinary content. Although there is room for improvement, FIS at the University of Ottawa is an example of creating possibilities where post-secondary education and bilingualism meet. It provides a model that can be emulated by other postsecondary institutions to invent for themselves, taking into consideration their own situation and context, and imagining new possibilities for bilingualism for their student population.

Appreciation

We wish to thank Dr Marjorie Wesche for comments and suggestions on an earlier version of this chapter. All errors and shortcomings remain the authors' responsibility.

Notes

1. Canadian Parents for French is a national network of volunteers dedicated to French learning opportunities for Canada's youth. Enrolment figures and more information can be found at: http://www.cpf.ca.
2. These numbers are reported on page 4 of a University of Ottawa fact sheet: http://web5.uottawa.ca/mcs-smc/quickfacts/documents/quickfacts-2009.pdf.
3. The report may be accessed at: http://www.ocol-clo.gc.ca/docs/e/uni_e.pdf.
4. More information about the programme at Simon Fraser can be found at: http://www.sfu.ca/baff-offa/en/History/.
5. The Immersion Admission Test was based on the University of Ottawa Proficiency Test, which was used for over a decade as an exit requirement for all undergraduates, with Anglophones needing to demonstrate French proficiency and Francophones, English proficiency. The French cut-off score was calibrated with the University's FSL courses; students who pass demonstrate the same proficiency as students who complete the high-intermediate-level courses, and are therefore deemed 'low-advanced'.
6. The Second Language Certification Test was designed in 2003 as an optional test for undergraduates who wished to document their level of mastery in their second official language, so as to have a credential in applying for bilingual jobs after graduation. Passing grades range from level 2 ('Almost complete global comprehension and comprehension of many explicit details; communicates somewhat effectively, with some imprecision'.) to Level 4 ('Complete global comprehension; comprehends all explicit and implicit details; communicates very effectively, with ease and precision'.).
7. Antidote is a French language editing programme developed by Druide Informatique, Inc. Antidote and other products are available at: http://www.druide.com/antidote.html. Accessed 2.2.10.

References

Allen, P., Swain, M., Harley, B. and Cummins, J. (1990) Aspects of classroom treatment: toward a more comprehensive view of second language education. In B. Harley, P. Allen, J. Cummins and M. Swain (eds) *Development of Second Language Proficiency* (pp. 57–81). Cambridge: Cambridge University Press.

Bayliss, D. (2009) The implementation of a program of immersion courses: What we have learned so far. In L. Yu (ed.) *Bilingual Instruction in China: A Global Perspective—Papers from the Symposium on Canadian Immersion Education and Bilingual Instruction at the Tertiary Level in China* (pp. 22–40). Beijing: Foreign Language Teaching and Research Press.

Bourassa, M., Philion, R. and Chevalier, J. (2007) L'analyse de construits, une co-construction de groupe. *Association canadienne d'éducation de langue française. Éducation et francophonie* 35, 78–116.

Brinton, D.M., Snow, M.A. and Wesche, M.B. (2003) *Content Based Second Language Instruction* (2nd edn). New York, NY: Newbury House.

Burger, S. (1989) Content-based ESL in a sheltered psychology course: Input, output and outcomes. *TESL Canada Journal* 6, 45–59.

Burger, S. and Chrétien, M. (2001) The development of oral production in content-based second language courses at the University of Ottawa. *The Canadian Modern Language Review* 58, 84–102.

Burger, S., Chrétien, M., Gingras, M., Hauptman, P. and Migneron, M. (1984) Le rôle du professeur de langue dans un cours de matière académique en langue seconde. *The Canadian Modern Language Review* 41, 397–402.

Dansereau, M.C. (2010) *Guide du professeur de langue: Régime d'immersion en français.* Document interne. Ottawa: Institut des langues officielles et du bilinguisme, Université d'Ottawa.

Dansereau, M.C. and Buchanan, C. (2009) (eds) *Recueil d'activités: Compréhension écrite et orale d'un cours de discipline suivi en français langue seconde.* Document interne. Ottawa: Institut des langues officielles et du bilinguisme, Université d'Ottawa.

Edwards, H., Wesche, M., Krashen, S., Clément, R. and Kruidenier, B. (1984) Second language acquisition through subject-matter learning: A study of sheltered psychology classes at the University of Ottawa. *Canadian Modern Language Review* 41, 268–282.

Fraser, G. (2009) Notes for an address to the French as a Second Language Contest at the University of Ottawa. On WWW at http://www.ocol-clo.gc.ca/html/speech_discours_15052009_e.php. Accessed 28.4.10.

Genesee, F. (1987) *Learning through Two Languages: Studies of Immersion and Bilingual Education.* Cambridge: Newbury House.

Harley, B., Cummins, J., Swain, M. and Allen, P. (1990) The nature of language proficiency. In B. Harley, P. Allen, J. Cummins and M. Swain (eds) *The Development of Second Language Proficiency* (pp. 7–25). Cambridge: Cambridge University Press.

Hauptman, P., Wesche, M. and Ready, D. (1988) Second language acquisition through subject-matter learning: A follow-up study at the University of Ottawa. *Language Learning* 38, 433–475.

Lambert, W.E. and Tucker, G.R. (1972) *The Bilingual Education of Children: The St. Lambert Experiment.* Rowley, MA: Newbury House.

Office of the Commissioner of Official Languages (2009) *Two Languages, A World of Opportunities. Second Language Learning in Canada's Universities.* Ottawa, Canada: Minister of Public Works and Government Services.

Lapkin, S., Swain, M. and Argue, V. (1983) *French Immersion: The Trial Balloon that Flew.* Toronto: The Ontario Institute for Studies in Education.

Mougeon, F. (2009) Beyond Immersion: The post-secondary challenge. Linking student experience and community-integrated learning. Paper presented at the CCERBAL Conference, Ottawa.

Peters, M., Chevrier, J., Leblanc, R., Fortin, G. and Kennedy, S. (2007) L'utilisation de l'analyse de construits dans un groupe de recherche pour définir le concept d'accompagnement métacognitif. *Association canadienne d'éducation de langue française. Éducation et francophonie* 35, 172–191.

Philion, R. (2007) L'analyse de construits au service de la co-construction de sens chez les étudiants mentors. Association canadienne d'éducation de langue française. *Éducation et francophonie* 35, 192–216.

Ready, D. and Wesche, M. (1992) An evaluation of the University of Ottawa sheltered program: Language teaching strategies that work. In R. Courchêne, J. Glidden, J. St John and C. Thérien (eds) *Comprehension-based Second Language Teaching/L'enseignement des langues secondes axé sur la compréhension* (pp. 389–405). Ottawa: Ottawa University Press.

Rebuffot, J. (1993) *Le point sur l'immersion au Canada*. Montréal: Éditions CEC.

Ryan, W., Courcelles, P., Hope, A., Buchanan, C. and Toews Janzen, M. (2007) *Evaluation of the French Immersion Studies Academic Stream: Year 1*. Document interne. Ottawa: Centre de recherche sur les services éducatifs et communautaires, Université d'Ottawa.

Ryan, W., Gobeil, M., Hope, A. and Toews Janzen, M. (2008) *Evaluation of the French Immersion Studies Academic Stream: Year 2*. Document interne. Ottawa: Centre de recherche sur les services éducatifs et communautaires. Université d'Ottawa.

Swain, M. (1985) Communicative competence: Some roles of comprehensible input and comprehensible output in its development. In S.M. Gass and C.G. Madden (eds) *Input in Second Language Acquisition* (pp. 235–253). Cambridge: Newbury House.

Swain, M. (1988) Manipulating and complementing content teaching to maximize second language learning. *TESL Canada Journal* 6, 68–83.

University of Ottawa (2005) Vision 2010 – Academic Strategic Plan. Online document: http://strategicplanning.uottawa.ca/vision2010/home.html. Accessed 28.4.10.

Weinberg, A. and Burger, S. (2010) *University level immersion: Students' perception of language activities*. Les cahiers de l'ILOB/OLBI Working Papers 1, 111–142. Ottawa: Institut des langues officielles et du bilinguisme, Université d'Ottawa.

Weinberg, A. and Burger, S. (2007) *Guide à l'intention des professeurs de langue: Cours d'encadrement linguistique*. Document interne. Ottawa: Institut des langues officielles et du bilinguisme, Université d'Ottawa.

Weinberg, A., Burger, S. and Hope, A. (2008) Evaluating the effectiveness of content-based language teaching. *Contact Research Symposium Issue* 34, 68–80. On WWW at http://www.teslontario.org/uploads/publications/researchsymposium/ResearchSymposium2008. pdf. Accessed 28.4.10.

Wesche, M.B. and Ready, D. (1985) Foreigner talk in the University classroom. In S.M. Gass and C.G. Madden (eds) *Input in Second Language Acquisition* (pp. 89–114). Cambridge: Newbury House.

Part 3

Language Use and Assessment Practices in Immersion Programs

Chapter 8

'I Thought That We Had Good Irish': Irish Immersion Students' Insights into Their Target Language Use

P. Ó DUIBHIR

Introduction

Irish is the first official language of the Republic of Ireland with English being the second. Despite its official status, it could be classified as a minority or lesser used language (Ó Catháin, 2001). All students in Ireland are required to study Irish commencing with their entry to school at age four/five and continuing until they leave high school (age 16–18). The result of this policy is that 1.66 million people, representing 41.9% of the population, responded in the most recent census that they are able to speak Irish (Central Statistics Office, 2007). The vast majority of these, 68.5%, however, reported that they never speak Irish or speak it less than once per week. The vast majority of the remainder are those who speak it within the education system. When the census responses are further analysed it emerges that there are only 72,148 daily speakers of Irish outside the education system (Punch, 2008). Thus, there is a relatively small number of daily speakers of Irish in Ireland that are thinly dispersed, and there are a substantial number of passive bilinguals.

Education through the medium of Irish has been a feature of the Irish education system since the Irish Free State was founded in 1922. The new independent Irish government wished to establish Irish as the main vernacular of the people (Ó Tuathaigh, 1991), and it identified schools as central to its policy of reversing the language shift from English back to Irish (Ó Riagáin, 2007). It announced in 1922 that Irish would be taught and used as the medium of instruction for at least one hour per day in all National (elementary) schools (National Programme Conference, 1922). It also decided that Irish should be the sole medium of instruction in infant (kindergarten) classes (Coolahan, 1981). Despite certain misgivings from teachers, this policy was initially quite successful, and by 1937 there were 288 National schools, outside the Irish-speaking areas, teaching all subjects except for English through the medium of Irish. There were 2032 schools where Irish was the sole medium of instruction in certain grades (An Roinn Oideachais/The Department of Education, 1937). These schools were in effect employing a total or partial immersion policy for their English-speaking students, although that term was not used. Following an initial period where this state-led initiative flourished (Coolahan, 1981), there were only 10 schools continuing to teach through the medium of Irish by 1972. These schools became known as 'all-Irish schools' because all subjects, except for English language arts, were taught through Irish. A new parent-led movement seeking Irish-medium education grew during the 1970s, and there has been sustained growth in the number of all-Irish schools since then. There are now 139 primary 'all-Irish' immersion schools in the Republic of Ireland, with more added each year. Today, approximately 5% of students receive their primary education through the medium of Irish in these schools and a further 2.5% attend *Gaeltacht* schools in Irish-speaking communities (Máirtín, 2006). The majority of Irish immersion schools employ an early, total immersion policy for the first year of Junior Infants (Junior Kindergarten, age four/ five). This is followed by the introduction of English language arts in Senior Infants (age five/six) representing almost 15% of the instructional time. The early introduction of primary language (English) instruction is similar to the practice followed in Swedish immersion programmes in Finland, as described by Björklund and Mård-Miettinen (Chapter 2). The remaining 85% of instruction is through the medium of Irish, and this percentage remains constant throughout the students' schooling to the end of high school. This high language intensity model, consistent across Irish immersion schools, is parallel to the model developed at Nāwahī Hawaiian Immersion School (Wilson & Kamanā, Chapter 3). Student attrition is not perceived as a problem, although there are no official statistics available to confirm this. The students attending these schools come, predominantly, from English-speaking homes with a small number, estimated to be less than 3%, from Irish-speaking homes. In more recent years, students whose home language is neither English nor Irish have chosen to attend Irish immersion schools.

Irish is the communicative language of the school, and students are expected to converse in Irish at all times within the school environment including the school playground at break time, providing students with opportunities for output and social interaction outside the classroom. This expectation is consistent with practices at Nāwahī School (Wilson

& Kamanā, Chapter 3). Teachers report that students by and large comply with this expectation, particularly in Grades 1–4 (Ó Duibhir, 2009). Students develop functional proficiency in Irish in the first two years of Junior and Senior Kindergarten. By Grade 1, they have developed some communicative competency, and teachers encourage them to use Irish at all times even if this requires some code-mixing. In the pre-adolescent years of Grades 5 and 6 (ages 11–12), the influence of the peer group becomes stronger, and compliance with the wishes of the teacher can weaken. Irish can be perceived by the students as something that belongs to the domain of the school, and they may be more comfortable speaking English to their peers, particularly when they are not being monitored by a teacher. A similar pattern is described by Broner and Tedick (Chapter 9) for Grade 5 Spanish immersion students in the United States.

Background to the Study

For decades, research studies have consistently shown that immersion students achieve high levels of functional proficiency in the target language, and their receptive skills (listening and reading) are near native (e.g. Day & Shapson, 1996; Genesee, 1987; Harley, 1987; Lyster, 1987; Swain, 2000). Their productive skills (speaking and writing), however, contain many non-target-like forms that appear to persist over time (e.g. Genesee, 1987; Lyster, 1987; Swain, 2005; Swain & Lapkin, 2008).

In an early immersion programme where the predominant focus is on meaning (i.e. experiential learning), the addition of an analytic approach is likely to be successful in focusing learner's attention on form. Lyster (1998, 2007) has suggested that it is critical not just to focus learners' attention on form, but also to create opportunities for student reflection on their language use. This could be facilitated, for example, through a jigsaw task as in Lyster's (1998) study. The recording of students' speech as reported in the present study also provides a context for reflection on communication that can alert the learner to non-target-like features.

Research studies of Irish immersion programmes have been limited in number and scope. Nonetheless, they show that Irish immersion students achieve high levels of proficiency and comprehension, which considerably exceed those achieved by students taking Irish as a school subject (Harris, 1984; Harris *et al.*, 2006). These advantages are achieved without cost to their literacy skills in English (Parsons & Liddy, 2009). As has been the case in other immersion programmes, concern has been expressed that Irish immersion students' productive skills do not reach native speaker levels, and their speech includes a range of inaccurate forms that persist as they move through the grade levels (NCCA, 2006). No comprehensive study of the features of Irish spoken in Irish immersion, based on speakers from the full range of such schools, has yet been carried out. Neither has there been any systematic attempt to explore the origins and maintenance of these features or to establish students' views on their language use. This study, therefore, represents a first attempt to make good an important research deficit in Irish immersion and to offer insights to other immersion programmes.

Study Design

Study participants and research questions

The study reported here was part of a larger study whose aim was to document and analyse the features of Grade 6 Irish immersion students' spoken Irish and to gain student views about their proficiency. This chapter confines itself to the latter part. The research questions are as follows:

(1) What are the students' opinions of the variety of Irish that they speak?
(2) Do the students notice errors in their own and their peers' speech and are they able to correct those errors given time to reflect on them?
(3) Why do the students use non-target-like forms when they know more accurate forms?

A mainly qualitative design was adopted for this part of the study with some quantitative measures applied to a number of themes that emerged from the students' comments. The approach was ethnomethodological in character where an attempt was made to describe the situation from the perspective of the group members (Coolican, 2004). A purposive sample was chosen consisting of nine Irish immersion schools from a total of 130 such schools in existence in September 2006. The schools selected represent the full range of Irish immersion schools found in the Republic of Ireland and were carefully chosen against a set of criteria that represented their different characteristics. Summarised in Table 8.1, these criteria included school size, geographical location, number of years in existence, socio-economic status of students' parents and access to an Irish immersion high school. Sixty-five Grade 6 students were chosen from these schools. Grade 6 students were chosen because they were in their final year in elementary school and had experienced an average of 5750 hours of instruction through the medium of Irish.

Table 8.1 Characteristics of participating schools

School ID	Students F	Students M	Students Total	No. of groups	No. of minutes transcribed	Location: Small town/ City	No. of years established	Accessible to 2nd level Irish immersion school	No. of pupils in school	Disadvantaged status
School 1	2	4	6	2	40	Small town	<20 yrs	X	200–300	X
School 2	6	3	9	3	55	City	<20 yrs	✓	200–300	X
School 3	4	2	6	2	26	City	>30 yrs	✓	>300	X
School 4	4	5	9	3	60	City	>30 yrs	✓	200–300	✓
School 5	5	4	9	3	56	Small town	20–30 yrs	✓	>300	X
School 6	7	4	11	4	51	Small town	<20 yrs	X	<200	✓
School 7	3	3	6	2	40	Small town	20–30 yrs	✓	>300	X
School 8	3	3	6	2	31	City	20–30 yrs	✓	200–300	✓
School 9	1	2	3	1	21	Small town	20–30 yrs	X	200–300	X
Total	35	30	65	22	380 (6 hours, 20 minutes)					

Collaborative task

I was the sole researcher, and in order to gather samples of student speech, as close as possible to typical peer-to-peer interaction, I designed a whole-class activity where I divided students into groups of three (22 groups in total).[1] The activity took place during regular class time, and the teacher assisted in grouping the children. The students were asked to collaborate in designing a playground for an elementary school in Zambia. They were given a budget of €3000 and pictures of playground equipment with prices attached. They were asked to draw their design following discussion and negotiation. Up to three student groups in each class were randomly selected to be video recorded while engaged in the task.[2] As Table 8.1 shows, only one group was recorded in School 9, as this was the first school where data were gathered. Due to the fact that there were only eleven Grade 6 pupils in School 6, the students were divided into three triads and one dyad.

On average, the task took 25–30 minutes to complete. The initial analysis revealed that the first 20 minutes of speech from the selected groups yielded the greatest amount of discussion. Thus, the first 20 minutes were chosen for transcription, although it should be noted that a small number of groups succeeded in completing the task in less than 20 minutes, reducing the amount of transcribed speech. The transcriptions amounted to six hours and 20 minutes of student dialogue, generating a corpus of over 35,000 words.

The analysis of the corpus revealed that the most common features of Irish not yet mastered by the immersion students were use of the copula and verbal noun clauses. The incidence of code-mixing and the mapping of English syntax onto Irish were also established. These features formed the main topics for investigation in the stimulated recall interviews described in the next section. An explanation of two of these features is provided in an Appendix for the benefit of non-Irish speakers.

Stimulated recall

In the second stage of the study, immersion students' understanding and awareness of the most common non-target-like features of their Irish were examined. Excerpts of the video recordings of the collaborative task containing the most common features identified above were chosen and converted to DVD format. The rationale for choosing the most common features was that they provide the most reliable evidence of linguistic competence compared to low-frequency items (Chaudron, 2003). These

DVD recordings were then used to ask participants to explore their perceptions as they viewed themselves performing the task. The students were given an opportunity to reflect on their output and to correct it upon reflection, thus giving more reliable evidence of their underlying linguistic competence and providing additional data than would be available if one relied merely on the linguistic performance in the initial recording.

I returned to the school seven to 10 days after the initial recording, and invited the students in each group to participate in a stimulated recall of excerpts of their group work. Each group was withdrawn from the class to a quiet area in the school for this purpose. The stimulated recall interviews were audio recorded for analysis. There were three phases to the stimulated recall activity. Each phase took approximately 10 minutes, and one phase led naturally to the next with the result that the activity lasted no more than 30 minutes. There was also some overlap between the phases at times arising from the comments of a particular student. In the first phase, the students as a group, viewed recorded video excerpts in DVD format on a laptop computer and gave their general thoughts on the extracts. As they cited language-related issues, I focused the reflection on these issues, easing them into the activity in a non-threatening way to gain their confidence and trust. In this way, they were enabled to share their observations and insights into their thought processes with an interested enquirer.

In the second phase, the students were given a transcript of the excerpt that they had just viewed and shown the recording again. After the second viewing they were invited to comment on the quality of their Irish and to correct any mistakes that they had noted in the recording or transcript. The third phase focused on the errors that the students corrected. The issue of why they made mistakes when they knew the correct form was explored with them together with their thought processes as they were engaged in the collaborative task.

The audio recordings of the stimulated recall sessions were analysed using NVivo8 software. I listened to the recordings and identified different themes that emerged from the students' comments. I transcribed the exchanges between myself and the students and coded them under the different themes that emerged from the data.

Results

All aspects of the research were conducted through the medium of Irish; the views of the students quoted below have been translated to English for reporting purposes. The results arising from the three phases of the stimulated recall sessions are reported under the various themes that emerged.

Phases 1 and 2

Students' perceptions of the quality of their Irish

The students viewed selected excerpts containing non-target-like forms on a laptop computer. I then focused on how they had worked on the task as a group and on the general quality of their Irish. Regarding the latter, they generally responded in one of two ways. Eleven groups (50%) indicated general satisfaction with the quality of their Irish. As Student A (School 7) stated: 'It's all right.' The other 11 groups (50%) were more critical of their Irish. In many cases this lack of quality appeared to be a revelation to them: 'I thought that the Irish, it wasn't good. I thought that it was better when I was talking to someone.' (Student F, School 9).

In some cases, the students were even more critical of the quality of their Irish when they viewed it a second time in combination with the written transcript. It appears that until they saw their speech written down, they did not realise the level of code-mixing and the number of mistakes, as the following exchange from School 3 indicates:

Student J: I thought that we had good Irish.
Student N: Yeah, when you see it on the screen and when you can hear yourself.
Student S: And then when it is written out.

Correction of errors following reflection on output

In the second phase of the stimulated recall process, the students were invited to correct the errors that they noticed. Again, they received a written transcript and viewed the recording a second time. The initial reaction of all groups was to replace English words with their Irish equivalent or to remove discourse markers ('okay', 'so', 'like') completely.

The analysis of the student corpus in the first stage of the study revealed the students used incorrect forms of the copula 32.7% of the time. In the majority of these instances, students used the substantive verb *Bí* 'to be' where the copula *Is* 'is' should have been used. The stimulated recall sessions offered an opportunity to see if the students could correct some of these incorrect forms given an opportunity to reflect on them. I found that the students in almost every stimulated recall session failed to notice errors of this type. When their attention was drawn to them, they were still unable to correct the errors. When I prompted them, however, with an analogous example they could correct their deviant use of the copula in almost 85% of cases. The following exchange with Student J (School 7) illustrates the point. Student J made the following incorrect utterance while engaged in the original collaborative task. He used the substantive verb instead of the copula: *Agus tá sin an airgead go dtí an méid a bhí ceadaithe againn.* (And that be (substantive verb) the money to the amount that was allowed.) I drew his attention to this utterance and asked if he noticed any errors in it. When he did not notice the error I prompted him as follows:

Researcher: If you said to the teacher, 'That be the pencil.' (*Tá sin an peann luaidhe* – using substantive verb) What would she say?

Student J: 'That is a pencil.' (*Is peann luaidhe é sin* – using copula)

Researcher: [now referring to his error in the transcript] Is there a better way to say? 'That be the money.'

Student J: That is the amount of money that was allowed. (*Sin an méid airgead a bhí ceadaithe* – using copula)

When other students were prompted in this way they were able to reform their original utterances and use the copula correctly 85% of the time. It appears that the language input that Irish immersion students receive may not be sufficiently salient for them to acquire this form of the copula where there is not a single map from English onto Irish. This in turn may indicate a need to change the way in which the copula is taught. Based on the results of this study, it appears that Grade 6 students have partially mastered the use of the copula. They can produce the correct form when prompted to do so in a particular way. It appears, however, that it has not been internalised as part of their unmonitored spontaneous output.

The use of verbal noun clauses was noted as another area of difficulty for the students. The corpus analysis revealed that they were incorrectly used 61.4% of the time. This issue was explored with the students in the recall sessions in a similar way to the copula above. In general, the students did not notice their incorrect use of verbal noun clauses. When I drew their attention to them they could correct approximately 50% of them. On the other occasions when I prompted them with a similar phrase that used the same structure in a familiar context, they managed to see the connection and correct the verbal noun clause.

The following excerpt from School 4, illustrates a typical example where the students did not notice an error even when I drew their attention to it initially. When I followed up with a similar error that they might make with the teacher, they were able to correct it. It is interesting to note in the final three utterances that the reformulation Student B offered was not fully correct. Student D inserted the omitted word 'else' and Student N repeated him:

Original utterance by Student B: *An bhfuil cead againn déan rud éigin eile?* [May we (have we permission) something else to do?]

Stimulated recall:

Researcher:	Do you know B, or any of the rest of you, if you said to the teacher, 'May I a drink to get?' What would he say?
Student B:	May I get a drink? (*An bhfuil cead agam deoch a fháil.*)
Researcher:	If you said to the teacher, 'May we something else to do?' What would he say?
Student B:	May we do something? (*An bhfuil cead rud éigin a déanamh?*)
Student D:	Do something else. (*Rud éigin eile a déanamh?*)
Student N:	Do something else (with lenition). (*Rud éigin eile a dhéanamh?*)

Turning now to the issue of code-mixing, the corpus analysis revealed that 10% of the words uttered by the students were English words. Further analysis showed that the affirmative/negative particles, 'no' and 'yeah', and the discourse markers 'so', 'okay', 'just', 'like' and 'right' accounted for the majority of these, representing 6.35% of the total corpus. Students' reactions to this relatively high use of English words were explored in the stimulated recall sessions. In general, when students were questioned about this they repeatedly stated that they were not aware that they were using them and that it was a 'habit'. It was this aspect above all others that disappointed them regarding the quality of their Irish.

Phase 3

Using the reflections from Phases 1 and 2 as a starting point, the third phase of the recall sessions engaged the students in considering the reasons, in a more general way, why they had not spoken as accurately as they were capable of and why their Irish contained so many English words. Six themes emerged from the analysis: monitoring of output, correction of errors by peers, recycling of learner errors, translation from English, 'focus on forms' and exposure to Irish outside of school.

Monitoring of output

In the exchange below, following the correction of a verbal noun clause, the student (Student J, School 7) was questioned as to why, in her spontaneous speech, she makes mistakes when she knows the correct form.

Researcher: Why do you make a mistake like that when you know the correct language form?

Student J: Maybe you are just trying to say it, to get it out and you are not giving it a lot of thought.

This suggests that on occasions, mistakes are made because students are not monitoring their output, and once their attention is drawn to a problematical feature they know immediately that it is wrong. The issue of monitoring of output emerged in 19 of the 22 groups, in all cases the students indicated that they 'don't think' when they are engaged in spontaneous conversation with their peers. Student A (School 7) offered the view that they are influenced by their language behaviour outside of school:

Researcher: Why do you make a mistake like that when you know the correct language form?

Student A: Because when you are going around with your friends it is English that you speak and when you come to school it is Irish and you have to think about it.

Following responses such as this, I asked the students in 13 of the 22 groups about monitoring their speech when speaking to the teacher:

Researcher: Do you think more when you are talking to the teacher or to your friends?

Student C: When you are talking to the teacher, before you go up, you are thinking about what you are going to say to him. Like before you put up your hand you have to think. What is the Irish for the thing you are looking for?

Student D offered a similar response:

Student D: We make a big effort in class with the teacher but I think when we are with our friends that we don't make as big an effort.

It is clear that the norm of speaking Irish as accurately as possible with the teacher is well established. It is also clear that students must expend extra effort to maintain this 'standard', and they are not as inclined to do so when speaking to their friends.

Correction of errors by peers

It was noted in the corpus analysis that there were no instances where a student corrected a peer's inaccurate use of Irish. Notwithstanding this, the students in seven of the 22 groups were asked in the stimulated recall if they ever corrected each other. The responses of Student G (School 4) and Student J (School 3) to this question were typical:

Researcher: Do you ever correct one another?
Student G: No, it depends. Maybe if you are speaking English a lot you will be corrected.
Student J: Sometimes. You hear it when someone else speaks Irish that isn't accurate. But you don't hear that you are not speaking accurately yourself.

Student S (School 3) offered the following response when asked if it upset them in any way to be corrected by a peer:

Student S: Sometimes it upsets you if there is a person in the class who thinks that they know everything …. If your friends correct you they will be just telling you to be careful speaking like that because you will be in trouble. Your friends are looking out for you. You will feel embarrassed, because everyone is around and someone corrects you.

These comments underline the difficult task that immersion teachers have in striking a balance between encouraging students to speak the target language and in correcting their inaccuracies, which may cause embarrassment. Similarly, it is difficult for students to correct their peers' inaccuracies as they may worry that they might be seen as policing their peers. 'Looking out' for your friends, however, legitimises drawing their attention to the use of English words. It may also be the case that the immersion variety of Irish spoken by the students is seen as legitimate and the accepted norm and that students see no more need to correct it than they would correct a peer's English (de Courcy, 1997).

Recycling of learner errors

The effect of being exposed to incorrect Irish was also mentioned by a small number of students. Student K (School 2) explained how she 'picks up' on incorrect forms from her peers and uses them herself. She goes on to explain that she would not correct her peers when they use an incorrect form because she understands what they are trying to say. The emphasis is on communicating the message:

Student K: Because you hear people saying the wrong things and you just pick up on those things. And you just say them.

Researcher: When you are speaking among yourselves, if I say, 'It be a computer' (using substantive verb). You wouldn't correct me?

Student K: No. Because I know what you are like, trying to say, so I don't say anything.

It appears that once the students' output conforms to the implicit norms of their variety of Irish, a peer will not comment on it unless it leads to a breakdown in communication.

Translation from English

The issue of translation from English, the students' L1, was raised specifically with seven of the 22 groups. The students recognise that they translate words from English in some contexts when the source of their conversation is in English, such as a television programme in English or when doing a crossword, as explained by Student C (School 4):

Student C: Say if you are talking to your friend about a television programme and say if the programme is in English. You have to translate it in your head before you say it to your friend. But if you are just talking to your friend you say it in Irish. You are just thinking of the words in your head.

The use of English in this way is a type of 'translanguaging' where students hear or read something in English and produce it in Irish (Baker, 2001). Other students also reported translating from English when doing an essay in Irish, for example. Although it has been noted that immersion students appear to map English syntax onto the target language (Lapkin & Swain, 2004), the evidence from the responses of the students above and five of the other groups that participated in the stimulated recall is that the students do not consciously translate from English to Irish in the course of their everyday conversation. Thus, where the influence of English is detectable, it is very likely an embedded unconscious influence, not a transient effect of 'translation'. The only exception to this is where they are referring to material that occurred in English. The influence of English on the students' Irish appears to be at a subconscious level. If this is indeed the case, the students' attention may need to be drawn to it in order to change it.

Focus on forms

It was observed that students in two of the schools (School 3 and School 4) referred to grammar lessons more frequently than students in the other schools. In the case of School 3 it emerged that their teacher engaged in 'focus on forms' lessons with a particular emphasis on the irregular verbs in Irish. While it is beyond the scope of this study to assess the efficacy of these lessons, it was notable that the students from both School 3 and School 4 displayed a greater sense of awareness of the importance of grammatical accuracy than students from the other schools in the study. Although the students in Schools 3 and 4 had a heightened sense of awareness of certain features of Irish relative to their peers in the other schools in the study, it did not appear to translate into their communicative performance, as Student S explained:

Student S: You forget some of those things when you are speaking naturally. It must be very clear in your mind.

It may be the case, however, that this was an important first step in helping them to notice the gap in their accuracy (Skehan, 1998). It was noted that the students in School 3 outperformed all other schools in their ability to notice mistakes in the transcripts and to correct those mistakes. They may have access to declarative knowledge about some forms that has not yet been proceduralised.

Exposure to Irish outside of school
    The lack of exposure to Irish outside of school was offered as a reason by seven of the 22 groups, in five different schools, as to why the students' Irish contained errors and words in English. The students in School 6 were asked why they thought that their Irish contained mistakes when they knew the correct form.

Student A: 'Cos we are always like speaking English and when we are at school we speak Irish.
Student C: We have no Irish, it is just English at home.
Student L: There is no Irish anywhere in this town, it's just the Gaeltacht (Irish-speaking areas) like where you speak Irish outside of school.

Discussion

Half of the students in the selected groups were critical of their spoken Irish when they were given an opportunity to view a DVD of their interaction and to see their speech transcribed. The aspect that they were most commonly critical of was code-mixing. When students were given an opportunity to correct their Irish on reflection, their most common response was only to replace the English words. Student-expressed reasons for the use of English were that it was just a 'habit', that they were not monitoring their language, as they were focused on the task rather than on their language use, and that they lacked exposure to Irish outside of school.

Apart from code-mixing, the recall sessions focused on two grammatical features of the students' Irish in particular, namely the copula and verbal noun clauses. When the students were given an opportunity to correct their mistakes, they rarely noticed any problem with them until their attention was specifically drawn to possible alternative forms. As for the copula, they could correct the error 85% of the time if prompted. They corrected 50% of errors involving verbal noun clauses when their attention was drawn to them, but without the need for prompts. That students were able to correct many of their mistakes when their attention was drawn to them may reflect an underlying communicative competence that may not always be fully displayed in students' communicative performance.

There was evidence in the recall sessions that students monitor their output more carefully when they are speaking to the teacher than when speaking to peers. Use of Irish with the teacher, therefore, represents 'pushed output' (Swain, 2005: 473) where the students know that their inaccuracies will be corrected. The students indicate that they do not like being corrected publicly by their peers or the teacher, and that this can lead to embarrassment. They rarely negotiate form in interaction with peers. Broner and Tedick (Chapter 9) uncovered a similar finding with Grade 5 Spanish immersion students. In the cases where Irish immersion students do so, it is generally in instances where there is code-mixing or code-switching.

A factor that the students believe may affect the level of errors in their output is that they acquire inaccurate forms that they hear so often from their peers. As these deviant forms are comprehensible, they can go unnoticed or are tolerated, when the emphasis is on meaning rather than on form. The role of the teacher, therefore, is crucial in providing corrective feedback (e.g. Lyster & Ranta, 1997) to the students, as they are not exposed to native speakers outside of school who might fulfil the role of maintaining the kind of implicit social pressure that promotes native speaker norms.

There were examples in the transcripts where it appeared that English syntax was mapped onto Irish. When the students were questioned about this they stated that they did not consciously translate from English to Irish unless they were talking about a topic that was originally experienced in English, such as a movie or television programme. This may indicate that the inaccurate forms of copula and verbal noun clauses that they use have resulted from negative transfer from English and have stabilised in their interlanguage rather than the direct translation from English to Irish. If this is the case, it may be more difficult for them to notice and internalise the correct forms available to them in the input and may require specific pedagogic intervention. The research suggests that focus-on-form activities may help learners attend to form, leading to change in their underlying interlanguage (Lyster, 2007; Lyster & Ranta, 1997). If this issue is not addressed, the Irish immersion students' propensity to habitually produce inaccurate forms may become embedded and lead to a degree of permanency (Hammerly, 1989).

Conclusion: Exploring Pedagogical Possibilities

The study presented in this chapter leads to a range of pedagogical possibilities that may be implemented in all types of immersion programmes to improve the linguistic accuracy of immersion students' oral language. Convincing arguments have been made in the literature for a more analytic (form-focused) approach to L2 learning in immersion (e.g. Lyster, 2007). While not advocating extensive explicit teaching of grammar, some explanation of grammatical elements adjusted to the maturity level of the students with tasks focused on meaning *and* form are warranted (e.g. Lyster, 2004, 2007; Swain & Lapkin, 2008). There is a danger that by not addressing particular features at the appropriate time, the non-target-like forms will be stored in long-term memory and become automatised (Skehan, 1998), rendering them less susceptible to change.

Irish immersion teachers have suggested that inaccurate use of these forms is the result of translation from English (Ó Duibhir, 2009). While this assessment may be partially true, it appears more likely from the students' feedback that these forms were internalised at an earlier stage and that they have stabilised in the students' interlanguage. Another factor in their continued use is that both these forms do not have a single map from English to Irish. This raises the issue that the input students receive may not be sufficiently salient for them either to notice the correct form or to realise that the forms they are using are not target like and need to be corrected. Thus, certain grammatical forms in the immersion language may require enhanced input (Sharwood Smith, 1993) and/or explicit teaching (Spada & Lightbown, 2005) at an early stage in an attempt to prevent them from stabilising and becoming less susceptible to change. Such an intervention may help to counterbalance the over-reliance on the acquisition of these forms by means of exposure to content alone (Lyster, 2007). This speaks to the need to incorporate a language focus into content-based activities. Tasks that involve the preparation of oral presentations and materials for real audiences provide opportunities for pushed output and enable the teacher to integrate language and content objectives more effectively should be emphasised in immersion classrooms. Teachers should engage in more consistent monitoring of input to ensure that there is sufficient input of the correct forms and that it is sufficiently salient. In addition, corrective feedback that promotes self-repair of grammatical errors has been shown to be effective in immersion contexts (Lyster, 2007; Lyster & Ranta, 1997). This approach also encourages learners to be more responsible for their own learning and enhances learner autonomy.

The students in Schools 3 and 4 commented on the focus-on-forms lessons taught by their respective teachers. Although these lessons did not lead to significantly greater accuracy on the part of the students, the groups from these schools displayed a greater awareness of their errors in the stimulated recall. The two groups from School 3 in particular outperformed all other schools in their ability to notice mistakes and correct them. Further research into the pedagogy in these schools may lead to interesting pedagogical possibilities for improving accuracy.

The behaviour of the Irish immersion students in this study indicated that they interpret the school norm of speaking Irish as 'not using English words'. In immersion programmes, eventually the emphasis needs to shift to affirming students, not only for speaking the target language, but also for the quality of their output. In order to further improve students' accuracy, it may also be necessary to change the teacher–student power relationship. The students in this study demonstrated very good insight into their language use when given an opportunity to express their opinions. It also emerged that they would be reluctant to correct peers' language, as they might be perceived to be policing them. If a more collaborative approach towards speaking the immersion language with greater accuracy was promoted, students could be facilitated to support one another in providing a stimulus for pushed output. Students would need to have greater autonomy over their learning for this to happen (Little, 2007).

The stimulated recall activity in the present study demonstrates one way in which students can be more autonomous in their language learning. Viewing video excerpts allowed them to become aware of their errors and code-mixing. Teachers could record their students engaged in different activities and provide opportunities for the students to view the recordings, transcribe extracts and then be provided with a reformulation of this dialogue by the teacher. The transcription element appeared critical in this study in helping students notice errors. Various studies (Lynch, 2001; Swain & Lapkin, 2008) have shown that these strategies lead the students to notice gaps in their own interlanguage, and this has led to longer-term learning of targeted structures. It has also been shown that such collaborative dialogues facilitate students in engaging in 'languaging', where the students produce language to try to understand the difference between their original utterance and the reformulation (Swain, 2006). This process serves to mediate cognition by acting as 'a vehicle through which thinking is articulated and transformed into artifactual form' (Swain, 2006: 97). Indeed, Swain (2005) maintains that stimulated recalls can be viewed not just as means of collecting research data but as part of the learning process itself.

Finally, the stimulated recall interviews described in the study sought to give a voice to young immersion students about the quality and nature of their use of Irish. Their views provide valuable insights into their understanding of the accuracy of their target language use and offer interesting possibilities for immersion teaching. Indeed, the process of engaging students in stimulated recall activities heightens their awareness of the quality of their target language use and could be used as a first step towards greater agency on the part of the learner and learner autonomy.

Notes

1. One group contained two students.
2. Groups containing children who spoke Irish more often in the home, as identified by the teacher, were excluded from video recording.

Appendix

The copula Is and substantive verb Bí

An area of difficulty for English speakers learning Irish is the use of a substantive verb and a copula to express 'to be'. Irish is similar to Spanish in this respect, as Spanish has two verbs to express 'to be', *ser* and *estar*. The two lexical items in Irish to express the verb 'to be' are *Bí* (substantive verb) and *Is* (copula), posing difficulty for native English-speaking learners of Irish. *Bí* can be used to express 'it is ...' or 'he is ...' in cases, where temporary states are being described:

It is raining. = *Tá sé ag cur báistí.*
He is in the house. = *Tá sé sa teach.*

It cannot be used, however, where a permanent state is being described. In such instances the copula *Is* must be used.

He is a teacher. = *Is múinteoir é.*
It is a ball. = *Is liathróid í.*

To complicate matters further, when the copula is used with the demonstrative pronoun *sin* 'that', the copula and the personal pronoun can be omitted. Thus, the following three sentences are all acceptable ways to express the same thing, that is 'That is the table.'

(1) *Is é sin an bord.*
(2) *Sin an bord.*
(3) *Sin é an bord.*

Sentence (1) contains the copula *Is* and the personal pronoun *é*, sentence (2) omits both the copula *Is* and the personal pronoun *é*, while sentence (3) omits the copula *Is* but contains the personal pronoun *é*.

Word-order principles in verbal noun clauses

Another feature that differs from English and other languages is the word order of verbal noun clauses. In English the object generally comes after the verb, whereas that order is reversed in Irish with the insertion of the preposition *a* + lenition. Thus, the syntax in Irish is: object + *a* (preposition) + verbal noun.

You can draw it.
Is féidir leat é a tharraingt. (Literally: You can it to draw)

The tendency for learners is to use English syntax as in the following inaccurate utterance:

*Is féidir leat tarraingt é. (Literally: You can draw it.)

References

An Roinn Oideachais/The Department of Education (1937) *Tuarascáil Staitisticiúil 1935/36*. Dublin: The Stationery Office.
Baker, C. (2001) *Foundations of Bilingual Education and Bilingualism* (3rd edn). Clevedon: Multilingual Matters.
Central Statistics Office (2007) *Census 2006: Volume 9 – Irish Language*. Dublin: Stationery Office.
Chaudron, C. (2003) Data collection in SLA research. In C. Doughty and M.H. Long (eds) *The Handbook of Second Language Acquisition* (pp. 762–828). Oxford: Blackwell.
Coolahan, J. (1981) *Irish Education: Its History and Structure*. Dublin: Institute of Public Administration.
Coolican, H. (2004) *Research Methods and Statistics in Psychology* (4th edn). London: Hodder and Stoughton.
Day, E. and Shapson, S. (1996) *Studies in Immersion Education*. Clevedon: Multilingual Matters.
de Courcy, M. (1997) Benowa High: A decade of French immersion in Australia. In R. K. Johnson and M. Swain (eds) *Immersion Education: International Perspectives* (pp. 44–62). Cambridge: Cambridge University Press.
Genesee, R. (1987) *Learning through Two Languages: Studies of Immersion and Bilingual Education*. Cambridge, MA: Newbury House.

Hammerly, H. (1989) Toward fluency and accuracy: A response to Allen, Cummins, Harley, Lapkin and Swain. *The Canadian Modern Language Review* 45, 776–783.

Harley, B. (1987) *The Development of Second Language Proficiency. Final report. Volume II: Classroom treatment*. Toronto: Modern Language Centre, Ontario Institute for Studies in Education.

Harris, J. (1984) *Spoken Irish in Primary Schools: An analysis of Achievement*. Dublin: Institiúid Teangeolaíochta Éireann.

Harris, J., Forde, P., Archer, P., Nic Fhearaile, S. and O'Gorman, M. (2006) *Irish in Primary Schools: Long-term National Trends in Achievement*. Dublin: Department of Education and Science.

Lapkin, S. and Swain, M. (2004) What underlies immersion students' production: The case of avoir besoin de. *Foreign Language Annals* 37, 349–355.

Little, D.G. (2007) Language learner autonomy: Some fundamental considerations revisited. *Innovation in Language Learning and Teaching* 1, 14–29.

Lynch, T. (2001) Seeing what they meant: Transcribing as a route to noticing. *ELT J* 55, 124–132.

Lyster, R. (1987) Speaking immersion. *The Canadian Modern Language Review* 43, 701–717.

Lyster, R. (1998) Diffusing dichotomies: Using the multidimensional curriculum model for developing analytic teaching materials in immersion. In S. Lapkin (ed.) *French Second-Language Education in Canada: Empirical Studies* (pp. 197–218). Toronto: University of Toronto Press.

Lyster, R. (2004) Research on form-focused instruction in immersion classrooms: Implications for theory and practice. *French Language Studies* 14, 321–341.

Lyster, R. (2007) *Learning and Teaching Languages Through Content: A Counterbalanced Approach* (Vol. 28). Amsterdam: John Benjamins.

Lyster, R. and Ranta, L. (1997) Corrective feedback and learner uptake: Negotiation of form in communicative classrooms. *Studies in Second Language Acquisition* 19, 37–66.

Máirtín, C. (2006) *Soláthar múinteoirí do na bunscoileanna lán-Ghaeilge: Bunachar sonraí agus tuairimíocht phríomhoidí i leith gnéithe den staid reatha sa Ghaelscolaíocht*. Baile Átha Cliath: An Chomhairle um Oideachas Gaeltachta agus Gaelscolaíochta.

National Council for Curriculum and Assessment (2006) *Language and Literacy in Irish-Medium Primary Schools: Descriptions of Practice*. Dublin: NCCA.

National Programme Conference (1922) *National Programme of Primary Instruction*. Dublin: Browne and Nolan.

Ó Catháin, B. (2001) Dearcadh an teangeolaí ar chomharthaí sóirt Ghaeilge an lae inniu. In R. Ó hUiginn (ed.) *Léachtaí Cholm Cille XXXI* (pp. 128–149). Maigh Nuad: An Sagart.

Ó Duibhir, P. (2009) *The Spoken Irish of Sixth-Class Pupils in Irish Immersion Schools*. Dissertation thesis, Trinity College, Dublin.

Ó Riagáin, P. (2007) Relationships between attitudes to Irish, social class, religion and national identity in the Republic of Ireland and Northern Ireland. *The International Journal of Bilingual Education and Bilingualism* 10, 369–393.

Ó Tuathaigh, G. (1991) The Irish-Ireland idea: Rationale and relevance. In E. Longley (ed.) *Culture in Ireland: Division or Diversity?* Belfast: Institute of Irish Studies.

Parsons, C. and Liddy, F. (2009) *Learning to Read in Irish and English: A Comparison of Children in Irish-Medium, Gaeltacht and English-Medium Schools in Ireland*. Dublin: An Chomhairle um Oideachais Gaeltachta agus Gaelscolaíochta.

Punch, A. (2008) Census data on the Irish language. In C. Nic Pháidín and S. Ó Cearnaigh (eds) *A New View of the Irish Language* (pp. 43–54). Dublin: Cois Life.

Sharwood Smith, M. (1993) Input enhancement in instructed SLA: Theoretical bases. *Studies in Second Language acquisition* 15, 165–179.

Skehan, P. (1998) *A Cognitive Approach to Language Learning*. Oxford: Oxford University Press.

Spada, N. and Lightbown, P.M. (2005) The importance of form/meaning mappings in explicit form-focused instruction. In A. Housen and M. Pierrard (eds), *Investigations in Instructed Second Language Acquisition* (pp. 199–234). Amsterdam: Mouton de Gruyter.

Swain, M. (2000) French immersion research in Canada: Recent contributions to SLA and applied linguistics. *Annual Review of Applied Linguistics* 20, 199–212.

Swain, M. (2005) The output hypothesis: Theory and research. In E. Hinkel (ed.) *Handbook of Research in Second Language Teaching and Learning* (pp. 471–483). Mahwah, NJ: Erlbaum.

Swain, M. (2006) Languaging, agency and collaboration in advanced second language proficiency. In H. Byrnes (ed.) *Advanced Language Learning: The Contribution of Halliday and Vygotsky* (pp. 95–108). London: Continuum.

Swain, M. and Lapkin, S. (2008) Lexical learning through a multitask activity: The role of repetition. In T.W. Fortune and D.J. Tedick (eds) *Pathways to Multilingualism: Evolving Perspectives on Immersion Education* (pp. 119–132). Clevedon: Multilingual Matters.

Chapter 9
Talking in the Fifth-Grade Classroom: Language Use in an Early, Total Spanish Immersion Program

M.A. BRONER and D.J. TEDICK

Introduction

For decades, researchers around the world have demonstrated that one-way (foreign language) immersion education is one of the most successful approaches to teaching foreign languages in terms of overall academic achievement and majority language development (e.g. Genesee, 1987; Swain & Lapkin, 1982). At the same time, studies have shown that although immersion students develop near-native levels of proficiency in the receptive skills (listening/reading), their productive skills (speaking/writing) do not reach native-like levels (e.g. Genesee, 1987; Harley, 1992; Swain & Lapkin, 1982).

Tarone and Swain (1995) further observed that as immersion students progress through the grades, they abandon exclusive use of the second language (L2). They argued that while the L2 is 'the institutional language of academic discourse', the first language (L1) becomes the language for social interactions, hypothesizing that immersion classrooms become diglossic over time (Tarone & Swain, 1995: 170).

The present study grew out of Tarone and Swain's call to conduct research that systematically examines the role of L1 and L2 use in immersion classrooms. In this case study, we analyze the social and linguistic factors affecting patterns of language use in the discourse of three fifth graders attending an early, total one-way Spanish immersion program in a large US Midwestern city. The mixed methods study uses a combination of corpus, quantitative and qualitative analyses to describe the contexts of

L2 (Spanish) and L1 (English) use for these three students. Emphasis in this chapter is on the qualitative portion of the study.

Background to the Study

Studies conducted in the 1990s attempted to understand when and why children attending early, total immersion programs used L1 in classroom contexts demanding L2 use. Issues revealed included interlocutor effects (e.g. Broner, 1991; Carranza, 1995; Tarone & Swain, 1995), the effect of task type and content (e.g. Fazio & Lyster, 1998; Swain & Lapkin, 1998) and the impact of reflection on L2 form using L1 in collaborative discourse (Swain & Lapkin, 1998). Only a few studies have attempted to answer Tarone and Swain's (1995) call for research on students' L1 and L2 use through direct observations in immersion classrooms. Carrigo (2000) and Potowski (2004) conducted studies in two-way immersion (TWI) programs, while Fortune (2001) explored language use in a one-way program that enrolled some Spanish-dominant learners. A feature shared by those studies and the present study is the focus on fifth-grade learners' language. More recently, Huang and Rau (2007) explored language use by kindergarteners attending an English immersion program in Taiwan and found that language use was significantly affected by factors such as interlocutor, gender, social networks, context and teacher and parents' attitudes.

Carrigo studied language use in six TWI upper-grade classrooms, including fifth grade. Teachers were found to use more Spanish with students who spoke Spanish at home. Children tended to respond to teachers in the language in which they were addressed. Among peers, Spanish speakers used more Spanish with each other but more English with English speakers. In mixed groupings, all children used more English: '... more than 75% of conversations initiated by students began in English, and these all happened during Spanish instruction time' (Carrigo, 2000: 157). Spanish was seldom used when students interacted socially.

Following a sociocultural theoretical framework (Vygotsky, 1978), Fortune (2001) carried out a carefully crafted interpretive case study following the oral language use of four fifth graders, two English L1 speakers, one Spanish L1 speaker, and one child who was raised bilingually with an English L1 parent and Spanish L1 parent. Fortune found that all children used Spanish roughly only a third of the time during Spanish instructional time. Factors that encouraged more Spanish use were the proximity of the teacher and when lessons involved writing and math problem-solving tasks. Fortune also found that interlocutor factors impacted children's language use.

Finally, Potowski (2004) carried out a study exploring the role of L1 and L2 among four fifth graders (two Spanish L1 and two English L1) attending a Spanish–English TWI school. She found that overall, these children used Spanish 56% of Spanish instructional time. Potowski's findings led her to speculate that language choice was possibly impacted by gender, with girls accounting for more Spanish turns than boys. Interlocutors also had an impact on Spanish use. More than 80% of turns with the teacher were in Spanish, but only 32% of turns with peers were in Spanish. Potowski argued that Norton's (2000) notion of investment added an additional dimension to language use in TWI settings, noting that each child's identification with Spanish partially explained the choices behind their language use.

The Study

In this mixed methods case study, the following questions were explored:

(1) What languages (English L1/Spanish L2) do students use in peer–peer and student–teacher interactions?
(2) What factors (interlocutor, task factors, context, individual characteristics, etc.) impact student language choices?

Context of the study

Data were gathered in a one-way K–5 early, total Spanish immersion school in the United States. In this school, English is introduced formally in second grade when English language arts are taught for 30 minutes a day. The amount of time devoted to English reading and language arts increases from 30 minutes to approximately 60 minutes in Grades 3 and 4 and 90 minutes in Grade 5. This school ends at fifth grade, though students have the option of enrolling in a secondary continuation program.

The teacher was a nonnative speaker of Spanish with near-native proficiency who encouraged a classroom atmosphere that fostered creativity. She promoted small group interactions and emphasized Spanish use and critical thinking skills.

Focal students: Leonard, Marvin and Carolina

After a period of observation that took place between October and December, three fifth graders were selected as the focal students for this study, Leonard, Carolina and Marvin.[1] Leonard and Carolina were selected with teacher input based on gender and students' willingness to use language orally and participate in class activities. Leonard was well liked by others, bright, extroverted, talkative and highly active. Carolina was usually 'on-task' and typically took the initiative to complete group tasks. She was also talkative, extroverted and tended to be more comfortable with girls. Marvin was later added based on observations of his unusual L2 use; he was the only student who consistently used Spanish, even outside the classroom. Although not an outcast, Marvin was not popular with the other students.

Data collection

Data were collected during the Spanish portion of the day in a fifth-grade classroom through a variety of techniques: audiotapes, field notes, interviews with focal students and the teacher and questionnaires to families and all fifth graders. This chapter focuses on audiotaped episodes, field notes and interviews. Classroom observations occurred once a week (Monday mornings) for 23 weeks during Spanish class time between October and May. Taped activities were not selected *a priori*, and hence whatever activity was taking place during Spanish time that morning was the observed activity.

Each focal student wore a lapel microphone connected to a wireless transmitter device during taping sessions, allowing for mobility. Audiotaped data were obtained from each of the three children as they carried out different classroom tasks with each other, the teacher and other children. The focal students often sat together in groups that included other children.

Fifteen sessions, ranging between 25–80 minutes, were taped from January to May. The analysis presented here is based on 13 of the 15 sessions in which at least two of the three focal students were present. Once data were gathered, they were transcribed. A variety of data transcription coding conventions were adapted from Liu (1991) and Edwards and Lampert (1993), among others and used during analysis. The unit of data analysis was the utterance,[2] defined as a stretch of language bounded by pauses, generally a single semantic unit (Chaudron, 1988).

Data analysis

A sociolinguistic perspective was adopted to analyze the factors that may influence the language choice of focal students. A sociolinguistic, or variationist, view assumes that language choice will be conditioned by extralinguistic and linguistic variables (Preston, 1996; Young, 1991). According to Tarone and Swain adopting a sociolinguistic perspective to explain language choice:

> leads us to look at what *types* of L2 input and L2 output are involved in immersion classrooms and to identify the *purpose(s)* for which the L2 is used in those classrooms. (Swain, 1995: 167)

A sociolinguistic perspective presupposes that Leonard, Carolina and Marvin belong to the same classroom *speech community* where members share the same linguistic norms (Labov, 1972). A characteristic of a speech community is the presence of 'formal' and 'vernacular' speech styles. Tarone and Swain (1995) speculated that in immersion settings the L1 may be functioning as the vernacular (informal) and the L2 as the superordinate (formal) register. Another sociolinguistic notion that may help characterize language choice for the three children is 'speech accommodation theory' (Beebe & Giles, 1984), which seeks to explain the underlying motivations in changes of speech styles (or languages in this case). In choosing speech styles, speakers may choose to 'converge' or 'diverge' to the interlocutor's style or language depending on a number of contextual and interpersonal factors. Apart from interlocutors, contextual features are also assumed to have an impact on language choice. A sociolinguistic view is further based on the premise that discourse is multivariate and that we should expect interaction among the various factors that impact language use (Bayley & Preston, 1996; Sankoff, 1988; Young & Bayley, 1996).

Once data were collected, transcribed and coded, several levels of quantitative analysis were performed on 4843 utterances: analysis of percentages to characterize the data, a chi-square analysis and a multiple regression analysis using Goldvarb 2.0 software.[3] Additionally, in order to further characterize the data and capture factors not apparent in the quantitative analyses, a more holistic, qualitative analysis was conducted on the data set including an analysis of language-related episodes (LRE).[4] To establish interrater reliability for both quantitative and qualitative analyses, portions of the data were coded and analyzed by two separate raters (not involved in data gathering), who reached approximately 95% agreement.

For the quantitative analyses, the dependent variables were Spanish and English.[5] The conditions were interlocutor and task. Interlocutors included teacher, peer (other than focal students), self, overhearer, Carolina, Marvin, Leonard, teacher aide, other adults, unknown, microphone and public/whole class. Task was defined as 'a [goal-oriented] activity ... which participants, themselves, must carry out' (Pica *et al.*, 1993: 11–12). Each task had a goal and was related to a subject matter area. In addition, students' utterances were classified as either 'on-task' or 'off-task'.[6] Task goals were directions, main activity-desk work, main activity-whole class, follow-up and review; task content areas included math, science, creative writing, social studies, arts and crafts, etc. The full data set that was coded and analyzed included 13 linguistic and extralinguistic factor groups with 56 factors. The quantitative analysis has been described at length elsewhere (e.g. Broner, 2001) and is briefly summarized here. This chapter focuses instead on the qualitative analysis.

Results

Summary of quantitative analysis

Findings revealed that each of the children used more L2 (Spanish) than L1 (English) overall during Spanish instructional time. Specifically, Leonard used Spanish 58% of the time, Carolina 62% and Marvin 91%. The chi-square analysis established that L2 use was not independent of the variables of interlocutor, activity, content and on/off task. In order to achieve a more complete picture of focal student language use that takes into account all independent variables, a logistic regression was performed using Varbrul, a type of multiple regression analysis widely used in sociolinguistics (Tagliamonte, 2006), which is designed to deal with situations of multidimensional language variation (Young, 1991). Varbrul calculates the 'input probability', or the probability that Spanish will be used, independent of any factor present. The effect is expressed as a probability coefficient ranging between 0.00 and 1.00 (weight). It is used to identify the 'exact probability for a set of specific factor occurrences' (Preston, 1996: 11). Three modified factor groups (all assumed to be independent by Varbrul) emerged as conditions that promoted Spanish and English use for each focal student: (1) content of the task: language-related and non-language-related, (2) on/off task and (3) interlocutor.

The analysis revealed that there was a high degree of probability that the three focal students would use Spanish when the teacher was either the interlocutor or was in close proximity (1.00, or 100%, for all students). When adults were not nearby and when focal students were interacting with peers, there was a lower probability that Leonard (0.46) and Carolina (0.44) would speak Spanish during Spanish instructional time. However, both were more likely to speak Spanish when Marvin was the interlocutor (0.82 and 0.63, respectively). Marvin always spoke Spanish to Leonard (1.00), but he accommodated to Carolina by speaking much less Spanish (0.27).

Type of task was also found to have a statistically significant effect on language use. Despite individual differences, the three children were significantly more likely to use Spanish when they were engaged in tasks that had a clear language-related goal, such as creative writing and reading (>0.60). Non-language-related content, such as math and science, led to more English use (with the probability that they would use Spanish during math and science at just 0.34).

Finally, being on/off task also impacted language use. When Leonard, Carolina and Marvin were 'on-task', the tendency was to favor Spanish (0.65, 0.56 and 0.63, respectively). 'Off-task' classification was the factor that inhibited the children's use of Spanish in the classroom the most (0.25, 0.20 and 0.10, respectively). In other words, 'off-task' utterances were most likely to be carried out in English, while 'on-task' utterances were more likely to be in Spanish. The on/off task factor even impacted Marvin's language use. If Marvin was to use English, the probability that he would do so when he was 'off task' was greater than when he was 'on task'.

Qualitative analysis

The quantitative analysis helped describe students' language use patterns and the probability of whether their utterances would be in Spanish or English given a set of extralinguistic factors. However, it does not explain why more Spanish or English is predicted for each factor that emerged as statistically relevant. Reasons for explaining the observed behavior may be better revealed through qualitative analysis. Sources that inform the qualitative analysis are close examination of transcriptions of audiotaped data as described in terms of LREs and student interview data. Factors influencing L2 use that emerged in the qualitative analysis include (1) task type, task content and activity structure, (2) interlocutor factors, (3) individual factors and (4) impact of vernacular and cultural references.

Task type, task content and activity structure

The quantitative analysis showed that despite individual differences, all three children used significantly more Spanish when the task was creative writing. When the goal of the task included *focusing on* the L2, children used the L2 more, regardless of other factors.

In creative writing the final goal of the task is to produce some type of written manuscript, and this alone could account for increased use of L2 for this task. In other words, the children may perceive that using English (and then translating to Spanish) is inefficient because of the added step and that it is more efficient to use Spanish. The data included all verbal interactions that students produced during the task in order to co-construct the final written product. Interactions included both 'on-task' and 'off-task' utterances, and those that involved negotiation of meaning for a word, phrase, idea, etc.

During these activities the children had to focus on the L2, and had to work together to achieve the final product. Thus, small group work, when focused on a task that requires L2 production, also appears to be linked to increased L2 use. Small group creative writing tasks elicited more and longer (i.e. involving more 'turns' (Ellis, 1994)) LREs (Swain & Lapkin, 1998), as illustrated in Table 9.1.

There were 128 LREs present in the data and of these, 69% occurred during language-related subject matter learning (creative writing and reading). In language-related content, interactions between children were performed for the most part in L2, and there seemed to be more instances of scaffolding (Vygotsky, 1978), poetic language use and language play (cf. Broner & Tarone, 2001). In addition, more negotiation of meaning emerged in language-focused content areas than in any other content area, and most of these utterances were in the L2. Creative writing tasks pushed students' L2 output (Swain, 1993). Small group tasks such as col-laborative creative writing provided opportunities for students to test out hypotheses about their own and other's language learning. This is evi-dent in Extract 1, where Carolina and Leonard's group is developing ideas for a script based on a story they have been reading. In this extract, they had just started to share ideas on how to start the play. Carolina asks for the expression 'He was still in the printing business'. The LRE starts in turn 4 where she says '¿Cómo se dice?' and ends in turn 50.

Table 9.1 Number of LREs produced by content area and number of turns

Subject Area	< 3 Turns	3–5 Turns	6–10 Turns	10+ Turns	Total No. (%)
Math	8	9	4	1	22 (17)
Science	8	3	1	0	12 (9)
Arts and crafts	3	2	0	0	5 (4)
Creative writing	15	26	17	9	67 (52)
Reading	10	5	2	5	22 (17)
Total	44	45	24	15	128 (100)

Extract 1: Creative writing group activity based on reading
The Trial of Peter Zenger

4	Carolina:	He was still in the, ehm, business. He was still in the printing business. No sé cómo decir ésto en español. (*I don't know how-non-target – NT to say this in Spanish.*)
5	Boy:	¿Qué? *(What?)*
6	Carolina:	¿Estaba? (p) *(Was?)*
7	Carolina:	He was still in the printing business, how do you say that?
8	Boy:	What?
9	Carolina:	He was still in the printing business.
11	Boy:	Él estaba: *(He was)*
12	Leonard:	Ella está diciendo. *(She is saying)*
13	Carolina:	He was in the printing business, how do you say that? (impatient)
14	Boy:	Él estaba: él estaba/publaciando/[(*He was:, he was/ publishing/coinage – NT*)
15	Carolina:	[él (*he*)
16	Boy:	]el/poblano/ (*makes another hypothesis NT*)
17	Leonard:	/poblando/? (*laughs*) (*populating?*)
18	Carolina:	Él estaba/publaciando/, /publando/ (*writes it down*) (*He was /publishing/, /mix of **pub**lishing and **–ing** Spanish ending. NT*)
19	Leonard:	/publando/ no es u:n palabra. (*/publando/ is not a word— agreement error*) [*several seconds. Leaves group to get a dictionary.*]
20	Leonard:	(*looks it up in the dictionary*) (*silence*) imprime. Él imprime el papel. (*prints. He prints the 'paper'—English translation, NT, 'papel' should be 'periódico' for newspaper*)
22	Carolina:	Él imprime el papel. Él lo estaba /imprimando/ (*He prints the paper. He was publishing it. NT-form*).
23	Boy:	/publiciando/? (*attempt with the word 'publish' NT-coinage*)
24	Leonard:	No. Es imprime. (*No, it is 'prints'.*)
25	Boy:	Yo sé, pero < ... > (*I know, but...*)
26	Leonard:	Tú dice /publiciando/? (*You says NT-person /publishing NT-form/*)
27	Leonard:	A-huh?
28	Carolina:	I don't know what else to say?

29	**Boy:**	¿Qué es? (*What is it?*)
30	**Carolina:**	Estaba /imprimando/. (*He was /printing/NT-form but correct word root*)
31	**Leonard:**	/imprimie:-imprime/. /imprimé/ el papel. (*attempts several endings. All are NT-form/person*)
32	**Boy:**	Él está imprimiendo. (*He is printing.*)
33	**Leonard:**	Nó, él imprimí el papel. (*No, he printed NT-person the paper NT-false cognate*)
34	**Boy:**	Eso tiene sentido pero no sé. (*That makes sense, but I don't know.*)
36	**Carolina:**	Para el papel (*for the paper NT-false cognate*)
37	**Leonard:**	[cómo estaba él él estaba:: (*how was he, he, he was.*)
38	**Boy:**	Él estaba /imprimando/. (*He was /printing/NT*)
39	**Carolina:**	Esta:ba conti-estaba continuando: (*Was, continued, was continuing*)
40	**Leonard:**	Conti-conti-continuó. continuó.(*Cont-cont-continued. Continued*)
41	**Girl:**	Con-continuó. continuó. (*Cont-continued. continued*)
42	**Leonard:**	a imprimir el papel. (*to print the paper NT-false cognate*)
43	**Carolina:**	Sí, el periódico. (*Yes, the newspaper.*)
44	**Leonard:**	Continuó a imprimir el periódico. (*Continued to print the newspaper.*)
45	**Carolina:**	**Oh, cool!** tara tara tara.
46	**Leonard:**	Continuó. cont- (*continued. cont-*)
47	**Leonard:**	**XXX (girl's name) is pretty fast** (referring to typing). (p) a continuó a a imprimir. imprimir. (*dictating*) (*to continue to to print,. print*)
48	**Girl:**	el papel. (*the paper NT-false cognate*)
49	**Leonard:**	el papel. (*the paper NT-false cognate*)
50	**Carolina:**	el papel. el periódico. (*the paper, the newspaper*)

In this extract Spanish is used to a much greater extent than English. English is used as a task regulator in turns 7, 13 and 28, as predicted by Swain and Lapkin (1998). But Spanish is also used to mediate the task in turn 4, *No sé cómo decir eso en español*, and as a task regulator in turn 34, *Eso tiene sentido pero no sé*. In turns 14–16 there is lexical scaffolding and word coinage *publaciando*. The children are constantly testing hypotheses against their internalized knowledge of both L1 and L2 (Swain & Lapkin, 1998). They do so by trying out different word and morphological possibilities. In turns 19–22, Leonard uses an external source, the dictionary, to confirm a hypothesis. According to Swain, 'this modified (reprocessed) output may be considered to represent the leading edge of a learner's interlanguage' (Swain, 2000: 202). The extract also shows evidence of *languaging* as proposed by Swain:

> Languaging ... refers to the process of making meaning and shaping knowledge and experience through language. It is part of what constitutes learning. Languaging about language is one of the ways we learn language. (Swain, 2006: 98)

In addition, we can speculate that the linguistic scaffolding that takes place in these interactions provides examples of how language that occurs in the 'external plane' is becoming internalized (Vygotsky, 1978: 27). The LRE ends when the children arrived at a mutually acceptable solution in turn 44 through negotiation.

According to Kasper (2000), children at the same level of proficiency can help each other, as this LRE clearly shows. Throughout the episode, the children never sought the teacher's help to confirm their hypotheses, but relied on each other's judgments to reach their final conclusion.

Fourteen of 15 LRE examples that were longer than 10 turns occurred during creative writing and reading, while only one occurred in math (Table 9.1). An example of the type of LRE present in math appears in the following extract, where the children are reviewing different types of lineal graphs and providing examples of each. The teacher had asked them to discuss possible examples for different types of graphs and to write them down.

Extract 2: Math

1	**Carolina:**	el el lineal usan para el **stock market**. (*the, the lineal, they use for the stock market-NT*)
2	**Marvin:**	Yo iba a decir ese. (*I was going to say that ending-NT.*)
3	**Carolina:**	Yo dije. (*I said missing object pronoun-NT*) ....¿Tienes un papelito? (*Do you have a little piece of paper?*)
4	**Marvin:**	Voy a escribir. (*I am going to write*)
5	**Boy 1:**	¿Cómo dices **stock market**? (*How do you say 'stock market'?*)
6	**Leonard:**	/marqueto **stock**/. (*stock market/coinage-NT*)
7	**Boy 1:**	**Leonard, do you want this?** (*addressing Leonard*)
8	**Leonard:**	**No.**
9	**Carolina:**	ahm, ¿Señora Johnson? ¿Señora Johnson? ¿Señora Johnson. (*calling Mrs. Johnson*)

> *(Teacher comes to the group.)*

10 **Carolina:** ¿Cómo dices **stock market**? (*How do you say 'stock market'?*)

11 **Teacher:** Oh, la bolsa. (*Oh, the stock market.*)

12 **Boy 1:** La bolsa. *(repeats, 'The stock market') (teacher leaves the group)*

In this small group math lesson the children used more lexis-based LREs (e.g. ¿*Cómo se dice....?*) and fewer form-based LREs of the type seen in Extract 1. At the same time, they also used L2 for task mediation, as seen in turns 1–4 (though these turns are not part of the LRE *per se*). Thus, both the content of the task and activity structure (small group work) appear to influence L2 use, but it is evident in this extract from math (non-language-related content) that the language produced is not nearly as rich as the language produced during creative writing (language-related content).

Further analysis of these data suggest that one of the characteristics of the verbal output of Leonard, Carolina and Marvin while working out math problems was increased use of verb-less, one-word or short-phrase answers when discussing the content itself. Output of this type is especially prevalent in teacher-fronted, whole-class instruction, as illustrated in Extract 3. In this extract, the teacher is teaching how to calculate the area of a triangle.

Extract 3: Math: area and perimeter. (*Talking to the whole class.)

1 ***Boy:** Sesenta metros cuadrados. (*Sixty square meters.*)

2 **Teacher:** XXX, de esa figura. (*Boy's name, from that figure.*)

3 **Teacher:** ¡Un momento, XXX! Tienes que levantar la mano. (*One moment, Boy's name. You need to raise your hand.*)

4 ***Boy:** Sesenta metros. (*Sixty meters.*) (*speaks as he raises his hand*)

5 **Teacher:** [No, no te he llamado. ¿XXX? (*no, no. I did not call on you. Girl's name?*)

6 **Teacher:** (*to Girl*) El área de esta figura. De este rectángulo. (*The area of this figure, this rectangle.*)

7 ***Girl:** ¿Sesenta? (*Sixty?*)

8 ***Teacher:** Sesenta. Largo, diez. Por ancho, seis. Seis por diez, sesenta metros cuadrados, ¿okey? y el área de este rectángulo? ahm::: Carolina? (*Sixty. Length, ten. By width, six. Six times ten. Sixty square meters, OK?*) (*[while making the calculations] (uhm::::: Carolina?*)

9   ***Carolina:**   (s) (*takes time to think of the answer*) Doce. (*Twelve.*)
10 ***Teacher:**   Correcto, doce. Para: calcular el área de este rectángulo: tienes que saber el ancho: y el largo, ¿no? (*Right. Twelve. To: calculate the area of this rectangle you need to find out the width: and the length, right?*)

Turns 1, 4, 7 and 9 were produced by children but none included a conjugated verb or more than a one-word or short-phrase answer. The data suggest that the children do not need to use verbs or produce more complicated utterances to answer the questions; in math short answers suffice if they are correct.

In addition, the qualitative analysis revealed that there were very few verbs and limited language present in the teacher's input during math lessons. The pattern of language use in Extract 3 above is parallel to that found in Transcript 1 in Hoare's chapter (Chapter 11). Like the English immersion middle-school teacher in Hoare's example, this teacher also relies on the diagram she is using to teach the math concept and on the use of demonstratives (this, that) rather than specific vocabulary. She does not model more complicated Spanish for students, nor does she help them to produce utterances beyond the one-word or short-phrase answers.

Interlocutor factors

As revealed in the quantitative analysis, the interlocutor also influenced the students' choice of language. In this study, as in Ó Duibhir's (Chapter 8) study on Irish immersion student language use, focal students were asked to reflect on their language use during interviews. While the students in Ó Duibhir's study reflected on the actual language they produced, the students in this study reflected on the *reasons* for using one language rather than the other. Children shared a number of reasons for their language use choices, including the role of interlocutor. As the following excerpt of his interview illustrates, Leonard explained that he uses English with friends because it is easier or because he perceives they only speak English. He uses Spanish in class with the teachers.

Researcher: Y cuando estás trabajando en la clase, ¿alguna vez hablas inglés? (*When you are working in class, do you ever speak English?*)

Leonard: Cuando ahora, cuando hay trabajo que está muy aburrido. Y hablamos ahí, pero no deben. y::: ahm:: [*When now (NT), when there is (NT-verb choice) work that is boring. And we talk there but (they/we) shouldn't (NT-person). and, uhm..*]

Researcher:	Cuando estás en el colegio, ¿Cuándo usas español y cuándo usas inglés? Y ¿por qué? (*When you are at school, when do you use Spanish and when do you use English and why?*)
Leonard:	En recreo y almuerzo hablo inglés porque es más fácil, pero en la clase hablamos español porque a los profesores y tal como eso, ellos hablan español. Podemos hablar español con ellos. También podemos hablar español como, con los amigos pero no hablamos (*giggles*) español con ellos. [*In (NT) Ørecess andØ lunch I speak English because it is easier but in class we speak Spanish because the teachers and that, they speak Spanish. We can speak Spanish with them. We can also speak Spanish like, with our friends but we don't speak (giggles) Spanish with them*]
Researcher:	¿Por qué? (*Why?*)
Leonard:	Yo no sé. Muchos, sólo hablan inglés. (*I don't know, many only speak English.*)

Unlike Leonard, Marvin did not choose to speak English with peers because he found it easier or because he perceived that they did not know Spanish. In his interview, he explained that he spoke English during recess because his friends did not want him to speak Spanish. Thus, interlocutor influence takes different forms.

Individual factors

Leonard also explains in the interview excerpt above that he tends to use English when he is bored in class or, as pointed out previously, because it is simply easier. Carolina also explained that she speaks English because, as her native language, it is easier. If she wants to get a good grade, she speaks Spanish.

| Carolina: | Porque yo <u>vivió</u>, yo aprendí inglés cuando <u>tuvía</u> como un año y entonces también mis padres hablan inglés. Entonces muchas veces hablo inglés en la escuela porque es mucho más fácil. Y en español lo hablo para sacar buenos grados. [*Because I lived (NT-person), I (NT-redundant) learned English when I was (NT) like a year old and then also because my parents speak English. So, I speak English a lot of time at school because it is much easier. And Spanish, I speak it to get good grades (NT-false cognate)*] |

The factors that appear to impact Leonard's and Carolina's language choices were not expressed by Marvin, who emerged as quite an anomaly, as evidenced by the high probability that he would use Spanish in most contexts and with most interlocutors as revealed in the quantitative analysis. Different individual factors appeared to play a key role in Marvin's language use choices. For example, he pointed out that with his twin brother, also his best friend, he used Spanish at home when they did not want their mother to understand what they were talking about. At home Spanish functions like a secret code, and this may contribute to Marvin's commitment to Spanish. Another possibility, as Potowski (2004) speculated, is that Marvin may have been more 'invested' in his Spanish persona and therefore used more Spanish at the expense of social and peer interactions.

Impact of vernacular and cultural references

Apart from the variables explored above, the qualitative analysis revealed additional reasons why students used the L1 in this immersion classroom that were not evident in the quantitative analysis. Namely, the use of vernacular words accounted for 10% of the data for Leonard and Carolina (Marvin only produced five vernacular words). All vernacular words were in English (e.g. 'cool' in turn 45, Extract 1), with the exception of *chistoso (funny), estúpido (stupid)*, and *sip*—a coinage from the word *sí* (yes). *Chistoso* served as part of the children's 'pubilect',[7] even though it may not be perceived as 'slang' in many L2 speech communities.

The children also made many references to Anglo culture, with topics ranging from talk about boyfriends, movies, songs, TV commercials and personal diaries to kissing. When they talked about cultural issues and topics that were of personal interest, they always used English. Fortune (2001) also found that fifth-grade immersion students used English for slang expressions and most cultural references. Interestingly, Ó Duibhir (Chapter 8) found that when Irish immersion students talk in school about, for example, a TV program that they watched in English, they will translate English to Irish as they interact with their friends. Outside of school, however, they will use English with one another. The tendency for these Spanish immersion students to resort to English within the school setting may be due to any number of factors, such as the greater amount of instructional time in English at this grade (50% as opposed to 15% in Irish immersion), the limited language use expectations set by the teacher and school culture (in Irish immersion, students are expected to use Irish at all times within the school setting) or factors related to the different contexts

(Spanish being learned as a 'foreign language' within an English-dominant culture and society versus Irish being learned as the minority, heritage language of the country).

Discussion

Both the quantitative and qualitative analysis revealed that interlocutor alone predicted language use when it was the teacher, but that other variables come into play when the interlocutor is another peer. Task type and content and activity structure (e.g. small group versus whole class) also had an effect on L2 language use. Language-related content tasks, such as creative writing, and small group activity structures promoted L2 use. In contrast, non-language-related content areas and tasks did not promote L2 language use. Fortune also found that when the goal of the task included a written product, students were more likely to use Spanish. So much so, that her students 'repeatedly identified the need to create and produce a written product as particularly influential in promoting their use of Spanish' (Fortune, 2001: 258). In this study, the same pattern emerged when focal students used language during collaborative creative writing.

One constant in these activities is that students needed to interact and talk to each other in order to arrive at the final written product. In the process of interacting, L2 use increases and more opportunities to talk about language emerge as children create, confirm, or disconfirm hypotheses about what L2 is needed to accomplish the task. In this process at times L1 is used, as predicted by Swain and Lapkin (1998), but emphasis is on L2 use. With regard to non-language-related content tasks, Tarone and Swain (1995) had predicted that due to their academic nature, students would use L2 to complete the tasks. In this study, more L1 was used. It appears that content that is not heavily language related does not require students to use L2 to complete the task, especially during whole-class instruction. Thus, both the language-related nature of the task and the activity structure itself are important for students to maintain L2 use.

Both the quantitative and qualitative analyses revealed that students were likelier to use Spanish for 'on-task' interaction and English for 'off-task' interaction, particularly for socializing, using slang and making cultural references. Thus, Tarone and Swain's (1995) suggestion that immersion classrooms become diglossic environments is confirmed at least in part. At the same time, the qualitative analysis allowed for further exploration of L1 and L2 use, revealing that language choice is highly complex and is impacted by task and content variables, interlocutor variables, context and a range of individual factors.

Finally, it should be noted that the tendency for these Grade 5 students to use English with peers during Spanish time may be closely related to their age and developmental stages. Wilson and Kamanā (Chapter 3) report that Hawaiian immersion students in upper-elementary grades and throughout middle school tend to revert to English (Hawaii Creole English) for peer communication. However, in college and at times by the upper-high-school grades, they return to Hawaiian. While collecting data for this study, Broner observed 'Alicia,' a fifth grader who seemed to encourage L1 use at every opportunity. Years later, Alicia walked into one of Broner's college-level Spanish classes. She was a Spanish major and very strong student, and later studied to become a bilingual lawyer. In informal conversations, she consistently attributed her immersion education as one reason she continued with Spanish. Future research, thus, should take a more longitudinal look at student language preferences so that we can begin to understand the long-term impact of immersion education.

Pedagogical Possibilities and Concluding Remarks

The study presented in this chapter offers a host of possibilities for immersion pedagogy. The data strongly suggest that teachers should feel confident that their students will use more L2 if the task requires that they produce some type of product in the L2. Collaborative creative writing, in particular, emerged as a powerful, heavily language-related task type and activity structure that led students not only to use more L2 to complete the task itself but also to engage in 'languaging' (Swain, 2006), hypothesis formation and testing, and task mediation. A very similar pattern was reported by Fortune (2001), who also identified preparation for oral presentations and collaborative math problem-solving activities as equally effective tasks for eliciting the L2.

The data extracts presented in this chapter showed examples of students using the L2 to manage creative writing task requirements, negotiate form and vocabulary and correct one another. The language students need to produce to carry out these collaborative tasks has both academic and social characteristics and incorporates both academic and communicative functions. What pedagogical possibilities might immersion teachers embrace to maximize the language learning potential inherent in well-designed collaborative tasks?

Immersion teachers should have access to the necessary professional development to become more 'language-aware' (Hoare, 2001: Chapter 11: 196) so that content lessons also become language lessons. This involves thoughtful, purposeful task design that builds in both content and language expectations, for example, clear language and content objectives for particular tasks. Teachers must make those expectations clear to students and take the time to review necessary forms in meaningful and contextual ways before students begin group work. Teachers should also design tasks to bring students' attention to form, encourage their reflection on language and provide for the opportunity to identify errors and correct them. Tasks like these are described in more detail by Ó Duibhir (Chapter 8) and have been promoted by, for example, Lyster (1998, 2007) and Kowal and Swain (1997).

In addition, during whole-class instruction (even in non-language-related content such as math) teachers should further exploit language learning possibilities through modeling, giving corrective feedback and setting high expectations for language production rather than simply allowing demonstration of content learning through one-word or short-phrase answers. Examples of corrective feedback strategies and other focus-on-form techniques used by immersion teachers during whole-class instruction have been offered by Lyster (2007), among others.

Finally, Allwright (2005) makes a strong case for teachers to gather data in their own classrooms to explore the effectiveness of their pedagogical practices. Although time consuming, such an exploration can provide useful information about the kinds of rich interactions that take place among learners during collaborative tasks and may lead to the creation of strategies for enhancing language learning. This exploration might be accomplished also by teacher partners who agree to observe each other (e.g. with a specific language-related focus), give each other feedback and imagine together the possibilities for improved practice. In the process, these teachers may develop the 'language awareness' (Hoare, 2001; Chapter 11) so fundamental to effective immersion teaching. The pedagogical possibilities suggested above may help teachers to bring students' L2 beyond sentence-level utterances to paragraph-level discourse and beyond.

In conclusion, life in language immersion classrooms is highly complex, and student language use involves a multitude of variables. By examining naturally occurring data, we have demonstrated how individual variables influenced language choice for each focal student. The qualitative analysis allowed for a description of contexts of L1 and L2 use that are often overlooked by quantitative data analysis. It led us to understand that classroom language use is conditioned by the nature of the academic content and task, the identity of the interlocutor and other individual factors. While our analysis provides some evidence to support Tarone and

Swain's (1995) hypothesis that immersion classrooms become diglossic, it, more importantly, revealed that L2 and L1 use in the classroom is not influenced alone by academic versus social interaction but rather is impacted by myriad other factors, some of which may be addressed pedagogically.

Notes

1. Pseudonyms were used for study participants.
2. The utterance as the unit of analysis surfaced from the data itself and was not set *a priori*. It was deemed appropriate because these children speak in sentences rather than paragraphs.
3. Goldvarb 2.0 is the VARBRUL version for the MacIntosh computer (Rand & Sankoff, 1990).
4. An LRE is '... any part of a dialogue where the students talk about the language they are producing, question their language use, or others'.... [These] were classified as either 'lexis-based' or 'form-based'' (Swain & Lapkin, 1998: 326).
5. Goldvarb accommodates only two dependent variables.
6. It is important to note the challenge of characterizing an utterance as 'on/off-task' (Yonge & Stables, 1998). Ambiguous cases were treated as follows: if the children were focused on completing a task (even if they joked about it), it was considered 'on-task'; if the children were carrying out a task but lost focus to make an aside (e.g. talked of a movie or song, etc.), it was considered 'off-task'.
7. Pubilect is 'defined simply as the social dialect of puberty. It is a meta-code in the same sense that mainstream dress and musical styles are meta-codes' (Danesi, 1994: 97).

References

Allwright, D. (2005) Developing principles for practitioner research: The case of exploratory practice. *The Modern Language Journal* 89, 353–366.

Bayley, R. and Preston, D. (eds) (1996) *Second Language Acquisition and Variation*. Philadelphia, PA: John Benjamins.

Beebe, L. and Giles, H. (1984) Speech accommodation theories: A discussion in terms of second language acquisition. *International Journal of the Sociology of Language 46*, 5–32.

Broner, M. (1991) Report on observations on the use of Spanish at an immersion school. Unpublished manuscript, University of Minnesota, Minneapolis.

Broner, M. (2001) Impact of interlocutor and task on first and second language use in a Spanish immersion program. *CARLA Working Paper No. 18*. Minneapolis: University of Minnesota.

Broner, M. and Tarone, E. (2001) Is it fun? Language play in a fifth grade Spanish immersion classroom. *Modern Language Journal* 85, 363–379.

Carranza, I. (1995) Multilevel analysis of two-way immersion discourse. In J. Atlatis, C. Strahele, B. Gallenberger and M. Ronkin (eds) *Gergetown University Round Table on Languages and Linguistics* (pp. 168–187). Washington DC: Georgetown University Press.

Carrigo, D. (2000) Just how much English are they using? Teacher and student language distribution patterns, between Spanish and English, in upper-grade, two way immersion Spanish classes. PhD thesis, Harvard University.

Chaudron, C. (1988) *Second Language Classrooms: Research on Teaching and Learning*. Cambridge, MA: Cambridge University Press.

Danesi, M. (1994) *Cool: The Signs and Meanings of Adolescence*. Toronto University Press.

Ellis, N. (1994) *The Study of Second Language Acquisition*. Oxford: Oxford University Press.

Edwards, J.A. and Lampert, M.D. (eds) (1993) *Talking Data: Transcription and Coding in Discourse Research*. Mahwah, NJ: Lawrence Erlbaum Associates.

Fazio, L. and Lyster, R. (1998) Immersion and submersion classrooms: A comparison of instructional practices in language arts. *Journal of Multilingual and Multicultural Development* 19, 303–317.

Fortune, T. (2001) Understanding immersion students: Oral language use as a mediator of social interaction in the classroom. PhD thesis, University of Minnesota, Minneapolis.

Genesee, F. (1987) *Learning Through Two Languages: Studies of Immersion and Bilingual Education*. Cambridge, MA: Newbury House Publishers.

Harley, B. (1992) Patterns of second language development in French immersion. *Journal of French Language Studies* 2, 159–183.

Hoare, P. (2001) A comparison of the effectiveness of a 'language aware' and a 'non language aware' late immersion teacher. In S. Björklund (ed.) *Language as a Tool: Immersion Research and Practices* (pp. 196–210). Vaasa: University of Vaasa.

Huang, J.F. and Rau, D-H. (2007) Language use by English immersion kindergarten children. Master's thesis, Providence University, Taiwan.

Kasper, G. (2000) Four perspectives on L2 pragmatic competence. Keynote address presented at annual meeting of the American Association of Applied Linguistics, Vancouver, Canada.

Kowal, M. and Swain, M. (1997) From semantic to syntactic processing: How can we promote it in the immersion classroom? In R.K. Johnson and M. Swain (eds) *Immersion Education: International Perspectives* (pp. 284–309). Cambridge, MA: Cambridge University Press.

Labov, W. (1972) *Sociolinguistic Patterns*. Philadelphia, PA: University of Pennsylvania Press.

Liu, G. (1991) Interaction and second language acquisition: A case study of a Chinese child's acquisition of English as a second language. PhD thesis, La Trobe University.

Lyster, R. (1998) Form in immersion classroom discourse: In or out of focus. *Canadian Journal of Applied Linguistics* 1, 53–82.

Lyster, R. (2007) *Learning and Teaching Languages Through Content: A Counterbalanced Approach* (Vol. 28). Amsterdam: John Benjamins.

Norton, B. (2000) *Identity and Language Learning: Gender, Ethnicity and Educational Change*. Essex: Pearson Education Limited.

Pica, T., Kanagy, R. and Falodun, J. (1993) Choosing and using communication tasks for second language instruction. In G. Crooks and S.M. Gass (eds) *Tasks and Language Learning* (pp. 9–34). Clevedon: Multilingual Matters.

Potowski, K.J. (2004) Student Spanish use and investment in a dual immersion classroom: Implications for second language acquisition and heritage language maintenance. *The Modern Language Journal* 88, 75–01.

Preston, D.R. (1996) Variationist perspectives on second language acquisition. In D. Preston and R. Bayley (eds) *Second Language Acquisition and Linguistic Variation* (pp. 1–41). Philadelphia, PA: John Benjamins.

Rand, D. and Sankoff, D. (1990) *GoldVarb Version 2.0. A variable rule application for the Macintosh* (version 2.0) [Computer program] Montreal: Centre de recherches mathématiques, Université de Montréal.

Sankoff, D. (1988) Variable rules. In U. Ammon, N. Dittmar and K.J. Mattheier (eds) *Sociolinguistics. An International Handbook of the Science of Language and Society.* (pp. 984–997). Berlin: Walter der Gruyter.

Swain, M. (1993) The output hypothesis: Just speaking and writing aren't enough. *Canadian Modern Language Review,* Golden Anniversary Issue 50, 158–164.

Swain, M. (2000) French immersion research in Canada: Recent contributions to SLA and applied linguistics. *Annual Review of Applied Linguistics* 20, 199–212.

Swain, M. (2006) Languaging, agency and collaboration in advanced second language learning. In H. Byrnes (ed.) *Advanced Language Learning: The Contributions of Halliday and Vygotsky* (pp. 95–108). London: Continuum.

Swain, M. and Lapkin, S. (eds) (1982) *Evaluating Bilingual Education: A Canadian Case Study.* Clevedon: Multilingual Matters.

Swain, M. and Lapkin, S. (1998) Interaction and second language learning: Two adolescent French immersion students working together. *Modern Language Journal* 82, 320–337.

Tagliamonte, S. (2006) *Analyzing Sociolinguistic Variation.* Cambridge, MA: Cambridge University Press.

Tarone, E. and Swain, M. (1995) A sociolinguistic perspective on second-language use in immersion classrooms. *Modern Language Journal* 79, 166–178.

Vygotsky, L.S. (1978) *Mind in Society.* Cambridge, MA: Harvard University Press.

Yonge, C. and Stables, A. (1998) 'I am it the clown': Problematising the distinction between 'Off-task' and 'On-task' classroom talk. *Language and Education* 12, 55–70.

Young, R. (1991) *Variation in Interlanguage Morphology.* New York: Peter Lang.

Young, R. and Bayley, R. (1996) VARBRUL analysis for second language acquisition research. In D. Preston and R. Bayley (eds) *Second Language Acquisition and Linguistic Variation* (pp. 253–306). Philadelphia, PA: John Benjamins.

Chapter 10

Using Language Assessment to Inform Instruction in Indigenous Language Immersion

L. PETER, G. SLY and T. HIRATA-EDDS

Introduction

The number of programs developed for the purposes of maintaining or revitalizing endangered languages has grown significantly in the past two decades as speakers of those languages – or descendants of speakers – have recognized the cultural and intellectual loss that accompanies language death. Globally, groups of people tied together by a common linguistic heritage have pooled existing resources and expertise and reached beyond community boundaries to learn ways to document their language, teach the language to learners young and old, and encourage the use of that language in both traditional and contemporary domains in which the dominant language has taken over.

As successful language revitalization endeavors spread, programs for imparting linguistic and cultural knowledge to a new generation of speakers reflect common purposes, goals and approaches. This is particularly true for indigenous language immersion education, and local versions of immersion are being implemented globally with varying degrees of success. Most notably, the Māori of New Zealand (King, 2001; Smith, 2000) and Native Hawaiians (Wilson & Kamanā, 2001) have developed models of language and culture revitalization through immersion schooling that serve as prototypes for other indigenous groups. In their chapter in this volume, Wilson and Kamanā describe in detail the features and successes of the Hawaiian immersion Nāwahī School, an integrated Pre-K–12 laboratory school of the state Hawaiian language college. Nāwahī School includes, on the same site, a private preschool, a K–8 charter school, and a 9–12 program formally administered as part of a standard public high school located several miles away. Planners of language programs, such as

187

the Cherokee Nation immersion school described in this chapter, have drawn from the experiences of these successful heritage language immersion programs as the basis for their planning, though actual implementation has resulted in unique approaches within each community.

The nature and effects of language immersion as a means for endangered language revitalization have been the focus of much research in the past two decades. However, one aspect of indigenous language immersion that has, until recently, been largely absent in studies on and information about these programs is language assessment. Developing reliable and valid language testing instruments for less commonly taught indigenous languages holds the possibility for program improvement toward the goal of endangered language sustainability. And yet, it also poses a number of challenges. First, by virtue of being 'less commonly taught', little is known about the length of time that it takes for nonspeakers in an immersion program to master linguistic aspects of the language, thereby making it difficult, initially, to establish concrete proficiency goals. This is particularly true for languages such as Cherokee, a polysynthetic language characterized by a complex morphological system.

Second, very few existing materials are readily available for classroom use. In the case of Cherokee Nation's immersion program, for example, the addition of each subsequent grade level of immersion has required a massive undertaking on the part of teachers and curriculum staff to develop books and instructional materials specifically suited to the age and language abilities of the students. Thus, if we view assessment as a seamless feature of instruction, but instruction is limited by the availability of content resources in the indigenous language, then assessments that are geared toward an 'ideal' proficiency level rather than reflecting classroom realities may lack validity.

Third, the development of reliable and valid instruments requires a great deal of planning, pilot testing, analysis and revising. The nature of the test development process, then, is extremely time consuming and requires a good deal of human and financial resources. Finally, knowing how to use the results of an assessment can prove to be a more complex issue than it may seem. What do the results reflect, exactly? To whom should the results be reported, and how? What adjustments need to be made to the curriculum, the teachers' instructional approaches or the assessment itself to make the best use of the information gleaned from the results?

Despite these challenges, we argue, the dedication of time and energy to the creation of such instruments is crucial to understanding the results of particular pedagogical processes aimed at developing language proficiency. Without this knowledge, the work of teachers and curriculum planners can be vague and lacking in purpose, making the goal of language proficiency difficult to achieve. In the context of revitalizing endangered languages, any amount of purposelessness represents a loss of precious time.

This chapter highlights how Cherokee Nation in northeastern Oklahoma has made the development and administration of language assessments a central feature of its immersion programming. Curriculum planners, classroom teachers, administrative staff and consultants specializing in linguistics and second-language teaching and learning have worked from the inception of the program to create language assessments uniquely suited to the Cherokee language immersion context, to administer these assessments with children in the preschool through sixth-grade program, and to analyze the results for the purpose of better understanding the strengths and limitations of children's developing proficiency in Cherokee. Importantly, the results have had significant bearing on teachers' classroom practices.

Although the Cherokee language immersion school merges the acquisition of language with the learning of academic content such as mathematics, science and social studies, this chapter focuses on children's linguistic achievements and what they mean for Cherokee language immersion. We begin our chapter with a brief overview of the context of Cherokee language loss and revitalization in northeastern Oklahoma followed by a description of the immersion school and the principles that guide Cherokee language planning. From there, we describe the process by which language assessments were developed, including deciding what aspects of language to assess and how, and the manner in which the assessments are administered. We then illustrate, with specific examples, how the assessments have resulted in providing teachers with much needed information regarding their students' language skills, and how this information has modified their approach to teaching.

Lindholm-Leary (Chapter 5) makes the point that all immersion programs need valid and reliable measures to assess students' language proficiency development over time. We hope that Cherokee Nation's experience with language assessment will stimulate greater inquiry and research into the question of immersion students' attainment of proficiency in endangered indigenous and other languages.

Cherokee Language Loss and Revitalization

The history of Cherokee language loss parallels so many American Indian languages whose vitality has diminished due to centuries of language policies that have oppressed minority languages and disenfranchised and marginalized those who speak them (Hinton, 2001). Policies aiming to remove Indian peoples from traditional lands, break up families, destroy sacred grounds and impose European manners of dress, religion, customs and language have resulted in both the demise of many American Indian languages and the idea, even among tribal peoples, that the language of their heritage is 'evil or inferior to English' (Hinton, 2001: 41). While public policy regarding American Indians' loss of heritage language and culture has swayed toward more supportive measures with the passage of the Native American Languages Act of 1990 by the US government, language shift has been further precipitated through forces such as pervasive mass media, public education and English Only legislation in the United States (Crawford, 1996, 2000; UNESCO, 2003). The result has been that, of the estimated 300–600 languages existing in the United States and Canada at the time of European contact, only 210 remained in Krauss' 1998 count; and of those, only 34 were still being spoken by children (Krauss, 1998). Today, even the most viable languages among these are fighting for survival.

The Cherokee language has fared better than some, although the loss of language over time has had a devastating toll. A 2002 language survey of 300 Cherokee Nation members in northeastern Oklahoma revealed the dismal news that only about 6–10% considers him or herself to be proficient in Cherokee, and 70% are nonspeakers (Cherokee Nation, 2003). Given that the language is spoken nearly exclusively by the grandparental generation, it is highly conceivable that, without intervention, the language will be lost in the next few decades.

Recognition of the possible demise of the Cherokee language has prompted a widespread community effort – centered in Tahlequah, Oklahoma but reaching outward to the 16-county Cherokee Nation jurisdictional area – to take action to promote Cherokee language teaching and learning in a variety of settings, for learners of all ages, and through a range of approaches. Tribal legislative action has resulted in a 10-year plan for achieving language revitalization with three central goals: (1) to create language revitalization programs that ensure survival of the Cherokee language throughout the tribal communities; (2) to educate and certify language teachers to assure a qualified and knowledgeable workforce for program implementation; and (3) to document the language and develop appropriate instructional materials and curriculum (Cherokee Nation, 2003). Meeting these goals has involved a wide range of interrelated language planning activities, including outreach to reinforce language use in homes, community social settings and Cherokee Nation businesses; the creation of Master-Apprentice learning opportunities for adult learners; coordination with public school districts to increase the quantity and quality of Cherokee language classes for students at all grade levels; coordination with higher education institutions to offer courses and professional development for teacher aides, teachers and linguists; and the documentation of various forms of written and spoken Cherokee. The centerpiece of action toward meeting the 10-year Cherokee language plan has been the language immersion school.

Learning Cherokee through Immersion

The Cherokee language immersion school is the fulfillment of a vision shared by many Cherokee Nation members who, over the years, recognized that creating a new generation of Cherokee speakers was the only way to ensure the survival of the language. This same recognition has driven the ongoing development of Hawaiian immersion (Wilson & Kamanā, Chapter 3) and that of other indigenous immersion programs. Although Cherokee language classes had been available for decades, these classes rarely resulted in proficiency as they tended to focus mainly on learning vocabulary and the Cherokee writing system known as syllabary – a writing system developed by Sequoyah (George Gist) from 1809 to 1821 and officially adopted by Cherokee Nation in 1821. With the support and encouragement of current Chief Chad Smith, plans began in 2000 for an early total language immersion program.

The strategy adopted to jump-start a new generation of speakers was premised on a parsimonious yet far-reaching mission statement which proclaims: 'The ultimate goal [of total language immersion] is for children to acquire the Cherokee language in such a way that it will become an integral part of their lives and their knowledge about the world around them' (Cherokee Nation, 2003: 36). The long-range plan for achieving that mission was to build on the preschool immersion program already established in 2004 and then add a new classroom at the next grade level each year until 2012, when the program would extend from preschool to sixth grade. At that point, students would matriculate to Sequoyah High School, a Bureau of Indian Affairs (BIA)[1] grant school administered by Cherokee Nation. In all, the long-range plan is to maintain two preschool levels plus kindergarten through sixth grade for a total of nine levels of Cherokee immersion with 20 students per class each year, for an annual enrollment of 160 students.

The success of the program depends on a number of factors that are also addressed in the 10-year plan (Cherokee Nation, 2003). Six actions comprise the crucial elements of the strategy and include:

(1) Recruiting and retaining bilingual and biliterate teachers and teacher aides with prior classroom experience and who are willing to be prepared in an immersion language teacher education program.

(2) Providing professional development opportunities for immersion instruction in coordination with local colleges and universities, the Oklahoma Native Language Association, and consultants.

(3) Developing a family component to involve parents in immersion classroom activities, with opportunities for the parents to learn both the language and the ways to reinforce the language at home.

(4) Coordinating with Head Start and local schools to create immersion classrooms in public school settings with curricula that meet Oklahoma state standards.

(5) Soliciting proficient speakers from the community to visit immersion classrooms and to get involved in a variety of cultural activities so that the children have an opportunity to hear the richness of the language spoken by others.

(6) Developing and implementing an ongoing monitoring and evaluation protocol to assess all aspects of the immersion classrooms and to make necessary adjustments in a timely manner.

Still in the early stages of its implementation, the program has yet to achieve its lofty mission although all of the actions have been carried out to different degrees. Recruitment of qualified teachers has been an ongoing challenge, one that is clearly shared by all immersion programs, particularly indigenous immersion programs (Wilson & Kamanā, Chapter 3) and those that provide immersion in 'less commonly taught' languages such as Chinese (Lindholm-Leary, Chapter 5). In addition, the retention of children beyond pre-kindergarten has been less successful than anticipated, as children's families move or succumb to worries that their children will be at an academic disadvantage if they learn in a language other than English. Yet, the current instructional staff has received regular professional development (Hirata-Edds *et al.*, 2003; Peter & Hirata-Edds, 2006), including workshops on curriculum development, lesson planning, techniques for teaching language through immersion, language assessment and Cherokee linguistics. Most have been taking college courses through Northeastern State University, a partner college whose recently established Cherokee Language Teaching program has allowed for licensing and credentialing for current – and potential future – Cherokee teachers in elementary education and continues to build their Cherokee language proficiency through language courses taught in Cherokee.

Currently, the Cherokee immersion school consists of eight classes (i.e. preschool, pre-kindergarten, kindergarten, first, second, third, fourth, and fifth grades) in two buildings dedicated to the program. Each level has its own, well-equipped classroom headed by one-and-a-half or two teachers. Teachers are bilingual and, to varying degrees, biliterate. Most of them learned Cherokee as their first language at home and did not learn English until they entered public school, although most of them did not become fully literate in Cherokee until adulthood (Peter & Hirata-Edds, 2009).

Visitors to the immersion center are quick to remark that the school has the appearance of a familiar, mainstream school, albeit smaller. However, they soon discover that despite this appearance, the Cherokee immersion school is a unique and special place where children of mostly Cherokee descent learn, play, argue and joke all in the language of their heritage. Upon closer observation, one readily recognizes the imprint of Cherokee culture – in the images portrayed on posters; the presence of Cherokee artifacts such as stickball sticks, baskets and ribbon dresses; the stories read; and, more subtle yet ever-present, the behaviors and values modeled by the teachers themselves. Thus, although the mission of Cherokee immersion has yet to be fully realized, the vision shared by so many is finally being brought to fruition.

The Role of Language Assessment in 'Envaluing' Cherokee Language Immersion

As Action Plan 6 above suggests, the development and implementation of a monitoring and evaluation protocol is a necessary component of successful immersion programming, both for understanding various strengths and limitations of the immersion program and to make necessary adjustments for improvement. Yet, the grassroots nature of Cherokee language revitalization calls for an approach to evaluation that is responsive to local knowledge, experience and expertise in addition to being sensitive to the issues faced by a group of trailblazers who have never before attempted a language project of such proportion. So, early on in the immersion planning, the Cherokee concept of *idigoliyahe nidaduhnahui* (let us take a look at what we are doing) was adopted as a culturally appropriate way to step back and observe, or evaluate. Eventually, this process became known as 'envaluing', in which each aspect of the program is attributed value, whether that element successfully contributes to achieving the goals or not (Peter, 2003, 2007). Over time, envaluing would occupy a central role in immersion and include language assessments as a regular part of immersion programming, as illustrated in the Immersion Model (Figure 10.1).

Envaluing activities during the pilot year of the immersion program revealed some unexpected outcomes. On the positive side, Peter (2003, 2007) notes that the immersion program had far-reaching effects as teachers, parents and community members witnessed children speaking Cherokee for the first time in generations. Cherokee Nation members by and large embraced the immersion program and recognized its potential for reversing centuries of language shift. However, in terms of children's overall language abilities, the results did not measure up to expectations. As Peter and Hirata-Edds (2006) observed in the early years of the program, although teachers used Cherokee almost exclusively, children replied to their teachers and classmates predominantly in English. Even after 11 months in preschool immersion, their Cherokee production was mostly limited to naming vocabulary words, a few routine expressions such as *hesti* (stop) and *ahena* (come here) and a number of songs.

Figure 10.1 A model for Cherokee immersion planning

In order to better understand the nature of Cherokee second-language development and to envalue the progress that children were making, teachers, curriculum staff, Cherokee Cultural Resource Center staff and a team of consultants from the University of Kansas began the complex process of creating language assessments designed to measure the extent to which the children had achieved general social and academic language proficiency including knowledge of vocabulary, ability to comprehend verbal questions and commands and ability to respond appropriately either verbally or through action.

The first of these assessments, the Cherokee Preschool Immersion Language Assessment (C-PILA), was developed specifically for children aged three and four, to be administered at the end of each school year. Once these children reached kindergarten, a second oral assessment, the Cherokee Kindergarten Immersion Language Assessment (C-KILA), was developed to gauge the children's language development beyond the preschool years, and has been administered to kindergarten through fourth graders with several revisions. Most recently, a Cherokee Language Immersion Literacy Assessment (C-LILA) has been developed and administered to kindergarten through third-grade students. These assessments, although still works in progress, have provided valuable feedback to teachers and curriculum planners on what children are capable of doing with the language – as well as what they are not capable of doing – at certain points during their participation in the program.

Language testing occurs during one full week each spring, toward the end of the school year. Prior to that week, teachers review the testing materials, practice administering the tests and make any necessary changes to the administration procedures. During the week of testing, teachers work in pairs to administer the oral portions of the test to individual students, with one teacher acting as the tester and the other teacher recording the children's responses. The oral portion is also recorded for later playback to ensure scoring accuracy. The C-LILA is administered to K–3 classes as a whole, with one teacher reading the instructions and providing examples and the other teacher monitoring student work. Over the course of two days in the summer, teachers get together to score all of the assessments. The final scores are entered into a database for the purposes of analysis and the preparation of reports to CN Educational Services administrators, teachers and parents. Descriptions of the assessments can be found in Peter and Hirata-Edds (2006), Peter *et al.* (2008), and Peter and Hirata-Edds (2009), or can be requested by contacting the authors.

Since 2002, language assessment has assumed an important role in the overall programming of the Cherokee immersion program and serves a number of purposes, including:

- Providing feedback to teachers about learners' abilities.
- Giving feedback to learners and their parents.
- Planning for the future.
- Improving curriculum and instruction.
- Establishing credibility and accountability.
- Furthering understanding of second language acquisition of indigenous languages.
- Evaluating the effectiveness of the program in reversing language shift.

Ensuring the use of language assessment for the above purposes – rather than for the punitive purposes that high-stakes testing may promote – highlights the possibilities that thoughtfully designed and administered tests have for improving immersion as a viable programmatic option for revitalizing the Cherokee language.

Developing Cherokee Language Assessments

Cherokee Nation's experience with developing and implementing language assessments uniquely suited to the immersion school addresses the many challenges facing those who work in endangered language revitalization. The development of assessments for each level begins with the question: 'What should children be able to do in Cherokee by the end of the school year?' As groups of teachers and curriculum planners discuss outcomes for each level of immersion, they combine their ideal – what they hope students can do – with the reality of what children actually do on a day-to-day basis. In addition, consideration is given to the Oklahoma Department of Education's Priority Academic Student Skills (OSDE, 2003) for language arts as an indicator of the kinds of speaking, listening, reading and writing skills students in monolingual classrooms are expected to develop.

In the context of a language-focused, subject matter-driven immersion curriculum, the above activity necessitates familiarity with both the functions (the use of language to fulfill both social and academic tasks) and the forms of language (the morphology and syntax inherent in a given function) – and especially how these are different from their English counterparts. For example, the function of 'identifying family members' seems to be a straightforward and reasonable expectation for preschool children in an English-medium context, but this is far from the case in Cherokee, where kinship terminology requires grammatical forms that are quite complex for beginning-level students. The same can be said for other forms and functions, such as pluralizing nouns, naming body parts and requesting objects. The latter, for example, is a function whose form is complicated by its dependence on an understanding of Cherokee's rich noun classification system. Determining valid outcomes to measure in the Cherokee immersion context requires a great deal of input from teachers regarding the language functions that both they and their students use in the classroom, as well as the linguistic forms that children have mastered or are still developing. For the Cherokee test development team, this stage of the process has become more than simply an exercise in test preparation – with each session, the participants reach a deeper understanding of the composition of the Cherokee language, of the instructional practices they engage in and the degree to which these align with broader language goals (Peter *et al.*, 2008).

Once a list of expected outcomes is generated and prioritized, the next step is to create appropriate items to elicit sufficient evidence of the extent to which students have attained expected outcomes. This is partly achieved by involving teachers in the process and including in the assessment items that closely reflect the activities that their students engage in during the school day. For example, in developing the preschool assessment, the test development team recognized that a major expectation of the immersion approach at the early stages is that children respond appropriately to commands through action – known in second-/foreign-language-teaching literature as Total Physical Response (TPR) (Asher, 1982). Because so much of the preschool day is a lesson in learning routines through the guidance of teachers' instructions, the test planners decided to include a section on the C-PILA that measured the extent to which children understood basic classroom commands. For this portion of the test, a child is directed to a number of props displayed before him/her, such as crayons, a small blanket, a toothbrush, a bar of soap, a Cherokee ribbon shirt and a book. The child is then given a series of verbal commands and asked to respond to the command. For example, when she/he hears *tasuli* (wash your hands), the child should take the bar of soap and pretend to wash his/her hands. When she/he hears *witlvna* (go to sleep), the child should take the blanket and pretend to sleep. In this way, the test reflects what is done regularly in the classroom. At the same time, because the testing environment is different than the classroom context, it directly measures students' aural comprehension without the aid of observing and imitating what others are doing.

Another example of aligning test items to expected outcomes comes from the C-KILA. An expectation of kindergarten students is that they will understand prepositions of placement. So, the test development team constructed a comprehension test to measure their understanding of basic Cherokee expressions for on, under, behind, next to, in front of and in. The result is a TPR section in which children are given a toy train and a penny and are instructed to put the penny where they are told – in, under, in front of, behind, on or next to the train. Because this activity very closely mimics the kinds of activities teachers do in the classroom for the teaching of locatives, it directly measures students' achievement of instructional goals.

There are instances in which eliciting language to gauge students' acquisition of certain grammatical features poses challenges within the constraints of an assessment. For example, the test development team determined that by the end of first grade, children should be able to use Cherokee morphology to convey events that happened in the past, as well as events that will happen in the future. However, creating test items that reliably measure these grammatical forms has been difficult primarily because of the limitations of pictures to illustrate actions that occur in different periods of time. Several administrations of different versions of this section have not yielded desired results, making it difficult to determine if children simply do not have the language morphology necessary to perform these functions or if they do not understand the test items. The test development team continues to explore techniques for eliciting these grammatical forms and to create test items that are easily administered and readily understood by the students.

The test development process described above illustrates how, for indigenous languages, determining what immersion students should be capable of doing by the end of a year is necessarily a trial and error process. Therefore, assessments should be viewed as 'works in progress' requiring regular revising. Thorough and thoughtful analyses of test results have yielded important information not only about the abilities of the test takers, but about the test itself. Furthermore, the meaningful participation of teachers in the test development process has had a positive impact on their instructional approaches.

Using Assessment Results to Inform Instruction

Cherokee Nation's experience with language assessment provides a model of how assessment can be as much *for* learning as it can be *of* learning, a distinction that Stiggins (2002) regards as necessary for building healthy assessment environments and improving instruction. In this section, we share several examples of specific ways that the results of the C-PILA, C-KILA and C-LILA have provided useful evidence about the immersion students' developing language skills and how this knowledge has resulted both in measurable changes to teachers' instructional techniques and the establishment of more concrete grade-level expectations.

From comprehensible input to comprehensible output

As previously mentioned, the decision to develop a language assessment for the immersion preschool resulted from the observation during the early years of the program that toward the end of their first year in the program, children still appeared to be in a 'silent period' (Krashen, 1985), in which their output in Cherokee was nonexistent for some and consisting only of memorized phrases or isolated words for others. Although it was obvious through classroom observations and teachers' reflections that children were not passive learners and had attained some level of comprehension, this silent period extended beyond the expected few weeks or months, generating concern among parents, teachers and immersion planning staff (Peter & Hirata-Edds, 2006).

The C-PILA was administered at the end of the pilot preschool year with results that corroborated teachers' observations: after 11 months in immersion, children had much higher receptive skills than production skills. A closer examination of the different components of the C-PILA allowed for a more nuanced understanding of specific strengths and limitations of their developing language. For example, in an interview section, children were expected to exchange basic greetings and answer questions about their name and age; however, most children simply repeated the questions as though they had no understanding that they were supposed to be taking part in a conversation. In a different section of the test, their ability to point to pictures of objects upon hearing their names was their strongest skill with 57% accuracy overall, but their ability to name the same pictures proved much more difficult, with only 36% accuracy. Although they had some success answering basic information questions about pictures (yes/no, either/or, how many and what color) at 48% accuracy, none were able to say anything about a familiar storybook scene. Additionally, removed from the classroom, rich with daily routines, contextual clues and the ability to observe and imitate, children had difficulty understanding basic classroom commands on a TPR section of the test, with only 49% accuracy (Peter & Hirata-Edds, 2006).

Once teachers and language-teaching specialists examined the assessment results, they were able to identify not only strengths and gaps in students' linguistic repertoire, but also areas in which teachers needed instructional support. They realized, for example, that the rote drill technique they most relied on for teaching vocabulary and basic expressions was not resulting in students' ability to use those words and expressions in a meaningful context. Furthermore, the heavy emphasis on TPR did not provide sufficient opportunities for children to engage in two-way communication with their teachers and classmates. Teachers recognized that they needed more professional development in effective communicative language instruction and immersion-specific teaching techniques; they also needed more language- and age-appropriate storybooks, visual aids and other supplementary materials to enhance communication in the classroom.

The inclusion of thoughtfully designed language assessments in the Cherokee language immersion program has opened the possibility for evidence-driven professional development. Specifically, the insights gained from the test results have resulted in professional development workshops focused on communicative teaching that leads to what Swain (1985) has called *comprehensible output*, and how to create opportunities for 'pushed output', characterized by cohesion, appropriateness and accuracy in language use. Lyster (2007) and others have long maintained that input alone is not sufficient for language acquisition and that immersion teachers must learn to develop classroom tasks that strategically elicit student language use. And, as teachers have honed their skills and had more resources at their disposal, students have come closer to meeting their expected outcomes. For example, with each subsequent year, children in the preschool classroom have matriculated into prekindergarten with higher levels of both aural comprehension *and* verbal abilities. Figure 10.2 compares the C-PILA results of children in the first immersion preschool cohort with those in the third, illustrating the effect that test data had on driving higher levels of teacher performance.

Understanding the acquisition of Cherokee verb morphology toward form-focused instruction

By the end of second grade, a number of children enrolled in the Cherokee immersion program have had three or four uninterrupted years of schooling entirely in Cherokee. An analysis of the interlanguage of these children has been conducted based on language samples collected using the C-KILA (Peter *et al.*, 2008). In particular, an examination of first

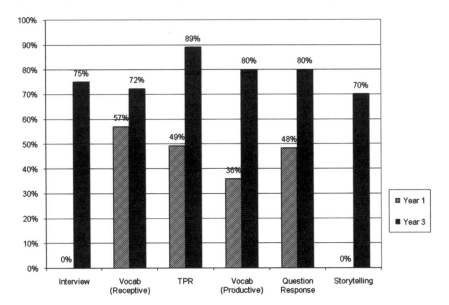

Figure 10.2 Comparison of the C-PILA results for preschool cohorts one and three

graders' usage of third-person singular and plural present tense verbs has yielded important information about immersion students' ability to use complex morphological markers accurately to convey information about actions being carried out in present time. These findings have had implications for teachers' instructional practices, and offer a detailed look at Cherokee second language acquisition by children.

The C-KILA tests both receptive and productive skills on a range of linguistic forms. Students are expected to demonstrate comprehension of a wide range of noun vocabulary, adjectives, prepositions of location, classificatory nouns and singular versus plural verb forms, and are expected to produce sentences describing present, past and future actions and to retell a short story. In reviewing the results of the initial administration of the assessment to first graders in 2007, it was revealed that, overall, children could not use the past or future tense of common verbs; moreover, most of them struggled to accurately produce present tense verb forms for third-person singular and plural forms. Closer linguistic analyses were necessary to identify specific ways in which children were – or were not – marking verbs to indicate person, number and tense. With the assistance of classroom teachers and a number of other fluent, native Cherokee consultants, three University of Kansas language specialists transcribed and analyzed acceptability of the 13 children's responses to the questions *do advne?* (What is he doing?) and *do anadvne?* (What are they doing?) for 24 verbs. They coded which of the three required parts of the verbs – the pronominal prefix (indicating the performer of the action), the root (indicating the verb meaning), and the stem (indicating the present tense and the continuous aspect of the verb) – children's utterances correctly supplied.

Analyses of accuracy in the children's utterances are described in detail in Peter *et al.* (2008). Simply put, children were able to label a picture using the correct verb root 51% of the time; however, they did not consistently mark that root using the correct pronominal prefix or aspect and tense markers. For example, when shown a picture of two boys jumping, most children could produce a Cherokee utterance that semantically indicated an action related to 'jump', even though that utterance did not include the appropriate pronominal prefix indicating 'they', or the accurate present continuous form for 'jumping'. Furthermore, children produced entirely accurate third-person singular verbs only 16% of the time, and only 6% of their plural verbs were completely accurate with respect to prefix, root and stem.

This detailed analysis of children's use of verbs on the C-KILA revealed specific knowledge of Cherokee grammar that children were lacking and suggested that simply immersing children in the Cherokee language – even for four years – was not sufficient for them to achieve the goal of language proficiency with grammatical accuracy (Peter & Hirata-Edds, 2006; Peter *et al.*, 2008). Research conducted in other immersion settings has revealed similar findings (Chaudron, 1986; Genesee, 1987; Harley, 1992; Lapkin & Swain, 2004; Lyster, 1987, 2004, 2007; Swain, 1985, among many others). Ó Duibhir (Chapter 8) offers a description of a more recent study focused on the language production of Grade 6 Irish immersion students and reports on aspects of the language that the students have not yet mastered, even though at least 85% of their instruction had been in Irish since preschool. These consistent research findings underscore the need for immersion teachers to balance natural, comprehensible input with planned opportunities for practice using specific (and both social and academic) language functions and their forms. Here again, evidence-based professional development opportunities for Cherokee immersion teachers and curriculum planners have focused on three major areas:

(1) Discovering linguistic rules for Cherokee grammar, especially verbs, which are the core of the Cherokee language, for the purpose of establishing clear language targets for each grade level.

(2) Planning lessons that target opportunities for children to practice a range of verb forms and other grammatical features through meaningful, functional activities.
(3) Preparing instructional books and other materials that expose children to a range of both social and academic language functions and encourage them to use the appropriate forms in a variety of fun and engaging ways.

A morphological analysis of the results of the C-KILA administered one year later indicates that an increase in form-focused instruction has led to greater overall proficiency and accuracy in children's production of a range of Cherokee verb forms.

Establishing more accurate grade-level targets

Over the seven years that the Cherokee immersion school has been operating, teachers and curriculum planners have become more knowledgeable about the principles and practices of immersion, the nuances of Cherokee morphology and syntax and techniques for encouraging communication while simultaneously focusing on linguistic forms. In addition, witnessing the acquisition of Cherokee by children over time has allowed for greater understanding of what children are able to achieve with each year of immersion. Establishing clear linguistic outcomes for each grade level has become a priority. To illustrate how assessment serves the purpose of refining curricular goals, we turn to a third example, the C-LILA and the results of the first administration of that assessment in May of 2008.

Briefly, like the C-PILA and C-KILA, development of the C-LILA was guided by the question, 'What Cherokee reading and writing skills should children be able to demonstrate by the end of each level of immersion?' Specific reading skills included on the multiple choice assessment measured students' ability to select syllabary to represent beginning and ending sounds, match isolated words and then full length sentences to pictures, find correct category labels for groups of words, select antonyms for cue words, choose sentences to predict what will happen next given a cue sentence and answer comprehension questions about a paragraph-length text. Writing test items included taking dictation of individual syllabary, whole words and complete phrases as well as writing sentences, and then a story about pictures. Included in both the reading and writing assessments were items to assess students' knowledge of specific morphological forms, particularly Cherokee verbs in both singular and plural forms. A single assessment was developed for kindergarten, first-grade and second-grade students in the hope that the results of the administration would provide clear breaks in scores between the grade levels, thus serving the dual purposes of gauging children's developing reading and writing skills and guiding teachers and curriculum staff in their goal setting and planning for each level. The results of the C-LILA are described in detail in Peter and Hirata-Edds (2009).

A glimpse of the reading results clearly shows limitations of the current curriculum and instructional approach to effectively delimit language objectives for each grade, particularly between kindergarten and first grade, as Figure 10.3 illustrates. Although the total score shows improvement from one grade to the next, first graders' average score was a mere 4% higher than that for kindergarteners. Additionally, on four sections of the test, kindergartners fared better than their first-grade counterparts.

The C-LILA results led to a closer examination of the first-grade curriculum and classroom instruction. We found that repetition and recycling of material across all grades had little, if any, facilitative learning value, and that this was particularly true for the first grade. In other words, the assessment results helped to show that the first-grade curriculum and the teacher's instructional approach did not adequately provide opportunities for children to build on the skills they had developed in kindergarten toward greater progress in their acquisition of Cherokee. Since then,

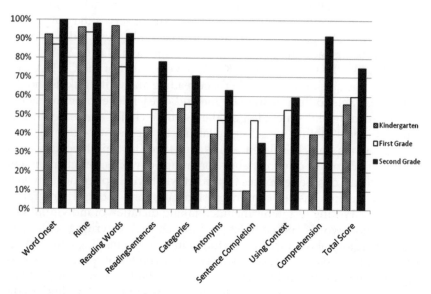

Figure 10.3 C-LILA grade-level comparisons

greater attention has been paid to building on, but not replicating, previously learned material so that learning progresses sequentially from preschool through, eventually, sixth grade. An initial attempt by teachers and curriculum planners to sequence the expectations for mastery of present tense Cherokee verbs appears in Figure 10.4. In this scaffolding model, each subsequent level includes the skills of the previous level but targets greater morphological proficiency.

It has taken years of testing and test analysis to reach a point at which realistic expectations can be established for children's acquisition of Cherokee as a second language – and there is still much to learn! A valuable lesson that the test development team has learned is that, in deciding what items to include in each assessment, it is not necessarily advantageous to balance ideal expectations with classroom realities. Rather, aiming high by including items that quite possibly none of the students will be able do, as well as items that they should be able to do with relative ease, allows children to demonstrate greater ranges of abilities and facilitates the establishment of clearer grade-level expectations. Moreover, the Cherokee immersion experience over time has shown that as teachers' instructional abilities improve and as more appropriate and effective teaching and learning aids are created, each cohort of students has attained a higher level of

PRESCHOOL: Evidence of
1st Person: "Me" in
accurate, complete phrases

PRE-K: Evidence of accuracy in 1st
Person Singular "ga/tsi", with common
verbs; with growing consistency

KINDERGARTEN: Evidence of use of some
accurate and appropriate 2nd and 3rd
singular verbs

FIRST GRADE: Mastery of 1st, 2nd, and 3rd person singular
forms of common verbs; some evidence of accurate use
of plural verbs

SECOND GRADE: Mastery of many plural forms, maybe not to the
degree of distinguishing between dual/plural

THIRD GRADE: Evidence of all person markings for present continuous
tense, singular, dual, and plural; evidence of some distinction between
inclusive/exclusive

Figure 10.4 Grade-level sequencing of targets for Cherokee present tense verb

proficiency more closely resembling the ideal. Thus, we see more concretely how the Cherokee Nation's language assessment program holds strong possibilities for improvement of both teacher instruction and student outcomes.

Insights for Other Immersion Programs

The Cherokee immersion curriculum and instruction staff has a lot of work to do in both refining the C-PILA, C-KILA and C-LILA and creating assessments for even higher levels of language attainment, in addition to establishing realistic benchmarks for Cherokee language proficiency among immersion children at each level of instruction. Still, attributing a central role to language assessment in the overall immersion programming has served to guide curricular and instructional planning in purposeful ways. It has given teachers valuable feedback on the strengths and limitations of their students, feedback that they have used to improve their teaching. It has helped curriculum planners sequence language objectives and prepare instructional materials with a richer language focus. Most importantly, it has provided evidence that immersion works, and that despite their limited production of complex morphological forms, children in the Cherokee immersion program have already achieved greater levels of proficiency than most any other second language learners of Cherokee previously documented. This bodes well for the possibilities of and potential for creating a generation of proficient Cherokee-as-a-second-language speakers to carry the language into the future.

We offer a few final insights that other immersion programs may find useful in guiding their development and use of language assessments:

(1) Language assessments provide just one piece of the overall picture and need to be combined with other sources, such as classroom observations, recording or noting conversations between children during informal interactions, using observation checklists to note specific strengths and limitations of students' language skills throughout different classroom activities and feedback and input from parents.

(2) Developing appropriate assessments is an ongoing process, and the assessment process should be revisited and revised regularly.

(3) The most important purpose of an assessment is not to prove, but to improve the quality and effectiveness of curriculum and instruction.

(4) For indigenous language immersion programs, culturally responsive and responsible language assessment requires full participation of a wide range of teachers, curriculum planners, parents, elders and fluent speakers and is respectful of their values and opinions.

Future Possibilities for Cherokee Immersion

As we look to the future, we are reminded that in order to ensure the survival of Cherokee, we must continue to strive to create a new generation of Cherokee speakers. This is a colossal project, and yet, as we have described in this chapter, the results of the Cherokee language assessments indicate that progress is being made. As an integral component of 'envaluing', the Cherokee language assessment has opened the possibility for purposeful immersion planning that proceeds from careful attention to what works, and what does not. With the future of the Cherokee language at stake, such knowledge could mean the difference between a minimally effective language immersion program and one that breathes new linguistic life for generations to come.

Note

1. The BIA was established in 1824 and is the oldest bureau in the US Department of the Interior. It provides services to nearly 2 million American Indians and Alaskan Natives. More information can be accessed at http://www.bia.gov/. Accessed 29.4.10.

References

Asher, J. (1982) *Learning Another Language through Actions: The Complete Teacher's Guidebook*. Los Gatos, CA: Sky Oaks Productions.

Chaudron, C. (1986) Teachers' priorities in correcting learners' errors in French immersion classes. In R. Day (ed.) *Talking to Learn: Conversation in Second Language Acquisition* (pp. 64–84). Rowley, MA: Newbury House.

Cherokee Nation (2003) *Ga-du-gi: A Vision for Working Together to Preserve the Cherokee language: Report of a Needs Assessment Survey and a 10-year Language Revitalization Plan*. (Final report submitted in fulfillment of FY 2001 DHS ANA Grant #90-NL-0189.)

Crawford, J. (1996) Seven hypotheses on language loss causes and cures. In G. Cantoni (ed.) *Stabilizing Indigenous Languages* (pp. 51–68). Flagstaff, AZ: Center for Excellence in Education Northern Arizona University Stabilizing Indigenous Languages.

Crawford, J. (2000) *At War with Diversity: US Language Policy in an Age of Anxiety*. Avon: Multilingual Matters.

Genesee, R. (1987) *Learning through Two Languages: Studies of Immersion and Bilingual Education*. Cambridge, MA: Newbury House.

Harley, B. (1992) Patterns of second language development in French immersion. *Journal of French Language Studies* 2, 159–183.

Hinton, L. (2001) Federal language policy and Indigenous languages in the United States. In L. Hinton and K. Hale (eds) *The Green Book of Language Revitalization in Practice* (pp. 39–44). San Diego, CA: Academic Press.

Hirata-Edds, T., Linn, M., Peter, L. and Yamamoto, A. (2003) Indigenous language teacher training seminars in Oklahoma and Florida. *Cultural Survival Quarterly* 27, 48–52.

King, J. (2001) Te Kōhanga Reo: Māori language revitalization. In L. Hinton and K. Hale (eds) *The Green Book of Language Revitalization in Practice* (pp. 119–128). San Diego, CA: Academic Press.

Krashen, S.D. (1985) *The Input Hypothesis: Issues and Implications*. New York: Longman.

Krauss, M. (1998) The condition of Native North American languages: The need for realistic assessment and action. *International Journal of the Sociology of Language* 132, 9–21.

Lapkin, S. and Swain, M. (2004) What underlies immersion students' production: The case of avoir besoin de. *Foreign Language Annals* 37, 349–355.

Lyster, R. (1987) Speaking immersion. *Canadian Modern Language Review* 43, 701–717.

Lyster, R. (2004) Research on form-focused instruction in immersion classrooms: Implications for theory and practice. *French Language Studies* 14, 321–341.

Lyster, R. (2007) *Learning and Teaching Languages through Content: A Counterbalanced Approach*. Philadelphia, PA: John Benjamins.

OSDE (2003) Priority academic student skills. On WWW at http://www.sde.state.ok.us/Curriculum/PASS/default.html. Accessed 29.4.10.

Peter, L. (2003) A naturalistic study of the Cherokee language immersion pre-school project. PhD thesis, University of Kansas, Lawrence.

Peter, L. (2007) 'Our beloved Cherokee': A naturalistic study of Cherokee preschool language immersion. *Anthropology & Education Quarterly* 38, 323–342.

Peter, L. and Hirata-Edds, T. (2006) Using assessment to inform instruction in Cherokee language revitalization. *International Journal of Bilingual Education and Bilingualism* 9, 643–658.

Peter, L. and Hirata-Edds, T. (2009) Learning to read and write Cherokee: Toward a theory of literacy revitalization. *Bilingual Research Journal* 32, 207–227.

Peter, L., Hirata-Edds, T. and Montgomery-Anderson, B. (2008) Verb development by children in the Cherokee language immersion program, with implications for teaching. *International Journal of Applied Linguistics* 18, 166–187.

Smith, G.H. (2000) Protecting and respecting indigenous knowledge. In M. Battiste (ed.) *Reclaiming Indigenous Voice and Vision* (pp. 192–224). Vancouver, BC: UBC Press.

Stiggins, R.J. (2002) Assessment crisis: The absence of assessment for learning. *Phi Delta Kappan* 83, 758–765.

Swain, M. (1985) Communicative competence: Some roles of comprehensible input and comprehensible output. In S. Gass and C. Madden (eds) *Input in Second Language Acquisition* (pp. 235–253). Rowley, MA: Newbury House.

UNESCO (2003) *UNESCO Intangible Cultural Heritage Unit's Ad Hoc Expert Group on Endangered Languages Programme Safeguarding of Endangered Languages: Language vitality and endangerment*. UNESCO.

Wilson, W.H. and Kamanā, K. (2001) Mai Loko Mai O Ka 'I'ini: Proceeding from a dream. The 'Aha Pūnana Leo connection in Hawaiian language revitalization. In L. Hinton and K. Hale (eds) *The Green Book of Language Revitalization in Practice* (pp. 147–176). San Diego, CA: Academic Press.

Part 4

Policy and Practice in Immersion Education

Chapter 11

Context and Constraints: Immersion in Hong Kong and Mainland China

P. HOARE

Introduction

In most Asian regions, the demand for additive bilingualism through schooling is immensely strong as a support for and a consequence of their rapid economic development. Language education and, in particular, the place of English within the school system, is high on social, political and economic agendas across the region, for example, South Korea, Philippines, Malaysia, Brunei and Singapore (e.g. Ho, 2002; Lee, 2008; Nunan, 2003). In Hong Kong, articles and letters about language education appear in the press on almost a daily basis. In Mainland China, the demand for more English is enormous (Hu, 2005). The debate on the place of English in education in the region is not one sided, however, as the 2009 retraction by the Malaysian government of its reintroduction of English as the language of instruction for mathematics and science shows (*The Star*, 2009).

In Hong Kong, the response to the demand has been a continuous stream of initiatives to enhance English teaching and learning stretching back over nearly 30 years.[1] The use of English as the medium of instruction has been a major, if controversial, feature of these initiatives and further 'fine tuning' is now underway to increase access to English in schools for all students.[2] In Mainland China, English has been introduced to primary schools (He, 2007), and universities are expected to teach 5–10% of their curriculum through a second language, nearly always English (Jiang *et al.*, 2009). A further significant initiative is the introduction of various forms of content-based instruction (CBI). Indeed, Hu has likened bilingual instruction in China to 'a juggernaut' (Hu, 2007: 94). In Xi'an the China–Canada–USA English Immersion (CCUEI) Project was the first 'immersion' programme in Mainland China (Yu, 2009). It began as a response to what was perceived as the inadequacy of the curriculum in meeting the needs of students for English.

In this chapter, I will explain how the policies within the educational contexts of Hong Kong and Xi'an have brought about different approaches to immersion. I will argue that the implementation of the curriculum is in many respects a result of the different policy contexts and that the two approaches, however unsatisfactory they may appear in some respects, are a coherent and pragmatic response to policy and societal factors. Nonetheless, the experience of and research in immersion from other parts of the world can suggest some directions for development which may, in turn, enhance students' learning.

Immersion Programming in Hong Kong and Xi'an

The core features of immersion education have been described by, among others, Fortune and Tedick (2008), Swain and Johnson (1997) and Swain and Lapkin (2005). Table 11.1 shows those features and the extent to which these are met in Hong Kong and Xi'an.

In Hong Kong, before 2010, students entered some 25% of middle and high schools at Grade 7 to be taught through English for most subjects for the next seven years. This late immersion programme met in principle the core features for immersion education (Table 11.1). English was used across the whole school rather than for specific classes. Classes were taught by academically and professionally trained subject teachers with Chinese as their first language who received the same initial training whether they were going to teach through English or Chinese. All students learned

Table 11.1 Core features of immersion education as manifested in secondary schools in Hong Kong and middle schools in Xi'an

*Core features of immersion education**	*Hong Kong*	*Xi'an*
(1) The immersion language is a medium of instruction.	Yes. English is used in most or all subjects except Chinese and Chinese history. It is used by most immersion teachers most of the time. Materials are in English.	Yes. English is the medium of instruction in the 'immersion' class. It is used by 'immersion' teachers all of the time. Materials are in English.

(*Continued*)

Table 11.1 (*Continued*)

Core features of immersion education*	Hong Kong	Xi'an
(2) The immersion curriculum parallels the local L1 curriculum.	Yes	No. The 'immersion' subject is separate from subjects in the formal curriculum.
(3) Overt support exists for the L1.	Yes	Yes
(4) The programme aims for additive bilingualism.	Yes	Yes
(5) Exposure to the L2 is largely confined to the classroom.	Yes. Hong Kong is bilingual in some senses, but students almost never engage with English outside school.	Yes
(6) Students enter with similar (and limited) levels of L2 proficiency.	Yes	Yes
(7) Teachers are proficient in language(s) used for instruction.	Yes. Proficiency varies but very few teachers have difficulty maintaining English in the teaching of their subjects.	Yes. Proficiency varies but very few teachers have difficulty maintaining English in the teaching of the 'immersion' class.
(8) The classroom culture is that of the local L1 community.	Yes	Yes
(9) The immersion language is the language of instruction for at least 50% of the day. As a secondary continuation programme, it is used to teach at least two year-long core subjects.	Yes	No. Only one subject is taught through English; that only takes up about 1½ hours per week.
(10) Clear separation of teacher use of L1 versus L2 for sustained periods of time.	Yes	Yes

*Based on Fortune and Tedick (2008) and Swain and Johnson (1997)

English as a subject for six years in primary school and continued to study the language as a school subject both in the immersion- and the Chinese-medium streams. The system is referred to locally as 'English/Chinese-medium instruction', usually abbreviated to 'EMI' or 'CMI'. It has evolved from the colonial education system and has been subject to serious critique in the context of post-colonialism (e.g. Lin, 2005). Entry to EMI schools or classes is a choice for those students who are considered academically equipped to benefit from it. In practice, however, very few parents turn down the opportunity for their children because the schools involved are the most prestigious, and English proficiency is a requirement for entry into higher education. The system has been widely criticised for being socially divisive, and that is one reason given for the 2010 'fine tuning'.

There exist a very small number of early total immersion schools within the public education system. The challenge for students of acquiring literacy in Chinese, however, together with the difficulty in providing sufficient suitably qualified teachers has made this approach impossible to offer on a wider scale. Hong Kong education is elitist by design, with students assessed as Band 1, 2, or 3 according to their academic achievement at Grade 6. The students who went on to full EMI education at secondary level before 1998 were almost all in Band 1 (highest academic performance), and EMI schools are invariably categorised by the public as 'Band 1 schools'.

The CCUEI Project was started in the late 1990s in a number of kindergartens in Xi'an (Chi, 2006). It was initiated by a group of local teacher educators with support from scholars from Canada and the United States, who suggested that immersion as implemented in Canada might prove an effective way of raising the English proficiency of learners in kindergartens and primary schools. It was later extended to some middle schools. The Project currently involves 18 kindergartens, 13 primary and four middle schools. In middle schools, the focus of this chapter, some 25 teachers and 2000 students, generally in classes of 50–60, are involved.

The CCUEI Project was introduced because it was felt that levels of English that students were achieving in schools were not sufficiently high to meet the needs and aspirations of the community. In an interview conducted for one of the studies (Hoare, 2010) which inform this chapter, Professor Qiang Haiyan, who initiated the programme, asserted that the original objective was:

> for English teaching reform, to deal with our problems of [the] inefficiency of traditional English teaching [...] We want to educate children to be capable to use English to study, to live, to work in the future. (Hoare, 2010: 73)

The project was intended to be an early partial immersion programme, meeting the core features of immersion education. For example, at the primary level, the programme originally covered 50% of the standard school curriculum. The implementation has come up against contextual constraints at different school levels, however, and schools, particularly at middle-school level, have had to accept a model which does not meet some core features of immersion (Table 11.1). One feature lacking is intensity, in that the amount of content taught through English is very low. Only one course is taught for no more than about one-and-a-half hours per week. Second, the content of the course is not part of the standard national curriculum. This means that the 'immersion' lessons are outside the mainstream curriculum, thus missing a core feature of immersion but allowing some flexibility of content. In some schools only students with better English are allowed to take the immersion programme. The challenge of creating secondary immersion continuation programmes is not unique to the CCUEI Project. (see, e.g. de Jong & Bearse, Chapter 6 and Lindholm-Leary, Chapter 5).

The middle school CCUEI programme provides points of contrast with immersion in Hong Kong and gives rise to consideration as to whether immersion is possible in mainstream schools in China at present and, if so, how contextual challenges might be met. Whether the middle schools concerned are ready to become immersion schools and the reasons why they cannot do so at present lie in the realm of public policy.

Programme Implementation in Hong Kong and Xi'an

Not surprisingly, the different policy contexts in Hong Kong and Xi'an have resulted in very different approaches being taken regarding programme implementation. Implementation in both places, however, can be considered unsatisfactory in relation to the curriculum demands and the consequent need for teachers' pedagogical skills to integrate and balance content and language learning. In this section I describe programme implementation in each context by first presenting a typical transcript of classroom discourse to illustrate the pedagogical skills used and then drawing on the findings of a number of studies to elaborate the discussion.

Hong Kong Grade 9 science: Lenses

The following transcript is typical of Hong Kong EMI classroom discourse in the more than 30-lesson database used in Hoare and Kong (2006). The discourse lacks the use of the language of the content by teachers and students to support students' learning of the language, thus defeating the purpose of immersion education. The transcript is taken from a Grade 9 science class on lenses. The teacher is an experienced and trained science teacher. The EMI students, all boys, have studied most of the curriculum through English for more than two years. The teacher has used their previous learning of refraction to explain the different effects of convex and concave lenses, and the boys have been drawing diagrams to illustrate the passage of light through different lenses. In the transcript, they are clarifying some additional ideas within the topic and reviewing terminology.

Transcript 1:

Teacher:	Let me ask you a question. How many principal foci are there? Ah, principal fo … foci? Foci is the plural form, OK. So here I got a principal focus.
Students:	One.
Teacher:	Can I have a second principal focus?
Students:	Yes. Yes.
Teacher:	Yes or no?
Students:	Yes. Yes.
Teacher:	Some say yes. Some say no. Can I have another principal focus?
Students:	No.
Students:	Yes, yes.
Teacher:	Can I have another principal focus?
Students:	Yes. Yes.
Teacher:	How many of you would say yes, there is another principal focus? OK, so. Ah, XXX [naming a student]. You think that there is another principal focus. Where … where can it be?
Student 1:	Opposite side
Teacher:	On the.
Student 1:	other side.
Teacher:	On the other side. On the opposite side, very good.
Students:	Woow … .
Teacher:	Do you agree?
Students:	Yes.
Teacher:	Yes, because we can have those parallel rays fall onto the lens from this side. Can you see? Can you see that?
Students:	Yes.
Teacher:	We can have the parallel rays [labelling another 'F' on the principal axis] fall onto the lens from this side and then

meet at <u>this</u> point. And still we can call it principal focus [changing the 'F' drawn earlier to 'F″']. OK, so we have two principal foci. OK, 'foci' is the plural form. F-O-C-I. Hm, so the principal axis can mean a line joining <u>F and F dash (F-)</u> [writing 'FF″' before 'principal axis']. OK. If you don't want to say that it is a line perpendicular to the plane of the lens passing through the optical centre, we can make it simple. And it is the line joining <u>F and F dash (F-)</u>. Do we have any terms which are known as the focal length? Do you think we can have a term known as focal length? Yes, we can have. It is the distance [drawing ←f→ above 'O' and 'F' on the diagram], ah, hm, between <u>F and O</u> [writing 'f: focal length' under the diagram]. It is focal length.

The teacher challenges the students to think about whether a lens has two principal foci but does not push them to articulate their thinking; she simply gives the explanation herself and moves on. The language is potentially complex, to explain the reasons why there can be two principal foci, but the teacher does not model that complexity. She relies more on the diagram, through the use of labels and deictics (such as *this*) (underlined in the transcript above), than on the use of language to explain. It is apparent from their work in the lesson that the students understand the physics, but the teacher does not help them put that understanding into English. The lesson may appear to be interactive but in reality it is transmissive in style, with a strong focus on facts and technical terminology, as shown in the last teacher turn. The questioning demands only yes–no or short-phrase answers. The teacher has neither modelled to students the English of the topic nor helped them use the language. This is parallel to the interactive pattern observed in Broner and Tedick's (Chapter 9) study during teacher-fronted, whole-class math instruction.

EMI classes in Hong Kong are teacher centred, with a focus on the transmission of rich and complex content. Technical terms abound, and teacher language may match the content in complexity. There is little sustained student talk. When complex student talk occurs, it is frequently in Chinese and many teachers accept Chinese even for one- or two-word answers. Some lessons are characterised by long teacher monologues (see Kong, 2009 for examples). Students' academic writing is of poor quality, characterised by memorisation of textbook extracts or plain copying (Kong, 2010). Assessment is frequent, rigid and traditional in format, and the implemented curriculum is dominated by public examinations administered in English in Grades 11 and 13, for which intensive preparation begins long before.[3]

Studies of immersion programme implementation in Hong Kong suggest that 'many Hong Kong immersion teachers do not have the pedagogical skills, nor the understanding of and commitment to immersion education, to integrate the teaching of language and content in the classroom in ways that can bring about the learning of both' (Hoare & Kong, 2008: 254). This weakness has been documented since the 1980s (e.g. Education Commission, 1990; Johnson, 1983, 1997). Studies of EMI classrooms since 1998, when a limit of 112 immersion schools was established, indicate that teachers use English much more consistently but they still lack language awareness and the related pedagogical skills to integrate the teaching of language and content and to support students' learning of both (e.g. Hoare, 2004; Hoare & Kong, 2006; Kong, 2010; Wannagat, 2007). That these aspects of implementation may not always be due to inadequate training is suggested by Hoare and Kong's (2006) study of the effectiveness of an in-service professional development programme. This indicates that school contexts, influenced by public policy and community pressures (particularly societal emphasis on examination success and the lack of any official language-related objectives or guidelines for EMI schools), inhibit teachers from making changes to their classroom practice despite an enhanced understanding of the rationale for and the pedagogy of immersion.

This view was supported in part by Kong (2010), who found that students' writing in four Grade 10 late immersion biology and history classrooms did not demonstrate the levels of content and language learning expected of immersion education. The purpose of writing was to help students achieve good results in public examinations rather than to learn. This view was confirmed in a survey of 68 immersion teachers.

Tsui *et al.* (2004) studied the use of questions in EMI classrooms and found that the usefulness of questioning as a pedagogical technique was constrained by lack of language repertoire (i.e. range and flexibility in language use) on the part of both teachers and students. Tsui (2004) confirmed that this lack greatly reduced the shared space of learning between teachers and students in EMI classrooms.

Since 1998, there has been little research comparing the English or subject content learning outcomes of immersion with those of CMI schools in Hong Kong. The most important evidence comes from a major three-stage longitudinal research project summarised in Tsang (2008), which involves student assessments from more than 50 schools. The findings show that after three years the academic achievement of EMI students is much lower than that of CMI students in science and social studies, though there is no significant difference in mathematics and Chinese. In English, the immersion students make significant gains (Yip *et al.*, 2003). After seven years, however, while the EMI students still have significantly higher levels of English proficiency than CMI students, there is no significant disadvantage in other subjects (Tsang, 2008). The way in which these results were publicised in 2008 suggested that, more than any other factor, it was the level of English when students left school which differentiated between EMI and CMI school students, and this influenced policy decisions leading to the introduction of 'fine tuning'. Despite these positive results for immersion, it remains to be shown whether the gains in English are what should be expected. Johnson states that EMI students 'fail to achieve the high levels of proficiency demanded by the community and assumed to be possible' (Johnson, 1997: 172). There is no evidence that the community's feelings have changed, and there is still widespread dissatisfaction in the community with English achievement.

Xi'an Grade 8 nature and society: Water

The transcript below exemplifies the classroom discourse typical of a CCUEI middle-school lesson. The transcript is taken from a Grade 8 class which takes *Nature and Society* as its 'immersion' subject. The teacher is a qualified teacher of English (not science trained) with seven years' teaching experience. The topic of the lesson is 'Water', and it is the only lesson that the class has on this topic. They have been asked to prepare for the lesson by finding out facts about water.

Transcript 2:

Teacher:	OK, so in your opinion, what is the best drink among those, coffee or tea? ... XXX (naming a student) What do you think?
Student 10:	I think cola, water and orange juice is ...
Teacher:	Is?
Student 10:	Are the best drink.
Teacher:	If you have to choose one, only one.
Student 10:	Cola.
Teacher:	Cola is the best. Thank you. Do you agree with him?
Students:	No.
Teacher:	Try to find some reasons. Why isn't cola the best drink among those? XXX [naming a student].
Student 7:	I think water is good for us.
Teacher:	So do you agree with him?

Students:	No.
Teacher:	Can you give him any reasons?
Student 7:	Cola is bad for us because cola has many, many, cola has water in [inaudible].
Teacher:	What? I don't know either. Sorry. So is it sweet? Is cola sweet I mean?
Students:	Yes.
Teacher:	Yes. So it has much sugar in it, right? So too much sugar is bad for our health, so cola is not the best drink. So what's your idea?
Student 7:	I think water is the best drink.
Teacher:	Water is the best drink, so why do you think so?
Student 7:	Drink water is healthy and now water is more expensive than before.
Teacher:	Water is more expensive than before. So?
Student:	So I think water is good for us.
Teacher:	It's more expensive than before so it's good for us. It has no smell, no taste. Ok, XXX [naming a student], please.
Student 4:	I think because water has a lot of [inaudible].
Teacher:	What do you mean? So colour, you mean colour. Because it has wrong colour, so maybe there are some chemicals in it, so thank you. XXX [naming a student].
Student 20:	I think milk is the best drink.
Teacher:	You think milk is the best drink.
Student 20:	Because milk make us strong and tall.
Teacher:	Milk can make us strong and tall. So that's your idea. Ok, please.
Student 10:	I think cola is the best drink.
Teacher:	[Laughter] You are very stubborn.
Student 10:	Because cola is useful, can get over illness long long ago.
Teacher:	Cola is used for getting over the illness.
Student 10:	Long long ago.
Teacher:	Long long ago.
Student 10:	In America.

It is difficult to see a clear content learning focus in Transcript 2 and it is apparent that the teacher has little content of any depth to impart to students. The content is mainly facts of a very general nature and there is no attempt to explore complex ideas or relationships around the topic. The teacher's language is relatively simple and the students are not pushed to explore more complex language use because the processing of the content does not demand this. However, the class participates very enthusiastically and students talk a good deal, both in answering the teacher's questions and in group discussions (not part of the transcript). This is noteworthy, as in mainstream English lessons in these schools, by the students' and teachers' own account, there are usually few chances for uncontrolled practice. In fact in the whole lesson from which this extract is taken there are 102 student turns. Furthermore, while the lesson lacks depth, the range of language used, particularly the vocabulary, is far richer than is likely in a mainstream English lesson, which takes a traditional, grammar-focused approach to teaching.

This extract typifies the findings of Kong (2009) and Hoare (2010), which show that CCUEI lessons are interactive, with a great many student turns and group discussions. Students are highly motivated and attentive. The content is generally superficial but factually loaded. Students are often familiar with some of the content as they are expected to learn independently in advance; the teachers then ask students to share these facts during lessons. The teachers supplement and reinforce these but do not exploit them to lead to further learning. If they perceive that the content is too demanding for students, they feel they can omit it as the content is, after all, not part of the formal curriculum. There is very rarely any explicit focus on language except, perhaps, vocabulary. Interviews and personal communication with teachers indicate that this is a result of teachers' beliefs that language acquisition in immersion is 'primarily incidental' (Lyster & Mori, 2008: 133). The English that teachers and thus students use matches the content in its lack of complexity, with no explicit focus on language–content relationships. Students tend to practice language they already know in talking about relatively undemanding topics, which leads to little new content and language learning (Kong, 2009). Hoare (2010) argues that the CCUEI lessons, however unsatisfactory in terms of the language and content learning goals, provide students with the much needed language practice opportunities they lack in mainstream English lessons.

To date, there have been no measurements of language gains by CCUEI students at the middle school level, but the staff at participating schools evaluate the project highly and are delighted with students' progress. Hoare (2010) reported that principals and teachers believe strongly that students benefit. In the data set analysed for this study, one principal claimed:

> The effect is very obvious. The goal that we expected has been achieved. Students' proficiency is higher than the other classes in the same grade through these two to three years.

The teachers have more nuanced views and point out that the gains are more in oral than written language, which is understandable given instructional emphasis on oral language, and they note particular gains in vocabulary. Observations and interviews with students and preliminary data from a study currently underway by Hoare and Kong (2010) suggest that students with weaker English skills may not benefit greatly, however, and that students do not acquire a great deal of complex academic discourse though this is not completely lacking in the data from some classrooms.

Parents also are convinced of the success of the programme, at least if school personnel are to be believed. One principal recounted that from the start of the programme 'Parents had very positive response towards it.' The expansion of the programme within schools, with more and more classes being opened, seems to confirm this.

While the interview data (Hoare, 2010) reveal general, though not comprehensive, satisfaction among stakeholders regarding the success of the Project, this is limited to English learning. Although internal school assessments include course content, it is apparent from interviews such as that quoted above that school personnel regard English learning as important above other outcomes. This emphasis on English learning contrasts with the content learning emphasis in Hong Kong's late immersion programmes (Hoare & Kong, 2008). These differences are undoubtedly linked to contextual factors and policy constraints.

Influence of the Sociopolitical Context on Implementation

The lesson transcripts, description of classroom implementation and perceived learning outcomes in both Xi'an and Hong Kong have revealed features which are far from those suggested as distinguishing 'well-implemented immersion programs' (Fortune & Tedick, 2008: 10). For example, Hong Kong classrooms are rarely 'language attentive' and Xi'an lessons rarely 'challenge students both cognitively and linguistically' (Fortune & Tedick, 2008: 10). In neither context is there a truly appropriate balance of content and language which requires students to engage with content and, thereby, learn new language. It would be easy to assume that the teachers simply lack the pedagogical skills to establish this balance, which is critical to the success of immersion teaching. This would be an oversimplification, however.

Hong Kong

Education in Hong Kong is highly valued by parents and society; it is moderately well resourced and teachers are conscientious and professional. English is considered immensely important. There is ample international experience to draw on and Hong Kong is not shy of doing this. Significant yet less obvious aspects of the sociopolitical context, however, may help explain what appears to be inadequate implementation of immersion. These contextual factors, largely the result of underlying educational and social policy, interact with and support one another.

The first and arguably most important influence on classroom implementation of immersion is the schools' narrow focus on academic success. Secondary schools operate in a selective educational environment in which parents have some choice over which schools their children apply for and schools can select the best and brightest. Immersion schools are among the most prestigious and have often been so since colonial days. Yet, school personnel know they will only attract the best students if their students are consistently academically successful as demonstrated by published results from public examinations. Schools are judged largely on academic success and, inevitably, so are teachers. The political decisions which govern these aspects of education may, therefore, militate against successful implementation of immersion. Teachers understandably focus on content as, despite some attempts to redress the balance, public examinations tend not to demand coherent, well-written English (Kong, 2010). Science subjects and mathematics, which make fewer demands on extended written English, are by far the most popular as examination subject choices (Hong Kong Examinations Authority, 2008). Interviews with subject teachers suggest that they see English proficiency as only marginally relevant to the goal of academic success (Hoare & Kong, 2006). Despite this, it would be wrong to say that immersion schools do not take English seriously. They frequently have policies to promote English use in school; they take measures which should enhance English learning and make it the main language of the school. They appear reluctant or unable, however, to insist on classroom strategies that teachers judge to be constraints on effective content teaching. Teachers feel that either it is not their responsibility or they lack the expertise to help their students focus on English use in the EMI classroom. They also know well that their individual success as teachers is not judged on this aspect of their teaching.

Second, the policy of allowing a substantial proportion of the age group to join immersion classes, largely in response to public pressure, has made immersion an alternative mainstream programme so that no special requirements have been considered necessary for teachers. Twenty-five percent of Hong Kong's secondary teachers worked in total immersion schools in 2009. It is improbable that all of these have the level of commitment that immersion teaching demands and perhaps it is unrealistic to expect that they should. Interview data (Hoare & Kong, 2006) reveal that many teachers simply do not feel the need to make the significant adjustments to their pedagogy that immersion demands. For example:

Teacher: I just follow the textbook. And I don't use any other teaching skills because of the time. There are six or seven points in the textbook. [. . . .] I'll explain to them step by step, point by point. Make sure that they understand.

Interviewer: How do you deal with vocabulary?

Teacher: I translate in Chinese.

It would be wrong to suggest that teachers do not do their best to teach well or that many teachers avoid English rather than immerse their students in it. As mentioned above, however, their initial teacher education has not prepared them for the role of immersion teacher (Hoare & Kong, 2008). This mirrors policy weaknesses found not only in Asia, but in other countries around the world (cf. Lindholm-Leary, Chapter 5; Tedick *et al.*, Chapter 1).

Xi'an

The limited effectiveness of lessons in the CCUEI Project, which is suggested by the discussion of the extract in the last section, is also partially a result of limitations imposed by the political and educational context within which the project operates. First of all, the language law of the PRC requires all school education to be through the national language (Kirkpatrick & Xu, 2001). The immersion subjects are, therefore, additional to the mainstream curriculum, within some time that can be scheduled at the school's discretion. This greatly limits the amount of time the schools can allocate to the Project. Approval for the project has had to be sought from the provincial education bureau and, interviews suggest, this has not always been easy to obtain. Although there may be ways around this limitation, as in Shanghai,[4] genuine immersion education does not seem to be possible in most of China within the current legal framework.

Second, the high-stakes assessment for high school selection in Grade 9 dominates the concerns of middle school personnel. Some teachers are unwilling to consider an immersion agenda because they do not believe that it would improve students' ranking in the province-wide assessment. The structure of the education system, therefore, limits the possibilities for immersion.

Furthermore, as immersion has never been on the national education agenda, schools have to choose between content-trained teachers with low levels of English proficiency or English-trained teachers with no academic background in a content area. As the overall focus of the project is English development, they naturally choose the latter. These are qualified teachers of English who usually teach the same students for their English subject. Inevitably they find some of the more complex content challenging to teach and may oversimplify or avoid this at times, particularly as they have few resources to support the curriculum (Hoare, 2010). At the same time, they do not feel accountable for students' content learning. This accounts in part for the lack of emphasis on content and their greater concern for language, even though their understanding of immersion inhibits them from including a language focus in their instructional planning.

Either directly or indirectly, therefore, the policy context of education in both Hong Kong and Xi'an militates against successful implementation of immersion. While there is frequently goodwill towards immersion among teachers and school management, this cannot overcome the weight of policies and hierarchical traditions which focus attention on publicly assessed academic achievement. In Hong Kong, these prevent all but the most committed content teachers from providing students with the balance of language and content that successful immersion demands. In Xi'an they prevent genuine implementation of immersion at the middle school level even if the current language policy is changed.

Future Possibilities for Hong Kong and Xi'an

Every educational context has its own priorities and possibilities and it is neither realistic nor desirable to expect that either the Hong Kong or Xi'an programmes will be transformed into immersion models such as those found elsewhere. Nonetheless, it is apparent that neither programme maximises students' language learning. Successes elsewhere may provide a source of theory, experience and inspiration to draw on, which can suggest adjustments that may enable these students to achieve their potential as language learners. Björklund and Mård-Miettinen (Chapter 2) and Wilson and Kamanā (Chapter 3) point out, for example, how immersion programme design adjusts to different contexts.

In Hong Kong, policy revisions in 2010 are intended to widen access to immersion from Grade 7 and, at the same time, to provide preparation for students who may transfer to immersion at Grade 10. One of the aims of these revisions is to delink immersion from school status and prevent labelling of schools and students. This aim accords with one of the principles espoused by Fortune and Tedick that immersion should develop 'more equitable and socially respectful student relationships' (Fortune

& Tedick, 2008: 10). The system of banding students has been maintained, however, and, effectively, the more high banding students a school can recruit, the more immersion (wholly English-medium) classes they are allowed to run. In addition immersion schools, there are immersion classes and non-immersion classes within the same school. Schools are also allowed to use English within the curriculum to a greater extent than before for non-immersion classes either subject by subject or in time set aside within several subjects. Some manifestations of this are CBI, similar to content-and-language-integrated-learning (CLIL) described briefly by Björklund and Mård-Miettinen (Chapter 2), which is spreading rapidly in Europe and elsewhere. Although not immersion, if implemented effectively, these classes provide a cline within the system ranging from very limited CBI for, perhaps, two years, to late total immersion for six years.

A great deal will depend on the professional development programme to be established and the long-term support given to schools and teachers. There are already 'language-aware' teachers in the system who are able to integrate language and content more successfully than occurs in the transcript quoted (see, e.g. the discussion of Lesson 2 in Kong, 2009). At present, however, it is hard to see what will bring about attitudinal changes in teachers towards integrating language and content, which are as important as instructional changes. The history of Hong Kong's language in education policies over the past 25 years or so suggests that 'fine-tuning' is unlikely to be the end of the story. The recognition of the need for teacher development may signal that immersion is finally being seen as a teaching specialism and this could mean that significant advances might be made over the medium term.

In Xi'an, the fluidity brought about by China's socioeconomic development opens up a range of possibilities. It is acknowledged that English language teaching has to develop quickly to keep up with societal changes (Hu, 2005), and this may lead to greater policy flexibility and more autonomy for schools. More resources are likely to become available as education becomes better resourced. Teacher supply for immersion in middle schools will, nonetheless, continue to be a limitation and only in particularly fortunate schools, perhaps those in coastal cities and other wealthier areas, are there likely to be subject-trained teachers with a sufficiently high level of English proficiency to become immersion teachers. The overwhelming demand for English will doubtless continue for some time, and if we consider what the CCUEI Project has achieved thus far in overcoming formidable obstacles, such as lack of teaching resources and teacher education (Hoare, 2010), it is possible that either this or some other initiative will evolve from the current CBI language course model into a more internationally recognisable form of immersion as the advantages are better understood.

In the meantime, professional development with English-trained teachers in Xi'an (Hoare & Kong, 2010) is bringing about a far greater understanding of how language and content interact in learning and the consequent need to provide greater content depth (see, e.g. Lesson 3 discussion in Kong, 2009). This understanding may prove invaluable to the provision of cross-curricular support if subject teachers become involved in immersion.

Conclusion

In this chapter I have described how the implementation of immersion education in two very different Asian educational contexts is influenced by policy constraints and community pressures to the extent that in Xi'an the term 'immersion' is inappropriate. These influences impact on both programme design and classroom implementation and limit students' likely language gains. I emphasise, however, that when evaluated on their own terms, the programmes may be successful and, in the vibrant socio-economic context of Asia today, may be able to draw on immersion theory and experience to develop further in future.

Notes

1. See the Hong Kong Education Bureau website http://www.edb.gov.hk/ index.aspx?nodeID = 1900&langno = 1 for details and links to many official documents and a list of government-sponsored research projects. See also Hong Kong Education Commission reports 1, 2, 4 and 6 at: http://www.e-c. edu.hk/eng/online/index_e.html. Accessed 23 February 2011.
2. For a more detailed description, see Hoare and Kong (2008). The situation described in this chapter has been in place since 1998 when only 112 schools were permitted to remain as EMI (i.e. late immersion) schools. The 'fine tuning' introduced in 2010 will allow some secondary schools to open one or more EMI classes for more academically able students rather than requiring that the whole school be English medium. All schools are now permitted to teach up to 25% of the non-language curriculum through English, either teaching one or two subjects wholly through English or up to 25% of any subject in discrete blocks of time.
3. Public examinations are available in Chinese or English versions (except for the two language subjects and Chinese history), but EMI students generally enter for the English version.
4. There have been pronouncements about plans to introduce immersion on a large scale in Shanghai but few reports of its implementation (Yu, 2009).

Economically advanced coastal cities in China, such as Shanghai, are sometimes given dispensations to try social and economic experiments not permitted elsewhere, which may be how they overcome the legal prohibition.

References

Chi, Y.P. (ed.) (2006) *English Immersion Pedagogy in Chinese Context*. Shaanxi: Shaanxi People's Education Press.

Education Commission. (1990) *Education Commission Report Number 4*. Hong Kong: Hong Kong Government Printer.

Fortune, T.W. and Tedick, D.J. (2008) One-way, two way and indigenous immersion: A call for cross fertilisation. In T.W. Fortune and D.J. Tedick (eds) *Pathways to Multilingualism: Emerging Perspectives on Immersion Education* (pp. 3–21). Clevedon: Multilingual Matters.

He, G.K. (2007) Thoughts on English teaching in primary schools – From the perspective of teachers. Paper delivered at the First National Symposium on Primary English Language Teaching: GDTCFLA, Guangzhou.

Ho, W.K. (2002) English language teaching in East Asia today: An overview. *Asia Pacific Journal of Education* 22, 1–22.

Hoare, P. (2004) The importance of language awareness in late immersion teachers. In M. Bigelow and C. Walker (eds) *Creating Teacher Community: Selected Papers from the Third International Conference on Language Teacher Education* (pp. 235–258). Minneapolis, MN: Center for Advanced Research on Language Acquisition.

Hoare, P. (2010) Content-based language teaching in China: Contextual influences on implementation. *Journal of Multicultural and Multilingual Development* 31, 69–86.

Hoare, P. and Kong, S. (2006) *Enhancing Teacher Education for English-medium Teachers: Report of a Teaching Development Project*. Hong Kong: Hong Kong Institute of Education.

Hoare, P. and Kong, S. (2008) Late Immersion in Hong Kong: Still stressed but making progress? In T.W. Fortune and D.J. Tedick (eds) *Pathways to Multilingualism: Emerging Perspectives on Immersion Education* (pp. 242–266). Clevedon: Multilingual Matters.

Hoare, P. and Kong, S. (2010) Cognitive content engagement in content-based language teaching. Paper delivered at the American Association of Applied Linguistics Annual Conference, Atlanta, GA.

Hong Kong Examinations Authority (2008) HKALE Analysis of male and female candidates by age and subject choices. On WWW at http://www.hkeaa.edu.hk/DocLibrary/HKALE/Release_of_Results/Exam_Report/Examination_Statistics/alexamstat08_4.pdf. Accessed 29.4.10.

Hu, G. (2005) English language education in China: Policies, progress, and problems. *Language Policy* 4, 5–24.

Hu, G. (2007) The juggernaut of Chinese–English bilingual education. In A. Feng (ed.) *Bilingual Education in China: Practices, Policies and Concepts* (pp. 94–126). Clevedon: Multilingual Matters.

Jiang, B., Nong, G., Zhang, R. and Liu, X. (2009) Study on problems and countermeasures of bilingual teaching. In L.M. Yu (ed.) *Bilingual Instruction in*

China: A Global Perspective (pp. 159–168). Beijing: Foreign Language and Research Press.

Johnson, R.K. (1983) Bilingual switching strategies: A study of the modes of teacher-talk in bilingual secondary classrooms in Hong Kong. *Language, Learning and Communication* 2, 267–285.

Johnson, R.K. (1997) The Hong Kong education system: Late immersion under stress. In R.K. Johnson and M. Swain (eds) *Immersion Education: International Perspectives* (pp. 171–189). Cambridge: Cambridge University Press.

Kirkpatrick, A. and Xu, Z. (2001) The new Language Law of the People's Republic of China. *ALM Articles* 14–15.

Kong, S. (2009) Content-based instruction: What can we learn from content-trained teachers' and language-trained teachers' pedagogies? *The Canadian Modern Language Review* 66, 229–263.

Kong, S. (2010) Writing in late immersion biology and history classes in Hong Kong. *Writing & Pedagogy* 2, 13–38.

Lee, T.J. (2008) Seoul moves to revamp English education. *Singapore: The Straits Times* 11 February.

Lin, A.M.Y. (2005) Critical transdisciplinary perspectives on language-education-policy and practice in postcolonial contexts: The case of Hong Kong. In A.M.Y. Lin and P. Martin (eds) *Decolonisation, Globalisation: Language in Education Policy and Practice* (pp. 38–54). Clevedon: Multilingual Matters.

Lyster, R. and Mori, H. (2008) Instructional counterbalance in immersion pedagogy. In T.W. Fortune and D.J. Tedick (eds) *Pathways to Multilingualism: Emerging Perspectives on Immersion Education* (pp. 133–151). Clevedon: Multilingual Matters.

Nunan, D. (2003) The impact of English as a global language on educational policies and practices in the Asia-Pacific region. *TESOL Quarterly* 37, 589–613.

Swain, M. and Johnson, R.K. (1997) Immersion education: A category within bilingual education. In R.K. Johnson and M. Swain (eds) *Immersion Education: International Perspectives* (pp. 1–16). Cambridge: Cambridge University Press.

Swain, M. and Lapkin, S. (2005) The evolving sociopolitical context of immersion education in Canada: Some implications for program development. *International Journal of Applied Linguistics* 15, 169–186.

The Star (2009) Math and Science back to Bahasa, mother tongues (Update). On WWW at http://thestar.com.my/news/story.asp?file=/2009/7/8/nation/20090708144354&sec=nation. Accessed 29.4.10.

Tsang, W.K. (2008) Evaluation research on the implementation of the medium of instruction guidance for secondary schools. *Hong Kong Institute for Educational Research Newsletter* 24. Hong Kong: The Chinese University of Hong Kong.

Tsui, A.B.M. (2004) Medium of instruction in Hong Kong: One country, two systems, whose language? In J.W. Tollefson and A.B.M. Tsui (eds) *Medium of Instruction Policies: Which Agenda? Whose Agenda?* (pp. 97–106). Mahwah, NJ: Lawrence Erlbaum Associates.

Tsui, A.B.M., Marton, F., Mok, I.A.C. and Ng, D.F.P. (2004) Questions and the space of learning. In F. Marton and A.B.M. Tsui (eds) *Classroom Discourse and the Space of Learning* (pp. 113–137). Mahwah, NJ: Erlbaum.

Wannagat, U. (2007) Learning through L2 – Content and language integrated learning (CLIL) and English as medium of instruction (EMI). *International Journal of Bilingual Education and Bilingualism* 10, 663–682.

Yip, D.Y., Tsang, W.K. and Cheung, S.P. (2003) Evaluation of the effects of medium of instruction on the science learning of Hong Kong secondary students: Performance on the science achievement test. *Bilingual Research Journal* 27, 295–331.

Yu, L.M. (2009) Comparing bilingual education models in China and Canada: Application of theory. In L.M. Yu (ed.) *Bilingual Instruction in China: A Global Perspective* (pp. 3–11) Beijing: Foreign Language Teaching and Research Press.

Chapter 12

US Immigrants and Two-Way Immersion Policies: The Mismatch between District Designs and Family Experiences

L.M. DORNER

Introduction

In the early 2000s, Engleville[1] – an elementary school district in the Chicago area – implemented a policy that made two-way immersion (TWI) the primary educational program for Spanish-dominant[2] English Language Learners (ELLs). Following this policy, equal numbers of students from predominantly English- and predominantly Spanish-speaking homes received content-area instruction in both languages, with about 80% in Spanish for the first few years. Research shows that TWI students like Engleville's become functionally bilingual and biliterate by the fifth grade (Howard *et al.*, 2003). Moreover, studies suggest that TWI is one of the most effective instructional models for ELLs (Lindholm-Leary & Borsato, 2006; Lindholm-Leary, Chapter 5; Thomas & Collier, 2002). However, minority-language immigrant families may resist such programs, finding it hard to believe that instructing young children in their native language for most of the day will improve their *English* language acquisition and academic achievement. How do families understand this seemingly counterintuitive finding? In general, what matters for immigrants' decisions about new language policies?

Schools that offer TWI need to solicit applications from a variety of families, including those who speak the minority language at home. Across the United States, many of these families are low-income Latino[3] immigrants, who may face economic, cultural or language barriers in

231

understanding educational policies or communicating with schools (Valdés, 1997) and whose children may be at risk for dropping out (Howard, *et al.*, 2003). To ensure that *all* families understand their educational options, policymakers need to know how families learn about policies and make their decisions. I took up this challenge with an ethnographic study that explored how Mexican immigrants in Engleville understood the implementation of their district's new TWI policy. This work is framed by sense-making approaches to policy analysis (Spillane *et al.*, 2002; Yanow, 2000). I argue that to understand how a policy is implemented and why it succeeds or fails, one needs to examine not only the interpretations and actions of those who implement it (e.g. teachers and district leaders), but also those who receive it (e.g. families) (Dorner, 2010a).

Specifically, in an ethnographic research project that included 18 months of participant observation with six Mexican immigrant families, I explored the following questions: How do immigrant families make sense of their district's new TWI policy? How do their contexts shape these sense-making processes? I start this chapter with a brief overview of relevant literature and argue for closer attention to all policy agents' sense-making processes. Then, drawing from the six case studies as well as field work documenting Engleville's implementation of TWI, I examine Mexican immigrants' sense-making processes in context. I conclude with possibilities for more fully engaging newcomers in the implementation of TWI policies.

Background: TWI and Immigrant Family Perspectives

As movements against traditional and transitional approaches to bilingual education in the United States have gained strength, an increasing number of schools have developed TWI programs, a form of dual-language education (see Tedick *et al.*, Chapter 1). The Center for Applied Linguistics had documented over 370 in October of 2010.[4] Such programs are designed to develop bilingualism and biliteracy in ELLs as well as in majority-language, English-dominant students. There are various TWI models, but all programs provide content-area instruction in two languages and integrate language-majority and language-minority speakers – usually striving for a 1:1 ratio – for all or most of the school day. Most programs in the United States are Spanish–English and have three goals for students: (1) bilingualism and biliteracy; (2) high academic achievement; and (3) positive crosscultural behaviors and attitudes (Howard *et al.*, 2003; Lindholm-Leary & Howard, 2008; Lindholm-Leary, Chapter 5; Tedick *et al.*, Chapter 1).

In the growing body of research on TWI, the majority of studies describe specific programs and the components necessary for effective programs, or analyze academic achievement and other TWI student outcomes, as in this volume's chapters by Lindholm-Leary (Chapter 5) and de Jong and Bearse (Chapter 6) (also see Lindholm-Leary, 2005; Lindholm-Leary & Howard, 2008). Relatively little research has examined TWI program implementation (cf. Freeman, 1996). Especially lacking are studies of parent involvement and recruitment, despite the fact that reviews consistently claim that family engagement is critical to program success and that overcoming politics is challenging, yet crucial (Lindholm-Leary, 2005; Valdés, 1997). This section briefly reviews the few studies that do examine immigrants' perspectives on immersion and bilingual education, arguing that researchers must go beyond *what* families think and examine *how* they interpret and take action regarding policies.

Many language-minority and language-majority parents choose TWI for their children because they believe in bilingualism. Some US studies have documented that Latino-immigrant parents, in particular, choose TWI programs because they want children to maintain their family's language and culture both for 'integrative' and 'instrumental' reasons (de Jong & Bearse, Chapter 6; Lindholm-Leary, 2001, Chapter 5). That is, immigrants want children to be able to communicate with the entire family and be proud of their cultural heritage (integrative) and to have successful futures as bilingual workers (instrumental) (Craig, 1996; Dorner, 2010a; Rhodes *et al.*, 1997; Shannon & Milian, 2002). De Jong and Bearse (Chapter 6) found that Latino students also emphasized the relationship between language and identity as an important reason for continuing with TWI into high school.

Studies of Latino immigrants and bilingual education in general demonstrate similar findings. Many US newcomers stress that knowing one's heritage language is important for cultural maintenance, while being bilingual or learning English is critical for children's future (Bayley & Schecter, 2005; Orellana *et al.*, 1999). However, research also points out that families' sociopolitical contexts matter for their ideas and decisions about policies. First and foremost, state policies may dictate what is possible; for example, Proposition 227 in California (Orellana *et al.*, 1999) and Proposition 203 in Arizona (González, 2005) effectively eliminated bilingual education programs for ELLs. Zehrbach (Chapter 4) explores the establishment of TWI charter schools in the United States in light of such legislation. Families' choices for language education are also shaped by other factors, ranging from the opinions of extended family members and local educators (Bayley & Schecter, 2005), as well as opportunities to use the heritage language and the sociopolitical context of the school district or town (Dorner, 2010b; Freeman, 1996).

These prior studies help us understand *why* immigrant families choose to enroll children in TWI, and suggest that each family's particular, local contexts matter for the educational and language decisions that they make. Extending this research to explore *how* immigrants make sense of TWI policies is necessary so that policymakers can effectively reach out to all their constituents. Moreover, understanding immigrants' sense-making processes may be especially critical for promoting TWI policies, as choosing an immersion model may seem counterintuitive to newcomers.

A Social-Interactional Approach to Studying TWI Policies

To better understand the implementation of educational policy, I take a sociocultural, bottom-up, interpretive approach. That is, I argue that policy agents' *interpretations*, which are influenced by *sociocultural* interactions and sociopolitical contexts, can shape a policy's implementation and results. Analyzing sense-making processes from the *bottom-up* – or 'on the ground', where policies' meanings are contested and actually created – is critical for understanding whether and how policies are carried out (Ball, 2006; Hornberger, 2003; Spillane *et al.*, 2002; Yanow, 2000).

Who are policy agents?

During any policy's implementation, the ideas and decisions of diverse 'policy agents' shape what a policy becomes. Besides state and federal legislators, teachers, administrators and other institutional players like funders and curriculum developers, educational policy agents include those who make choices for particular schools or programs (Lewis & Maruna, 1998). These include taxpaying citizens, families, parents and children, whose interpretations can influence implementation, and in fact, the policies that result (Dorner, 2010b).

Social-interactional sense-making processes

Scholars from across the disciplines have long argued that socially organized activity drives understanding (DiMaggio, 1997; Greeno, 1998; Lave & Wenger, 1991; Rogoff, 1990). Drawing from this work, Spillane and colleagues (2002) maintain that policy agents make sense of policies not only using their individual knowledge, beliefs and attitudes, but also drawing from their context and the socially situated learning inherent in those contexts.

In order to explore how policy sense making is situated, one must consider both the 'macro' and 'micro' aspects of contexts (Spillane *et al.*, 2002). At the macrolevel, the frameworks that people use to understand new information are dependent in part upon their 'thought communities' or worldviews. Such worldviews are generally developed through group membership and can be influenced by one's nationality, ethnic background, immigrant status, social class, religion or profession. These factors provide particular experiences, social interactions and, in turn, sense-making processes. The microlevel, in contrast, includes more immediate and daily practices. For example, the organizational arrangement of the workplace or the relationships developed at church can shape interpretations and sense-making processes 'in the moment'. None of these macro- or microfactors – from 'thought communities' to daily work and relationships – are static, as individuals shift contexts across time and place. Also, although they are separated here for analytical purposes, in everyday sense-making processes, 'macro-' and 'micro-' factors regularly interact as people interpret information and situations.

Drawing from these theoretical orientations, I contend that sense-making occurs in various contexts, shaped both by knowledge and belief systems developed as a result of macrogroup practices and experiences over time, as well as microinteractions and relationships within everyday life. I explore these processes for immigrant families, as they strive to understand US school systems, figure out what a TWI policy means, and make choices for their children's education.

Research Methods

To analyze policy agents' interpretations and sense-making processes, I designed a three-year ethnographic research project.[5] In this study, I examined TWI's public policy process based on field work that included interviews with district officials, participant observation at public policy meetings, and analyses of public documents, online listservs and media reports. Through participant observation, I also developed six case studies of Mexican immigrant families whose children were in TWI. In this section, I describe background information on Engleville and the specific data collection and analyses that inform this chapter.

A brief history of Engleville and its approach to bilingual education

Engleville is a large, diverse, resource-rich suburb of Chicago. At the time of the study, its public school district's demographics were approximately 40% Black, 40% White, 15% Hispanic and 5% other. The city's leaders seemed to take pride in Engleville's diversity, with a website that claimed to have citizens of many socioeconomic, religious and racial backgrounds and various social service institutions in place to serve low-income families.

Immigrants from Mexico started to settle in Engleville in the 1970s. Shortly thereafter, the elementary school district designed a Transitional Bilingual Education (TBE) program for its new population of Spanish-dominant ELLs. In TBE, ELLs initially received instruction and developed academic content knowledge in their native language (e.g. Spanish). They also studied the English language, often through English-as-a-Second-Language (ESL) instruction; then, after one to three years, they transferred to English-only, general-education classrooms (Christian, 2006). While TBE models provide instruction in the students' heritage language, just like TWI, the end goal is different: TBE *transitions* students to English-only instruction, whereas TWI *develops* and *maintains* students' bilingual and bicultural competencies (Christian, 2006).

In the 1990s, immigrant settlement in Engleville significantly increased. Reflecting the trends in suburban areas across the United States, an increasing number of immigrant families have made places like Engleville their 'first stop' (Richardson, 2000). The suburb's Hispanic population grew 90% from 1990 to 2000. As concerns mounted that TBE was not helping Spanish-dominant students succeed, a group of bilingual and English-speaking parents and educators in Engleville advocated for a TWI program. They claimed that this was in the best interest of all students, and that it would especially improve the academic achievement of ELLs.

After some years of debate, Engleville's school board decided to implement a pilot program; two schools started Spanish–English TWI 'strands'. Specifically, one kindergarten class at each school, with a mix of students from Spanish- and English-dominant backgrounds, had one teacher responsible for instruction in Spanish and one teacher responsible for instruction in English. In Engleville's case, the Spanish teachers were usually fluent, native Spanish speakers who were also fluent in English, while the native English-speaking teachers were not usually fluent in Spanish. After two years, in the early 2000s, the school administration and board decided that the program had been a success. Thus, the board voted to eliminate TBE entirely and resolved that 'Two-Way Immersion' would be the sole instructional model for Spanish-speaking ELLs in Grades K–5.[6] This new policy meant that elementary-aged children from Spanish-dominant families, whose performance on district tests classified them as

'Limited-English Proficient', would be enrolled in TWI. However, according to Engleville's policy, families could still choose English-only, general education for their children if they so desired.

Research participants and data collection

I began collecting data with six Mexican immigrant families, who all had children in TWI, after the district eliminated TBE and voted on the new policy. Three of these families had participated in a related research project, and so I knew some of the participants for over four years. The focal children who were in TWI ranged in age from five to nine, Grades K–3, and included three boys and five girls (Table 12.1). All children lived in two-parent families and had siblings, some older and some younger.

These six case study families had a range of experiences and viewpoints. This variety was important to the study because it led to understanding how different families made sense of the new policy, thus enabling broader theory building across cases. For example, each family

Table 12.1 Case study families

Names (pseudonyms)	Schooling (Completed level for parents; current grade for children)	Current education/ work
La Familia Balderas Señora Balderas	Some elementary in Mexico	Fast-food restaurant employee
Señor Balderas	Some college in Mexico	Landscaping services
Children (4)	7th grade, female	TBE through 2nd grade
	2nd grade, female	TWI starting in 2nd grade
	Preschool (3), female	
	Two years, female	Head-Start
La Familia Fernández Señora Fernández	Some elementary in Mexico	House cleaning/ childcare services
Señor Fernández	Relatively no schooling	Power lines/ landscaping services
Children (3)	Freshman, male	TBE through 2nd grade
	2nd grade, female	TWI, starting in kindergarten
	1st grade, male	TWI, starting in kindergarten

(Continued)

Table 12.1 (*Continued*)

Names (pseudonyms)	Schooling (Completed level for parents; current grade for children)	Current education/ work
La Familia Gutiérrez		
Señora Gutiérrez	Some elementary in Mexico	School lunchroom employee
Señor Gutiérrez	Some elementary in Mexico	Landscaping services
Children (3)	8th grade, female	TBE through 4th grade
	3rd grade, male	TWI, starting in kindergarten
	Preschool (4), male	Head-Start
La Familia Inez		
Señora Inez	Some in Mexico (unknown)	Preschool teacher's aide/childcare
Señor Inez	(unknown)	(unknown)
Children (2)	1st grade, female	TWI, starting in kindergarten
	Preschool (4), male	Nonprofit bilingual preschool
La Familia Navarro		
Señora Navarro	Some elementary in Mexico	House cleaning services
Señor Navarro	Some elementary in Mexico	(unknown)
Children (3)	8th grade, male	TBE through 2nd grade
	2nd grade, female	TWI, starting in kindergarten
	Kindergarten, male	TWI, starting in kindergarten
La Familia Pérez		
Señora Pérez	Some college in United States Finished high school in United	Preschool teacher's aide
Señor Pérez	States	
	1st grade, female	Own construction business
Children (2)		
	Preschool (3), male	TWI, starting in kindergarten Nonprofit bilingual preschool

experienced various approaches to language education over the years: the eldest children in some families were in TBE, while other families' eldest children started in TWI. Although all of the immigrants were generally of lower socioeconomic status (qualifying for free or reduced lunch), their work and education experiences also varied. Four of the mothers had completed only a few years of formal schooling in Mexico, while one had completed high school in Mexico and was attending a nearby community college. Her husband owned his own business, while most of the others worked in landscaping and other service industries. Three families owned their own modest homes, which they sometimes shared with other immigrants or relatives, while the rest lived in apartments.

This chapter analyzes data collected with families over 18 months during which Engleville's district made multiple decisions about the TWI policy. On average, I met monthly with each family, in order to probe their ongoing sense-making processes about immersion, the public debate about TWI's implementation and their general approach to education. I usually met families at their homes, but sometimes visited with them at school board meetings and other gatherings. During our visits, I set aside time to talk with the children, play games or work on homework together, activities that helped me become more of a *participant* observer in families' households. I always asked the young children in TWI (ages five to nine) if they wanted to speak in English or Spanish with me. Most chose English, although sometimes we spoke Spanish, too. I recorded most of the informal conversations that took place in families' homes and transcribed these into my field notes, of which I have over 100 sets.

To supplement the field work and conduct 'member-checks' on findings, I recorded a total of 11 semistructured interviews with five parents and three older siblings (ages 13–15). All interviews were one-on-one, semistructured conversations focusing on the families' educational experiences, especially in Engleville, and beliefs about language and education. I probed for stories about TWI and interactions with educators. The interviews with the teenage children were conducted in English, but I always spoke with the parents in Spanish. Two native Spanish-speaking, bilingual daughters of Mexican immigrants helped to transcribe and translate all audio recordings. They also provided linguistic and cultural insights during data analysis, which was critical since I am a nonnative speaker of Spanish and not a recent immigrant.

Data analysis

Guided by the theoretical framework, data analyses strove to examine: How do immigrants make sense of a new TWI policy? How do families' contexts shape these sense-making processes? Following a constructivist approach to grounded theory (Charmaz, 2003), I began analyses during later stages of data collection, iteratively coding and returning to the field to discuss proposed findings. Once fully immersed in analyses, findings were informed by the literature and analytical memos that I had written based on field work.

Specifically, I first coded field notes and transcribed interviews openly for 'how families learn about educational policy'. To look for patterns, I made domain charts of the ways that families found out information about schooling and language policies. This highlighted the various individuals with whom families interacted as well as the institutions from which they obtained information or services. Next, I constructed case study portraits or 'tales' of each family's education-related experiences in Engleville (as recommended by Saldaña, 2003). This allowed me to examine how each family learned and made decisions about educational policy in general and TWI in particular. Finally, I contrasted families' TWI-related experiences with their other educational experiences, as well as with the opportunities that the district provided for families to explicitly learn about the policy.

Findings: From Policy-Learning Opportunities to Sense-Making Experiences

Analyses demonstrate that 'policy-learning opportunities' designed by the district only sometimes turned into 'sense-making experiences' for immigrant families, who learned about TWI in various ways. Many attended district meetings, spoke with other immigrants and bilingual residents about language education, and went to social/community organizations in the town. Some families' situations, however, limited their sense-making experiences. Before explicating these issues in detail, it is necessary to provide more background on the implementation of Engleville's TWI policy.

Implementation of Engleville's new TWI policy

As described above, after two years of a pilot study, Engleville's school board voted to make TWI the official instructional method for Spanish-dominant ELLs. With this policy decision, the space needed for bilingual education doubled because TWI calls for an equal number of Spanish-dominant and English-dominant students, and those English speakers had not been in bilingual education before this. The implementation question became: Where should the district place the new TWI classrooms?

To help answer this, the school board and administration convened a Bilingual Education Committee made of Engleville residents, parents of school children and educators. Shortly into the school year, this committee proposed placing the entire program at Jefferson Elementary School, one of the schools that had historically housed the district's TBE program and currently held one of the pilot TWI strands. At this point, public debate erupted. If the district accepted the committee's recommendation and made Jefferson the sole site, the public felt that it would make Jefferson a TWI 'magnet school'.[7] They thought that Jefferson's current neighborhood students would then have to travel to other schools. In addition, many area residents, mostly White and Black English-dominant, were not interested in Spanish-language education for their children. These groups strongly argued against the proposal (Dorner, 2010b).

After some months of debate, numerous school board meetings, and various public town-hall gatherings, the school board decided against the committee's recommendation to house the entire program at Jefferson. Instead, the district placed strands throughout the district, which continued to grow one grade/year. Eventually, they had two strands of TWI at Jefferson, one strand at Harrison and two additional schools.

Policy-learning opportunities provided in Engleville

Early in the policy process, as the school district discussed and voted upon TWI, not many residents attended board meetings or other public gatherings about bilingual education reform in Engleville. Once the policy was set and public debate erupted about how to implement it, however, English- and Spanish-dominant families of varying races/ethnicities and immigrant status attended and regularly spoke at meetings about TWI. At these gatherings, I often saw mothers from the six case study families. In this section, I first provide a general picture of what occurred in Engleville, and in the next, I analyze where and how the immigrant case study families made sense of it all.

As with many school districts, there were a number of spaces for the public to gain information about Engleville's educational programs and policies. First and foremost, public debate was held at school board meetings, which were later broadcast on a local cable channel. District documents were sometimes posted on its website. The district also hosted a number of 'town-hall meetings' on weekday evenings at various schools to describe the program and implementation process to residents. In addition, the two local newspapers reported on the reform regularly (in English). In addition to these three typical outlets, the site at the heart of the debate – Jefferson Elementary School – had an active Parent–Teacher Association (PTA) and bilingual staff members and parents, who hosted informational meetings about TWI. This PTA also had an email 'listserv', on which some parents debated the new policy and its implementation. Finally, Engleville had a small group of advocates for TWI, most of whom were bilingual; they formed a parent group to lobby for consolidating the program at a limited number of sites.

Despite all this, there were few opportunities for the public to gain information about TWI *in Spanish*. Only the Jefferson School PTA and parent-advocacy meetings were led by bilinguals, who purposefully solicited participation from Latino immigrant families. In contrast, the school district did not provide formal translation at either school board or town-hall meetings, although there was usually at least one bilingual district official who would whisper her interpretations to small groups of Latinos. Recordings of board meetings were broadcast in English and most district documents were only in English, as was the discussion on Jefferson's email listserv. At the town-hall meetings, district officials spent most of their time fielding questions and concerns from White and Black English-dominant residents. Finally, as mentioned above, the local newspapers reported on TWI, but only in English; there was no Spanish-language newspaper in Engleville at the time of this study.

Immigrant families' sense-making experiences

Given these opportunities to learn about the policy and engage in public debate, how did immigrant families make sense of TWI? This section demonstrates that, despite the lack of opportunity to discuss the policy publicly in Spanish, many immigrants attended district meetings and followed the debate, which they then understood (1) through having conversations with other immigrant parents, (2) through relationships they formed with US-born and bilingual community members and (3) at community organizations. In the following paragraph I describe these three contextual factors in a general sense, and then illustrate these patterns in more depth, drawing from four of the case studies.

First, families spoke about TWI with other immigrant parents. In fact, studying what mothers said to other 'Hispanos' (see Note 3) provides one lens into what families understood about the new policy. Such comments also build upon what previous research has shown: Mexican immigrants in Engleville wanted their children to be bilingual for both instrumental and integrative reasons (Dorner, 2010a; de Jong & Bearse, Chapter 6). Second, many Mexican families in Engleville made sense of the new policy by speaking with US-born and South-American-born bilingual community members, including several women who were teachers at Chicago-area universities and schools. These women often served as advocates for the immigrant community: they started Spanish-speaking parent groups, served on school district committees and tried to address immigrants' concerns, and contacted the district for Spanish-speaking families. Third, most Mexican families became connected to two key organizations in Engleville: the 'Family Foundation' and 'San Marco' (a local Catholic church). The nonprofit 'Family Foundation' had a mission to promote the well-being of children by strengthening families, and in recent years, the organization had begun to offer new services, including: support groups for Hispanic mothers, ESL courses, and educational programming for ELL children. At different points in time, some children from each case study family attended the Foundation's 'field trips' and 'homework help' sessions. All of the case study families also attended St. Mark's, or what they called 'San Marco'. Like the Foundation, San Marco had changed over the years, and now offered church mass and various workshops in Spanish, and ESL courses for adults.

The Fernández and Gutiérrez families: Well-connected sense-making

Many of the case study mothers found themselves convincing other 'Hispanos' that TWI was the best educational model for their children. Sra. Fernández reported having multiple discussions about language education. One time, she told me about typical conversations she had with other 'Hispanos':

> ... me dicen muchas personas ... 'el puro inglés es mejor, por que ... se le va a hacer bolas y no va a saber ni diferentes, se le va a enredar todo y que'. Les digo, 'No, para mí es mucho mejor que sepa de los dos idiomas, a que no más sepa de, de uno'. *Many people tell me, 'English-only is better because ... they're going to get confused [in TWI] and they're not going to know the difference; everything will be too complicated.' I tell them, 'No, for me it's better that they know two languages, not just one'.*

Similarly, Sra. Gutiérrez reported that 'Hispanos tienen miedo de que se atrasen'. *Hispanics fear that their children will fall behind (in the TWI program).* She explained that parents were worried that children would not succeed because of all the Spanish instruction – rather than English – in the early grades. However, both mothers repeatedly told others not to worry. They both signed up their younger children for the pilot program, with some help from bilingual staff members at Jefferson and their elder children.

The Gutiérrez and Fernández families made sense of TWI and came to these conclusions in multiple contexts. First, Sra. Gutiérrez learned about TWI through some channels designed by the district; she regularly attended board and town-hall meetings, even if she could not always understood what was discussed in English. Second, she had many conversations with Jefferson's bilingual principal, who convinced her that instruction in English *and* Spanish would be beneficial, not detrimental, for ELLs. In sharing this message with other Hispanos, Sra. Gutiérrez relied on her eldest daughter's language education and experience to prove her point. She told them that her daughter had had some Spanish instruction through fourth grade in TBE and was now doing fine, in 'puro inglés' (*English-only*) courses, in middle school. Third, Sra. Gutiérrez took advantage of multiple learning opportunities for her family. Her youngest child was in the district's Head-Start preschool program. She attended the Hispanic mothers' support group at the Family Foundation, where her eldest daughter went for tutoring and homework help. Finally, Sra. Gutiérrez worked at a nearby school as a 'lunch lady' and studied ESL at San Marco. She specifically mentioned learning about the TWI policy at church, when petitions about making Jefferson the sole site for the program were explained and distributed by Spanish-speaking and bilingual members. In such spaces, she not only heard about the policy, but also had a chance to discuss it – to make sense about it – with fellow immigrants.

Like Sra. Gutiérrez, Sra. Fernández made sense of the policy in multiple contexts. Besides attending a few public meetings – she went to fewer than Sra. Gutiérrez because she could not always arrange or afford childcare for her two youngest children – she also had conversations with community members and at various organizations in Engleville. Although the Fernández family struggled to make ends meet financially, they were rich in social capital. Most significantly, Sra. Fernández was friends with the bilingual, White mother who led the original push for TWI in Engleville, who formed a Spanish-speaking parent group at that time and who used to be a TWI teacher in Chicago. Later, the Fernández family became neighbors with a bilingual family, whose father was from Central America and whose bilingual US-born, White mother was a professor at a nearby university. When Sra. Fernández was confused about her eldest son's shift out of TBE and into English only, this professor helped her contact the superintendent. The Fernández children also attended Family Foundation activities and took part in the summer library program and other similar educational events.

The Pérez and Balderas families: Struggling to enroll in TWI

Sense-making processes about TWI may be further examined through the experiences and contexts of the Pérez and Balderas families, who both struggled to enroll their daughters, despite their different backgrounds and access to resources. The Pérez family lived in the Jefferson Elementary School area and was keen to enroll their eldest daughter, Madison. Like other Mexican parents in Engleville, Sra. Pérez wanted TWI for her children because: 'Quiero que ella conserve las dos lenguas en un nivel parejo'.

I want her to conserve the two languages at a similar level. However, when they attempted enrolling her, they discovered that Madison apparently performed too well in English on the kindergarten entrance exam and was not considered in 'need' of bilingual education. That is, she was not 'Limited-English Proficient', and so the district initially denied her enrollment in TWI. Sra. Pérez questioned the district's actions: Why would they deny Madison enrollment because she knows some English? Would they not want a bilingual child in a bilingual program? In the end, after further testing and many stressful meetings with school officials, Madison enrolled in TWI.

Multiple contextual factors likely influenced this result. The family regularly attended Family Foundation events, where they got general advice about educational opportunities. More important, Sra. Pérez had the support and advice of a South American bilingual community member, the director of the Spanish immersion preschool where Sra. Pérez worked as a teacher assistant. Like Sra. Fernández, she also had bilingual friends who helped her communicate with the superintendent when she had concerns. Finally, with her level of education and growing knowledge of English, from taking ESL courses at San Marco and the local community college, she had the confidence and wherewithal to make demands upon the school system.

The Balderas family's experiences stand in strong contrast. Their neighborhood school (Wilson) did not have TWI or even an ESL program when their second daughter, Jasmine, was enrolling in kindergarten. Nonetheless, Jasmine could have been bused to a TWI school, which is what the family desired. Like the others, Jasmine's parents wanted their children to be bilingual for integrative and instrumental reasons. Sra. Balderas wanted Spanish maintained in the household, and Sr. Balderas pointed out that bilingualism was important because, 'en muchas oficinas ya se necesita que hablen los dos idiomas.' *In many offices, already one needs to speak the two languages.*

The summer before Jasmine's kindergarten year, Sra. Balderas went to Wilson, where her eldest daughter attended, to inquire about enrollment; she was given a general application packet. From the Head-Start where Jasmine attended, she also obtained enrollment forms, but for TWI. The parents were unsure what to do, and so with their eldest daughter's help, they submitted both packets. Shortly before the school year began, the family received a welcome letter from Wilson. A few weeks later, they also received a welcome letter from Jefferson's TWI program. By this point, however, they had already made arrangements for Jasmine to attend Wilson's general education program in English. Even though they originally wanted TWI, they decided that placing their shy daughter (as they described her) at her older sister's school would be best for everyone. No one advised them otherwise.

The next two years were difficult ones for Jasmine. Although she had attended the English-only Head-Start program, her English skills were not high enough for her to perform very well academically, according to her teachers. They also said Jasmine had 'behavior problems'. Both Sr. and Sra. Balderas reported many confusing phone calls with English-speaking teachers. School officials eventually said that Jasmine needed bilingual services, such as TWI, but, according to Sr. Balderas, they never followed up to complete a transfer. Finally, at the start of second grade, Jasmine entered the TWI program at Jefferson, and her spirits and academic performance improved, but only after much heartache and confusion.

Again, multiple contextual factors likely played into this situation. The Balderas' lower economic standing was similar to that of the Fernández family, but they were much more isolated in terms of their social ties. Unlike Jefferson Elementary School, the Balderas' neighborhood school, Wilson, did not have any bilingual personnel. Also, perhaps in part because they lived in a low-income neighborhood very close to much higher income housing, they did not have many interactions with middle-class, bilingual community members like the two case study families above. (Wilson's school demographics were about 60% White, 25% Black, 5% Hispanic, and 20% free/reduced lunch, in comparison with Jefferson's 30% White, 30% Black, 35% Hispanic and 50% free/reduced lunch.) In addition, both Sr. and Sra. Balderas worked long, hard hours and could not attend public meetings about TWI, and the family was unable to take advantage of many Family Foundation or San Marco events because of work schedules and young children. The Balderas' experiences did not match the district's designed policy-learning opportunities, and they did not have very many informal sense-making experiences either.

In summary, all of the families involved in this project wanted TWI for instrumental and integrative reasons (Dorner, 2010a). Many learned about the program and discussed it (1) with friends and neighbors, (2) with middle-class, bilingual community members and (3) at community organizations, especially the Family Foundation and San Marco. Having access to TWI discourse through their connections, many families found themselves convincing other Hispanos that TWI would help them reach their common goal: high levels of proficiency in two languages. However, the Balderas family, representative of the most disadvantaged in mixed communities like Engleville's, had little access to both the district-provided opportunities and the informal sense-making experiences of other families.

Possibilities for Implementing TWI Policies and Engaging Families

This chapter has detailed some of the complexities of implementing a TWI policy in a suburban public school district, highlighting how Mexican immigrant families made sense of the policy in context. Most notably, across Engleville, immigrants' sense-making experiences went beyond the spaces designed by the district (Dorner, 2010b). Indeed, Engleville's community was, in some ways, ideal for newcomers' informal sense-making processes, with various organizations providing some services in Spanish and bilingual community members and advocates.

However, since most 'policy-learning opportunities' occurred outside the spaces created by the district, there is room for improvement in the actions taken by school districts. Mexican immigrants in this study, even if they had Internet access at home, did not examine the school district web site, which included many complicated documents explaining TWI and TWI's implementation in English only. Only once did a family tell me that they had read a newspaper article about TWI, and none participated in Jefferson's email listserv. Moreover, although some Hispanic parents attended public meetings on TWI, their participation was limited since the district did not usually provide Spanish interpretation. District policy-makers generally neglected the places where immigrant families were already making sense of TWI and educational policies: with their friends, extended family, and bilingual neighbors, at the Family Foundation and San Marco. Finally, the most disadvantaged families who were not connected to alternate contexts were left behind entirely.

What does this study say about the possibilities for TWI policies in US public schools, for recruiting immigrant families and engaging *everyone* in implementation processes? The study points to a number of actions that could improve opportunities for immigrants to make sense of new policies, access critical information and make informed decisions for their children's education. Educators and policymakers should remember that context – and language – matters. They should hold educational forums about program choices in immigrants' native languages at times and places that working families can attend, such as after heritage language services at local churches. They might survey community organizations to find out where and when newcomers congregate and already 'make sense' of education and language policies, like Engleville's Family Foundation and San Marco. School districts might also identify who already advocates for and communicates with immigrants – for example, bilingual community members, ESL teachers, educational administrators or pre-school teachers – and use these connections to disperse information in culturally sensitive ways. Districts such as Engleville should also make sure that *all* district staff (even at schools that do not offer policies such as TWI) are informed about program choices, so that they can provide the proper information to families during enrollment.

Finally, it is key to engage newcomers in conversations about TWI program goals and methods. Immigrant families are concerned that extensive instruction in their heritage language may be detrimental for English language development. Fortunately, for Engleville, community brokers – from bilingual professors to immigrant mothers – worked to allay Hispanos' fears. School districts should make sure that they broadly and bilingually communicate the goals and potential benefits of TWI, to help immigrant families make the best educational decisions for their children, given their contexts. TWI will realize its goal of serving students from immigrant communities only if policymakers reconsider implementation processes and take steps to reshape the linguistic and contextual mismatch between district-designed policy-learning opportunities and families' actual sense-making experiences.

Notes

1. All names of people and places in this chapter are pseudonyms.
2. When I describe students as 'English-dominant' or 'Spanish-dominant', this means that they use and feel most comfortable in that language, and that it is probably their native and home language. However, a child of native Spanish-speaking parents from Central or South America may be English dominant; we cannot assume race or ethnicity based on the 'dominance' of a person's heritage language, language choice or linguistic abilities, nor can we assume language dominance based on ethnicity.
3. I interchangeably use such terms as 'Latino', 'Hispanic' and 'Hispano'. I choose terms based on the ones used by each respective study or research participant, in my attempt to reflect the particular perspectives and practices of different peoples, times and places.
4. The Center for Applied Linguistics maintains a directory of TWI programs in the US. The directory can be found at: http://www.cal.org/twi/directory/index.html. Accessed 01.10.10.
5. For a study of the public policy process, see Dorner (2010b). For a report focused on TWI students' and their families' perspectives, see Dorner (2010a).
6. The district added one TWI grade level per year in each strand, and so students in the upper grades continued with TBE, while new, younger students entered TWI. Also, to keep up with growing demand, they eventually started new strands in two additional schools. Most strands had enough interested English-dominant students to maintain a 50–50 balance.
7. In the United States, 'magnet' schools are different from neighborhood schools in that they draw students from an entire public school district, not just those who live nearby.

References

Ball, S.J. (2006) *Education Policy and Social Class*. New York, NY: Routledge.

Bayley, R. and Schecter, S.R. (2005) Family decisions about schooling and Spanish maintenance: Mexicanos in California and Texas. In A.C. Zentella (ed.) *Building on Strength: Language and Literacy in Latino Families and Communities* (pp. 1–12). New York, NY: Teachers College Press.

Charmaz, K. (2003) Grounded theory: Objectivist and constructivist methods. In N. Denzin and Y.S. Lincoln (eds) *Strategies of Qualitative Inquiry* (pp. 249–291). Thousand Oaks, CA: Sage.

Christian, D. (2006) Introduction. In F. Genesee, K. Lindholm-Leary, W.M. Saunders and D. Christian (eds) *Educating English Language Learners: A Synthesis of Research Evidence* (pp. 1–13). New York, NY: Cambridge University Press.

Craig, B.A. (1996) Parental attitudes toward bilingualism in a local two-way immersion program. *Bilingual Research Journal* 20, 383–410.

DiMaggio, P. (1997) Culture and cognition. *Annual Review of Sociology* 23, 263–287.

Dorner, L.M. (2010a) English and Spanish 'para un futuro' – or just English? Immigrant family perspectives on two-way immersion. *International Journal of Bilingual Education and Bilingualism* 13, 303–323.

Dorner, L.M. (2010b) Contested communities in a debate over dual language education: The import of 'public' values on public policies. *Educational Policy*. Advance online publication. DOI: 10.1177/0895904810368275.

Freeman, R.D. (1996) Dual-language planning at Oyster Bilingual School: 'It's much more than language.' *TESOL Quarterly* 30, 557–582.

González, N. (2005) Children in the eye of the storm: Language socialization and language ideologies in a dual-language school. In A.C. Zentella (ed.) *Building on Strength: Language and Literacy in Latino Families and Communities* (pp. 162–174). New York, NY: Teachers College Press.

Greeno, J.G. (1998) The situativity of knowing, learning, and research. *American Psychologist* 53, 5–26.

Hornberger, N.H. (ed.) (2003) *Continua of Biliteracy: An Ecological Framework for Educational Policy, Research, and Practice in Multilingual Settings*. Clevedon: Multilingual Matters.

Howard, E.R., Sugarman, J. and Christian, D. (2003) *Trends in Two-Way Immersion Education: A Review of the Research*. (Rep. No. 63). Baltimore, MD: Center for Research on the Education of Students Placed At Risk (CRESPAR).

Lave, J. and Wenger, E. (1991) *Situated Learning: Legitimate Peripheral Participation*. New York, NY: Cambridge University Press.

Lewis, D.A. and Maruna, S. (1998) Person-centered policy analysis. *Research in Public Policy Analysis and Management* 9, 213–230.

Lindholm-Leary, K.J. (2001) *Dual Language Education*. Clevedon: Multilingual Matters.

Lindholm-Leary, K.J. (2005) Review of research and best practices on effective features of dual language education programs. On WWW at http://www.lindholm-leary.com/resources/review_research.pdf. Accessed 29.4.10.

Lindholm-Leary, K.J. and Borsato, G. (2006) Academic achievement. In F. Genesee, K.J. Lindholm-Leary, W. Saunders and D. Christian (eds) *Educating English Language Learners* (pp. 176–222). New York, NY: Cambridge University Press.

Lindholm-Leary, K.J. and Howard, E.R. (2008) Language development and academic achievement in two-way immersion programs. In T.W. Fortune and D.J. Tedick (eds) *Pathways to Multilingualism: Evolving Perspectives on Immersion Education* (pp. 177–200). Clevedon: Multilingual Matters.

Orellana, M.F., Ek, L. and Hernández, A. (1999) Bilingual education in an immigrant community: Proposition 227 in California. *International Journal of Bilingual Education and Bilingualism* 2, 114–130.

Rhodes, N., Christian, D. and Barfield, S. (1997) Innovations in immersion: The Key School two-way model. In R.K. Johnson and M. Swain (eds) *Immersion Education: International Perspectives* (pp. 265–283). New York, NY: Cambridge University Press.

Richardson, P. (2000) Skipping the city: More immigrants are opting for the burbs instead of Chicago. *Crain's Chicago Business* 23, 15, 18–20.

Rogoff, B. (1990) *Apprenticeship in Thinking: Cognitive Development in Social Context.* New York, NY: Oxford University Press.

Saldaña, J. (2003) *Longitudinal Qualitative Research: Analyzing Change through Time.* New York, NY: Altamira Press.

Shannon, S.M. and Milian, M. (2002) Parents choose dual language programs in Colorado: A survey. *Bilingual Research Journal* 26, 681–696.

Spillane, J.P., Reiser, B.J. and Reimer, T. (2002) Policy implementation and cognition: Reframing and refocusing implementation research. *Review of Educational Research Quarterly* 72, 387–433.

Thomas, W.P. and Collier, V.P. (2002) *A National Study of School Effectiveness for Language Minority Students' Long-Term Academic Achievement.* Washington, DC: Center for Research on Education Diversity & Excellence.

Valdés, G. (1997) Dual-language immersion programs: A cautionary note concerning the education of language-minority students. *Harvard Educational Review* 67, 391–429.

Yanow, D. (2000) *Conducting Interpretive Policy Analysis.* Thousand Oaks, CA: Sage Publications.

Chapter 13

Struggling Learners and the Language Immersion Classroom

T.W. FORTUNE

Introduction

Immersion educators and researchers in the United States know how difficult it can be to convince parents, teachers, principals or superintendents that immersion works. It seems counterintuitive that teaching young English-speaking children the school curriculum in a new language will result in their learning subject content as well as same-background peers who are schooled in English *and* developing a high level of proficiency in that new language. Even more challenging is winning over the parents and educators of English language learners (ELLs) who are enrolled in two-way immersion (TWI) programs. The message that intensive and sustained schooling in a child's first (non-English) language and literacy development in that language are what is needed to open the doors to long-term academic success and higher levels of language and literacy *in English* just does not seem possible.

As hard as it is to cogently deliver this empirically documented information, arguing for the participation of children who are likely to struggle or are struggling in school is harder still. If a child enters the classroom with low levels of language or ability, known risk factors such as low income and a diverse linguistic and cultural background, or language and learning disabilities, is one language not hard enough? How could a language immersion program be an appropriate option for these learners? Such questions and the underlying beliefs they communicate about the learner profile required for successful immersion schooling are still commonplace.

Is the immersion program intended for a specific type of student? Official policies of the vast majority of US immersion programs state that the program is an appropriate option for all children regardless of socioeconomic circumstances, intellectual ability or ethnic background. However, anecdotal evidence suggests that parents with children who have been diagnosed with language delay or disability, attention deficit hyperactivity disorder and autism, among other developmental disorders, may be privately discouraged from enrolling in immersion.

Moreover, a family's choice to begin their child's schooling in immersion does not ensure success or continuation in the program. Several Canadian studies have reported a high incidence of attrition both within the elementary grades and between elementary, middle- and high school levels (see Cadez, 2006 for review). The persistent challenge with student attrition in one-way programs, and the discrepancy that sometimes exists between public policy and anecdotally reported practice, strongly suggest that immersion education is not necessarily perceived as appropriate for all children. Zehrbach (Chapter 4) offers further support for this idea with his finding that most TWI charter school programs in the United States enroll fewer students with special needs than other schools in area districts and the state.

Pertinent findings from studies carried out in immersion contexts are limited, and in some cases, inconsistent (see Genesee, 2007 for review). There is a need for more research in this area; however, securing funding, designing and carrying out high-quality longitudinal research remains difficult. Many communities in the United States lack a sufficient number of students and programs to create an adequate sample size of struggling learners for experimental research. While the Center for Applied Linguistics (CAL, 2006, 2010) reports some 360 one-way and over 370 TWI programs, as a group immersion students still comprise a minute percentage of the total US student population.

Absent more robust research findings, administrators, teachers, parents and other specialists are left to make decisions about the type of learner the program can best serve and what to do with low-achieving children who struggle with language, literacy and learning based on insufficient information and few, if any, guidelines. Not surprisingly, practices and policies regarding student groups that may struggle or are struggling vary greatly from one program to another. What research-based information is available to inform program policy and practice with children from a wide range of backgrounds and developmental profiles? What learning possibilities exist in immersion programs for children who struggle?

In the remainder of this chapter I briefly review academic and linguistic outcomes for typically developing learners and those who struggle with language, literacy or learning and may be developmentally atypical. I then underscore several issues related to the crux of the challenge for many immersion practitioners: Is the learner experiencing a typical delay or evidencing some kind of language and/or learning disorder? This section includes a discussion of common sources of misdiagnosis, useful parameters for distinguishing between delay and disorder and assessment possibilities to assist in determining language disorders. I then specify a set of principles that can serve as guideposts when developing program policies and tackling the day-to-day issues that surround struggling immersion learners. I end the chapter by urging educators in immersion programs to implement research-supported policies and practices that will more fully realize the possibilities of this program model as enrichment for all.

Immersion Outcomes

Typically developing learner profiles

Canadian and US research finds that immersion programs are able to support typically developing students' achievement at or above the levels of demographically similar students participating in non-immersion programs (cf. Genesee, 1987; Lindholm-Leary, 2001; Turnbull *et al.*, 2001). This finding holds constant with learners of varying ability levels, diverse linguistic and ethnic backgrounds, and those who receive free/reduced lunch services (Bruck *et al.*, 1975; Caldas & Boudreaux, 1999; Holobow *et al.*, 1991; Lindholm Leary, Chapter 5). In other words, a broad range of families who place their children in an immersion setting will find this program able to support academic development as well as, or in some cases, somewhat better than an English-medium program. The added bonus for these children is the opportunity to develop high levels of proficiency in a second, foreign, heritage or indigenous language.

Struggling learners[1]

Background information: Monolingual learners in the United States
Based on findings from studies on monolingual children, researchers calculate that between 5% and 10% of immersion learners are likely to struggle with language disorders (Kohnert, 2008). The National Center for Learning Disabilities (Cortiella, 2009) reports that in 2007 9% of all public school students were identified as eligible for additional educational assistance by the Individuals with Disabilities Act (IDEA, 2004). Four percent of all children received services under the category of specific learning disabilities (SLD) and two percent were identified for speech or language impairment (SLI). Eligibility for SLD-related services among certain ethnic

groups was found to be higher, for example, 5% of Hispanic children, 6% of African Americans and 7% of Native Americans were eligible. Additionally, researchers predict that some 30% of children who are learning to read in their first language (L1) will struggle with literacy development at some point between kindergarten and third grade (Bender & Larkin, 2009). Given the percentages of children who struggle while learning to read in their L1 and the numbers of monolinguals who are found to be language and/or learning disabled, immersion educators should expect to encounter children who will struggle with language, literacy and learning in their classrooms; among these struggling learners, between 5% and 10% will likely have language and/or learning disorders.[2]

Immersion learners with underdeveloped L1 skills

Students who enter school with low language skills or have struggled with L1 development are likely to find the immersion setting challenging. Boschung and Roy (1996) and others have cited poor L1 acquisition as a risk factor for low achievement in immersion. Based on her longitudinal studies, Bruck (1978, 1982) reported that L1 and pre-literacy skills predict immersion language achievement such that children who begin the program with lower levels of proficiency and less developed pre-literacy skills in L1 will demonstrate lower proficiency and progress more slowly with literacy development in L2.

The finding that children with underdeveloped L1 skills will struggle more in an academic environment that uses a new language for instruction relative to peers whose L1 is average or above average is not surprising. Schooling revolves around understandings that evolve through language and language-based literacy. The more important question is whether such children would be better served in an L1-medium program. To date, Bruck (1978, 1982) provides the most relevant findings. When comparing language-disabled children in Canadian French (L2) immersion to language-disabled children in the English-medium (L1) program, she found that both groups of learners made similar academic progress over time and concluded that French immersion learners were no worse off than their language-disabled peers who were learning in L1. Moreover, because the French immersion group was also learning to read, speak and comprehend a new language, they were overall at an advantage. Bruck noted that such learners would be less likely to successfully acquire L2 proficiency in a more traditional foreign language environment that made greater use of memorization and emphasized analytical language learning.

Immersion learners with reading difficulties

Very few studies have looked specifically at struggling immersion readers and no studies to date have been carried out on reading-impaired immersion learners and/or effective intervention strategies for readers who struggle. However, in their review of the literature on reading difficulties and French immersion learners, Genesee and Jared (2008) concluded that:

- Immersion students who read well in L2 were very likely to read well in L1, just as those who read poorly in one language were apt to read poorly in the other.
- When compared with L1 readers of English, French immersion students were less likely to be as fluent or independent with reading, had greater difficulty recalling details about what they read, and displayed a harder time integrating prior knowledge while reading in L2.
- Tests that predict good readers in English (e.g. word-level skills such as phonological awareness (degree of success with sound blending tasks), phonological access (speed of retrieving name of letter/sound/object/color), verbal memory (ability to repeat sentences and recall tasks)) also predict good readers in French, a finding that points to a strong similarity between foundational skills for learning to read in French (L2) and English (L1).

Most recently, Canadian French immersion programs have begun to investigate individual differences in reading achievement among primary students. Erdos *et al.* (2010) are conducting a comprehensive, longitudinal research project in this area with early total French immersion students in Montreal who began the program as either monolingual English speakers or English dominant. In line with a few other studies, data from K–1 students have offered additional evidence that kindergarteners' letter–sound knowledge in L1 (from fall testing) and letter–sound knowledge and phoneme blending skills in L1 (from spring testing) significantly predict word and pseudo-word decoding *in the* L2 when these same students are first graders. In contrast to earlier studies, French immersion kindergarteners' prior knowledge of French words was also found to be a significant predictor of Grade 1 decoding.

Among other things, findings from this study suggest that (1) it is possible to tentatively identify children who are likely to struggle with L2 reading (and begin to offer early intervention) by reviewing kindergarteners' performance on early literacy indicator assessments given in L1 and that (2) explicit word-knowledge development of L2 is an important focus in initial literacy development in addition to building skills in phonological awareness and phonological access.

The Crux of the Challenge: Identifying Delay versus Disability

According to the American Speech-Language-Hearing Association (2008), language and/or learning disabilities are rooted in a biological deficit in the brain that manifests itself in an inability to receive, send, process or comprehend concepts of verbal, nonverbal or graphic symbol systems. Language and learning delays, in contrast, are often the result of sociocultural influences on the learner's development. A lower performance level than what is typically expected may result because of a mismatch between a student's actual background and the background presumed by the schooling environment.

Durgunoglu and Öney (2000) argued that political, economic and social forces can affect literacy development given that the majority of a student's language experiences take place outside of school, normally in the home, making it a critical environment for language development. Research has shown, for example, that students from homes that receive welfare benefits are exposed to 10 million words by age three. This pales in comparison with the 20 million words heard by working-class children and the 30 million by children of professional parents (Hart & Risley, 1995). It is not only the quantity of input but also the nature of the language input. For example, professional parents' children receive eight times as many encouragements as children of parents on welfare by age two (Hart & Risley, 1995).

A student's attitude can also impact his/her acquisition of language skills. A learner's negative attitude toward a language, which results in unwillingness to use and/or learn that language, is often mistaken for a delay in language acquisition (Durgunoglu & Öney, 2000). When learners see a particular language as making demands that they cannot meet, they may move away from that language, identifying more with one in which they find success (Fradd & McGee, 1994). In the immersion setting, this influence is further compounded as a learner's attitude toward the subject matter can also be reflected in limited, if any, language use.

Common sources of misdiagnosis

Once enrolled, when a child begins to struggle, one of the first questions to arise involves the issue of distinguishing between a delay due to instruction in a new language and a disorder or disability.[3] This question is even more perplexing for English proficient immersion learners in early total (one-way) or 90:10 (two-way) programs who are learning to read first in the minority language. There are a variety of reasons that educators and families might incorrectly identify a language or learning disability.

Look-alike behavior

Educators who work with children learning through an L2 often describe specific language and learning behaviors that resemble those of language-impaired children. For example, Petzold (2004) referenced a number of general behaviors in students with a language disorder and/or learning disability that are also typically exhibited by non-disordered learners still acquiring the language of instruction. These behaviors may include a short attention span, shyness or timidity, nervousness, speaking infrequently, not volunteering information, appearing confused, low levels of comprehension and inappropriate comments.

Other traits shared by language and/or learning-disabled and L2 learners include, but are not limited to, difficulties in expression (including articulation), low vocabulary and comprehension, difficulty following oral directions, reading below grade level, confusion in sound/symbol associations, reversing words and letters, and poor recall of syllable sequences (Kohnert, 2008). Delays and disorders may manifest themselves in multiple academic areas for older learners as language proficiency is closely tied to measures of academic achievement, intelligence and general cognitive abilities. Developing language skills can impact a student's ability to think, organize and structure ideas as well as generate meaning from language (Fradd & McGee, 1994).

Research corroborates the observations of many immersion practitioners about the language use similarities between L2 learners and language-impaired monolinguals. Scholars have examined and compared specific grammatical features (e.g. Håkansson & Nettelbladt, 1996) and vocabulary development (e.g. Peña *et al.*, 2001) in the language produced by L2 learners and L1 learners with language disorders. Findings have shown a strong similarity between the linguistic abilities demonstrated by these two groups of children.

More recently, Gutiérrez-Clellan *et al.* (2008) examined the performance of English L1 children with and without specific language impairment, Spanish–English bilinguals with and without SLI, and typical ELLs on accurate use of verb morphemes and use of subject pronouns in English. Of their many results, one important finding was that the accuracy rate of Spanish-dominant ELLs was similar to that of language-impaired children, both English L1 and Spanish–English bilinguals (who were English dominant). Researchers concluded that, 'children whose English is the weaker language have the potential to be misdiagnosed as impaired in that language' (Gutiérrez-Clellan *et al.*, 2008: 16).

Lack of understanding of typical bilingual development

Another source for misdiagnosis of bilingual individuals stems from a lack of understanding among educators and specialists of typical bilingual development. For example, research finds that the language knowledge of bilinguals will be distributed across the two languages, and both languages will interact with the cognitive and social development of the learner. Oft-encountered characteristics such as code-mixing (speech that draws from both L1 and L2), gaps in word knowledge in one language or the other and other cross-linguistic influences on language production, such as following word order rules from the L1 to express something in the L2, are typical. Interaction among these developmental systems and the resultant behaviors do not evidence or *cause* impairment or disability (Genesee *et al.*, 2004; Kohnert, 2008). Further, the degree to which such characteristics occur is likely related to the levels of L1 and L2 proficiency and the intensity of instructional time spent in each language.

Developing high levels of language and literacy is a complicated process for all students, both monolinguals and developing bilinguals. After reviewing several studies on oral language development of L2 learners, Genesee *et al.* challenged the 'children soak up language like a sponge' myth, concluding that, 'one striking facet of children's acquisition rates in their L2 is the degree of variation among individuals' (Genesee *et al.*, 2004: 136). They further stated that such findings were consistent across all child L2 research.

Durgunoglu and Verhoeven (1998) also showed that children's achievement and rate of learning to read and write vary to a much greater degree among L2 learners when compared with native speakers. Given the strong link between oral language and initial literacy development, teachers should expect greater variability among L2 children and extend the timeline beyond one to two years for language and reading to develop.

Lack of understanding of typical language and literacy development for immersion students

Program model differences. English-proficient children participating in one-way early total immersion programs receive all subject-related instruction and are taught to read first in the immersion language. Despite this practice of withholding instruction in language majority children's L1, in some cases until fourth or fifth grade, research has consistently found no difference in English reading and math achievement when immersion and non-immersion students' test scores are compared *at the end of the elementary grades* (Turnbull *et al.*, 2003).

Certain studies have pointed to a limited period of time in which an early total immersion learner's L1 and literacy skills may test lower than same-age peers who have received all literacy instruction in their L1. Specific skills found to evidence lower test scores include word knowledge, word discrimination, spelling, capitalization and punctuation (Swain & Barik, 1976). However, this relatively brief lag was found to disappear within one to two years after the immersion learner received L1 literacy instruction, typically between Grades 4 and 6.

Large-scale studies on reading achievement of immersion learners in the United States are few, but their findings parallel those reported in Canada. US immersion students are reading at a level that meets or exceeds state and district standards. Most of these assessments measure English reading (e.g. Anderson *et al.*, 2005; Lindholm-Leary, 2001); some also consider reading in the student's L2 (e.g. Fortune & Arabbo, 2006; Klimpl *et al.*, 2007; Lindholm-Leary, 2001, Chapter 5).

Recently, Montgomery County Public Schools (MCPS) reported on the L2 reading performance of students in French and Spanish immersion. Over several years, MCPS has collected data on reading achievement in French and Spanish, the language of initial literacy for these one-way students. With these data, French and Spanish reading benchmarks have been established to measure student progress. They align with English reading benchmarks used with non-immersion students in the district. Data from K–2 reading benchmark assessments indicate that:

- French immersion students' performance on L2 benchmark assessments is lower than English language program students' performance on L1 benchmark assessments in all but the final quarter of K–2.
- By the final quarter of K–2, French immersion students as a group perform at the same benchmark *in French* (L2) as grade-level peers schooled in English only do *in English* (L1).
- Spanish immersion students' performance on L2 benchmark assessments is the same as English language program students' performance on L1 benchmark assessments during the K–2 years. The difference in reading performance between French and Spanish immersion students is thought to be linked to the high degree of sound–symbol transparency in Spanish.

(D. Gouin, personal communication, October 9, 2008; Klimpl *et al.*, 2007)

In contrast to findings from early total programs, research studies carried out in partial immersion contexts, where language majority children are usually taught to read in L1, do not indicate this lag in English literacy and language arts. At the same time, there is no research-evidenced advantage to introducing instruction in English earlier because the English language development of partial immersion students has been found to be no different from that of total immersion students, despite the greater number of instructional hours in English (Swain & Lapkin, 1982; Turnbull *et al.*, 2001), and the immersion language proficiency of partial immersion students is reportedly less well developed.

Students' language background differences. In Spanish/English TWI programs research indicates a somewhat different language development and academic achievement trajectory for each group of learners. Research on Spanish home language (SpHL) students has indicated that (1) academic achievement at or above grade level norms on standardized tests given in English may take six to eight years of participation in the program through middle school, (2) SpHL students develop a more balanced bilingualism in Spanish and English, and (3) in general, their language and literacy skills are similar in both languages (Howard *et al.*, 2004; Lindholm-Leary & Howard, 2008). In a study based on student self-assessment data, de Jong and Bearse (Chapter 6) also found that Latino (SpHL) learners perceive their reading skills to be equally strong in both languages.

On aggregate, English home language (EgHL) students display a somewhat different language and learning profile. Similar to their SpHL partners, students from EgHL backgrounds demonstrated academic achievement at or above same-background peers on tests given in English and Spanish. However, EgHL students typically exhibit a lower level of oral proficiency in Spanish relative to English and prefer using English (Lindholm-Leary & Howard, 2008).

Lack of understanding of language proficiency demands for success in school

The research literature distinguishes between two main types of language that L2 learners encounter in schools, social–interactional and academic–transactional (Brown & Yule, 1983). Social–interactional language is developed most quickly, generally within six months to two years, although Hakuta *et al.* (2000) reported that developing oral language proficiency can take between three and five years for ELLs in US schools. Academic–transactional language and literacy skills, however, are *fundamental* for long-term school success and take longer to develop, usually between four and seven years or longer.

Because of the period of time necessary for developing academic-transactional language skills, many L2 learners are unable to demonstrate grade-level achievement on standardized tests given in the L2 once the language and literacy demands of the curriculum have outpaced their language and literacy skills. Thus, when L2 and immersion learners are given normed assessments in their L2, individual student performance cannot be reliably used as a valid measure of delay or disorder.

Useful parameters for distinguishing between delay and disorder

Viewing language impairment as language general, not language specific

A clear guideline states that if atypical language development is exhibited in all languages, language impairment may be a possibility (Genesee *et al.*, 2004; Kohnert, 2008). Besides that helpful guideline, few defining behaviors exist to assist educators in sorting out delay and disability.

Using findings with high school and post-secondary foreign language learners Ganschow and Sparks (2000) concluded that most struggles in foreign language learning result from difficulties with the rule systems of language in general, not with one specific language system. The Linguistic Coding Differences Hypothesis (LCDH, see Sparks, 1995) accounts for this phenomenon, proposing that a learner's L1 skills (phonological, syntactic and semantic) provide the basis for L2 learning. If a learner has language impairment in the L1, this will also be evident in subsequently learned languages; the LCDH does not account for why these phonological, syntactic and/or semantic deficits exist in the L1.

Observation of language and literacy development in all languages

Howard and Sugarman (2007) make reference to a 50:50 TWI teacher who noted an advantage to being the observer of a learner's language development and literacy acquisition in both languages because she could directly compare the learning process in both L1 and L2. Immersion educators working in programs that begin with half of the instructional day in one language and half in the other may have a slight advantage in teasing delay apart from disorder in the early primary grades.

Educators in 90:10 TWI programs and early total one-way programs, on the other hand, spend the vast majority of K–2 instructional time teaching EgHL students through the L2. Because of this, they may find it more challenging to differentiate between a language/learning delay and a disorder since they typically observe language and literacy development in one language only.

Additional factors to consider

First, certain language learning differences observed in immersion learners may be language dependent. For example, Escamilla (2000) pointed out that Spanish speakers learning to read in Spanish will learn about the vowel system earlier than children developing literacy skills in English. Because Spanish-language vowel sounds are far more transparent than vowel sounds in English, they tend to be introduced and learned earlier. Likewise, consonant sounds are typically acquired later when learning to read in Spanish, and earlier when learning to read in English. Thus, an observed difference in early reading performance may be linked to the language and/or the learning experiences, not to the learner.

Second, it is possible for an individual to have language impairment yet not appear to have a disability because he/she has learned to accommodate it using self and social supports (Kohnert, 2008). In such cases it is likely that the impairment was never noticed nor did it become problematic in the L1 for these children. With the added linguistic and cognitive demands of an L2, however, learners who have impairment but compensate for it in their L1 may demonstrate a disability in the L2. What may look like a delay in the acquisition of the immersion language may actually be a language learning disability that has been overcome in the L1, and can similarly be overcome in the L2.

Assessment possibilities to assist in determining language disorders

Gutiérrez-Clellen and Peña (2001) advocated Dynamic Assessment (DA) as an alternative type of assessment for determining language delay versus disorder with linguistically diverse children. Based on Vygotsky's model of the zone of proximal development (ZPD), DA focuses on determining a student's potential language-learning skills and/or ability. It can help speech language pathologists make inferences about underlying learning processes and determine appropriate intervention strategies.

While all DA methods are effective, Gutiérrez-Clellen and Peña (2001) suggested that the test–teach–retest method is best suited for differentiating between language disorders and delays. In this approach, the evaluator first identifies a weak skill (test) and then provides the student with intervention (teach) before retesting the student. The idea is that students who are 'typical' language learners will make significant changes with meaningful language experiences that occur in the learner's ZPD, whereas students with language impairment will show few quantitative changes during post-testing.

Kohnert (2008) discussed two different types of measurement used to shed light on a child's language development: experience-dependent and processing-dependent measures. Experience-dependent language measures can provide a snapshot of an aspect of language development such as grammatical accuracy or vocabulary size, and this snapshot is strongly tied to prior knowledge and experience with language. In contrast, processing-dependent measures aim at limiting the impact of prior language experiences by measuring the speed of processing high-frequency words (more than likely known by all) and/or nonsense words (more than likely known by none). Because processing-oriented measures reduce the role of prior knowledge, they may be particularly appropriate for linguistically and culturally diverse learners such as those found in immersion classrooms.

Petzold (2006) has recommended that immersion programs quantify the degree of difference or discrepancy necessary to be considered learning disabled using curriculum-based measures (CBMs). This tool was developed at the University of Minnesota to measure academic skill development as an alternative to standardized testing; its emphasis is on the direct observation of a student's read aloud and on fluency (both rate and accuracy of performance), measuring performance repeatedly over a period of time to show progress. Petzold proposed that for learners to qualify as disabled (significantly discrepant) they must attain correct answers at a rate that is half or less than half of the rate of their peers in both L2 and L1.

Guiding Principles for Program Policies and Practices

Based on selected research findings and the collective experiences of veteran immersion educators summarized above, I offer the following principles for use in guiding program policy and practice.

Become familiar with typical L1 and L2 development for immersion students. For example, research shows that early total one-way immersion learners may experience a lag in English language arts until instruction has occurred in English for one to two years.

Consider the learner as a unique individual. The personality, strengths, weaknesses and educational needs of each student differ and thus influence an individual's success in an immersion program in varied ways. Researchers and practitioners have emphasized the importance of deciding each case on an individual basis, taking into consideration the many facets of a learner's make-up.

Secure specialist staffing and appropriate materials to address language and learning difficulties within the program itself. Transfer into a non-immersion program may be the only solution available to learners who struggle when there is a lack of intervention resources and remediation services available in the immersion program. By ensuring access to language and learning support services and materials within the program, educators may enable learners to stay and continue learning through the immersion language.

Respond proactively if delay is perceived. Once teachers and family members have communicated concern about a possible language or learning delay, immersion teachers are best advised to begin gathering samples of student work, keeping anecdotal records and monitoring student progress at specific intervals. If the program already implements a variety of assessment tools to measure learner progress, these may suffice. If not, it is vital to begin collecting supportive evidence of student progress, which can later be used as part of a more comprehensive assessment process.

Consider all potential sources of difficulty. It is important to look at the whole child, taking into account his/her language-learning background and experiences. Growing up bilingual does affect language development and does not predict disability. Diagnosis of a language-learning disability in bilinguals, as in monolinguals, requires multifaceted assessment including nonverbal measures of intelligence, achievement, language and literacy development, and basic psychological (information) processing abilities. The source of a learner's struggles with language must be identified, be it environmental, instructional, inherent to the learner or some combination of the above.

Assess struggling L2 readers earlier in their L1. While most programs have opted to put off testing early primary immersion students who exhibit difficulty acquiring word-level reading skills in their L2, research suggests that early assessment of foundational skills in a child's L1 can help to identify students who will need additional reading support services and give the teacher a head start on focusing on the students' specific needs (e.g. phonological awareness).

Compare, compare, compare! Kohnert (2004, 2008) has recommended comparing students not only to *standardized norms* but also to *other students with similar experiences.* Language learning experiences can vary because of within-the-learner (endogenous) as well as outside-the-learner (exogenous) factors. Thus, when making comparisons, it is necessary to take both types of influences into consideration, seeking out comparison groups for each of the different factors. Kohnert suggests comparing *siblings* as one possible way to control for some of the exogenous factors that may have an impact, as siblings may have had comparable home language experiences.

Making comparisons with other *students who have had similar educational experiences* is useful; establishing developmental benchmarks as well as achievement norms for learners in immersion programs is beneficial in the assessment process as bilingually schooled learners have educational experiences that differ greatly from their monolingual peers. It is advantageous for individual school districts and schools to develop their own norms in order to account for common academic language experiences as well as the interaction of bilingualism with cognitive and social development. Petzold (2006) has recommended collecting data every three years in order to reevaluate and more accurately reflect students' current language experiences, given inevitable curricular changes.

Expand beyond the standardized, norm-referenced assessment. To account for exogenous and endogenous influences on a learner's language development as well as those that reflect interaction between these two influences, educators should be wary of relying too heavily on formal evaluations, such as nonverbal IQ tests and standardized assessments. Also, because student performance will vary across tasks, it helps to include a broad range of assessment types.

For school psychologists, CBMs, as described above, are recommended.

For speech language pathologists, a recommended alternative to traditional assessments to assist in distinguishing between a language delay and a language disorder is DA (described above). Such assessments provide an important link to actual teaching and learning in the classroom.

Finally, as Kohnert (2008) argues, complementing *language experience-dependent measures* with *language and nonlanguage processing-dependent* measures holds great promise in current efforts to differentiate between bilinguals with and without a language disorder.

Involve the perspectives of multiple teaching professionals and specialists. In addition to employing a wide variety of formal and informal assessments, it is essential to involve the perspectives of multiple teaching professionals and specialists when deciding between difference and disorder or disability. Input from the school psychologist, principal, classroom teacher, school nurse, music/art/media/physical education specialist, speech language pathologist and so on should be included in the comprehensive assessment of a student (Woelber, 2003). Conflicts between a student's learning style and a teacher's instructional style can be revealed in this manner; a student's attitude and personality may also be exposed through this multifaceted input. In this way, a team approach guards against premature decision-making based on partial information and an overly simplistic view of the learner and the learning process, and a comprehensive assessment is ensured.

Believe in and remain committed to the immersion philosophy. Only when all who are involved with immersion students recognize, value, and work to uphold the philosophy of the program is success for all students promoted.

Specialists, resource teachers, psychologists, administrators, teachers and parents all play an important role. A level of trust and support needs to be developed between the school and the home, which requires that schools not only educate parents about options and resources but also provide them with high quality ones.

Trust the universal human capacity for language learning. When discussing issues of program-learner suitability, keep in mind that under the right circumstances, all children, even those with language impairment, are able to acquire and learn in two languages (Genesee *et al.*, 2004; Gutiérrez-Clellen *et al.*, 2008). Language-impaired learners educated in immersion settings will still exhibit impairment and function below normal, and they will do so in all languages, not just one.

Conclusion

Immersion education in pre-K–12 schools has fostered academic achievement and moderate to high levels of bilingualism and biliteracy among a wide variety of school children. Successful learner profiles include language majority and language minority students, ethnic majority and ethnic minority students, and students from a wide variety of socioeconomic backgrounds and cognitive abilities. While there is a clear need for more research with low language and language and/or learning-disabled students, evidence to date supports the inclusion of these learners as well. Indeed, it is difficult to argue in favor of whole program policies that would uniformly deny admission to any child.

Ensuring access to immersion education for all children and families who are interested in and committed to the program goals is still an unrealized possibility in the United States. More and more, administrators and teachers are wary of implementing programs that strongly promote L2 development and limit attention to L1 in the early primary grades. Pressure to demonstrate achievement on standardized tests given in English is unrelenting. Because of this and other concerns, a few programs or districts have unofficially adopted checklists or assessments that screen for a certain level of L1 language proficiency prior to admission; others discourage families who have children with diagnosed language and learning challenges from enrolling their child. Such practices serve to limit the program's possibilities.

While immersion may not be the best match for every learner, best practice suggests that any decision to restrict admission or recommend that a child transfer to a non-immersion program be given a great deal of thought, discussion and expert attention by a team of skilled professionals. Educators and specialists involved in such decision-making will need to sort through the complex issues related to language, literacy and learning for immersion students and be willing to work in tandem with family members for the long-term success and well-being of each and every child. Until we have strong evidence that shows that learners with certain language and/or learning disabilities are better served when schooled through one language only, there is no reason to deny the enrichment possibilities of an immersion education to any child.

Notes

1. I use the term 'struggling learner' to describe a child who exhibits difficulty with language, literacy and/or learning relative to the average performance of classroom peers. The learner's struggles may involve academic, linguistic, social–emotional and/or behavioral issues. Such learners may or may not have a diagnosed language and/or learning disability.
2. Sections of this chapter have been recently published by the University of Minnesota's Center for Advanced Research on Language Acquisition in a more comprehensive handbook on this topic titled *Struggling Learners & Language Immersion Education* (Fortune with Menke, 2010) and are reprinted in this volume with permission.
3. The terms 'disorder' and 'disability' are not consistently differentiated in the literature; different authors use these terms in different ways at different times. Consequently, these words are used interchangeably throughout this chapter.

References

American Speech-Language-Hearing Association (2008) Impairment, disorder, disability. On WWW at http://www.asha.org/public/hearing/disorders/impair_dis_disab.htm. Accessed 1.4.09.

Anderson, M., Lindholm, L., Wilhelm, P., Ziegler, M. and Boudreaux, N. (2005) Meeting the challenges of No Child Left Behind in immersion education in the US. *ACIE Newsletter* 8 Bridge Insert, 1–8.

Bender, W.N. and Larkin, M.J. (2009) *Reading Strategies for Elementary Students with Learning Difficulties: Strategies for RTI* (2nd edn). Thousand Oaks, CA: Corwin Press.

Boschung, S. and Roy, N. (1996) *Appendix A: Issues Surrounding Transfer Out of French Immersion: A Literature Review*. Nanaimo, Vancouver Island, Canada: University of British Columbia Modern Language Department.

Brown, G. and Yule, G. (1983) *Discourse Analysis*. Cambridge, MA: Cambridge University Press.

Bruck, M. (1978) The suitability of early French immersion programs for the language-disabled child. *Canadian Journal of Education* 3, 51–72.

Bruck, M. (1982) Language impaired children's performance in an additive bilingual education program. *Applied Psycholinguistics* 3, 45–60.

Bruck, M., Tucker, G.R. and Jakimik, J. (1975) Are French immersion programs suitable for working class children. *Word* 27, 311–341.

Cadez, R. (2006) Student attrition in specialized high school programs: An examination of three French immersion centres. Master's thesis, University of Lethbridge, Alberta, Canada.

Caldas, S. and Boudreaux, N. (1999) Poverty, race, and foreign language immersion: Predictors of math and English language arts performance. *Learning Languages* 5, 4–15.

Center for Applied Linguistics (2006) Directory of foreign language immersion programs in US schools. On WWW at http://www.cal.org/resources/immersion. Accessed 19.4.10.

Center for Applied Linguistics (2010) Directory of two-way bilingual immersion programs in the US. On WWW at http://www.cal.org/twi/directory. Accessed 25.3.10.

Cortiella, C. (2009) The state of learning disabilities. On WWW at http://www. LD.org/stateofld. Accessed 11.7.09.

Durgunoglu, A.Y. and Öney, B. (2000) Literacy development in two languages: Cognitive and sociocultural dimensions of cross-language transfer. In US Department of Education, Office of Bilingual Education and Minority Language Affairs (OBEMLA) (eds) *Proceedings of A Research Symposium on High Standards in Reading for Students from Diverse Language Groups: Research, Practice & Policy* (pp. 78–99). Washington, DC: US Department of Education.

Durgunoglu, A.Y. and Verhoeven, L. (eds) (1998) *Literacy Development in a Multilingual Context: Cross-Cultural Perspectives*. Mahwah, NJ: Erlbaum.

Erdos, C., Genesee, F., Savage, R. and Haigh, C. (2010) Individual differences in second language reading outcomes. *International Journal of Bilingualism*. DOI: 10.1177/1367006910371022.

Escamilla, K. (2000) Teaching literacy in Spanish. In J.V. Tinajero and R.A. DeVillar (eds) *The Power of Two Languages 2000* (pp. 126–141). New York: McGraw-Hill.

Fortune, T.W. and Arabbo, M.A. (2006) Attending to immersion language proficiency at the program level. Paper presented at the Dual Language Immersion Pre-Conference Institute of the National Association of Bilingual Education, Phoenix, AZ.

Fortune, T.W. with Menke, M.R. (2010) *Struggling Learners and Language Immersion Education: Research-Based, Practitioner-Informed Responses to Educators' top Questions* (CARLA Publication Series). Minneapolis: University of Minnesota, The Center for Advanced Research on Language Acquisition.

Fradd, S. and McGee, P. (1994) *Instructional Assessment*. Reading, MA: Addison-Wesley.

Ganschow, L. and Sparks, R. (2000) Reflections on foreign language study for students with language learning problems: Research, issues and challenges. *Dyslexia* 6, 87–100.

Genesee, F. (1987) *Learning Through Two Languages: Studies of Immersion and Bilingual Education*. Rowley, MA: Newbury House.

Genesee, F. (2007) French immersion and at-risk students: A review of research evidence. *The Canadian Modern Language Review* 63, 655–688.

Genesee, F., Paradis, J. and Crago, M. (2004) *Dual Language Development and Disorders: A Handbook on Bilingualism and Second Language Learning*. Baltimore, MD: Brookes.

Genesee, F. and Jared, D. (2008) Literacy development in early French immersion programs. *Canadian Psychology* 49, 140–147.

Gutiérrez-Clellen, V., Simon-Cereijido, G. and Wagner, C. (2008) Bilingual children with language impairment: A comparison with monolinguals and second language learners. *Applied Psycholinguistics* 29, 3–19.

Gutiérrez-Clellen, V.F. and Peña, E. (2001) Dynamic assessment of diverse children: A tutorial. *Language Speech and Hearing Services in Schools* 32, 212–224.

Håkansson, G. and Nettelbladt, U. (1996) Similarities between SLI and L2 children: Evidence from the acquisition of Swedish word order. In I. Gilbert and C. Johnson (eds) *Children's Language* (pp. 135–151). Mahwah, NJ: Erlbaum.

Hakuta, K., Goto Butler, Y. and Witt, D. (2000) *How Long does it Take English Learners to Attain Proficiency?* (Policy Rep. No. 2000-1). University of California Linguistic Minority Research Institute.

Hart, B. and Risley, T.R. (1995) *Meaningful Differences in the Everyday Experience of Young American Children*. Baltimore, MD: Paul H. Brookes.

Holobow, N.E., Genesee, F. and Lambert, W.E. (1991) The effectiveness of a foreign language immersion program for children from different ethnic and social class backgrounds: Report 2. *Applied Psycholinguistics* 12, 179–198.

Howard, E.R., Christian, D. and Genesee, F. (2004) *The Development of Bilingualism and Biliteracy from Grade 3 to 5: A Summary of Findings from the CAL/CREDE Study of Two-Way Immersion Education*. Research Rep. No. 13. Santa Cruz, CA and Washington, DC: Center for Research on Education, Diversity & Excellence.

Howard, E.R. and Sugarman, J. (2007) *Realizing the Vision of Two-Way Immersion: Fostering Effective Programs and Classrooms*. Washington, DC: Center for Applied Linguistics and Delta.

Individuals with Disabilities Education Improvement Act (2004) Public–Law 108–446, Office of Special Education Programs (OSEP). Washington, DC: US Department of Education.

Klimpl, J.I., Amin, I.A., Gouin, D.M. and Sacks, R.I. (2007) Elementary immersion programs and assessments in Montgomery County Public Schools. Paper presented at American Council on the Teaching of Foreign Languages (ACTFL), San Antonio, Texas.

Kohnert, K. (2008) *Language Disorders in Bilingual Children and Adults*. San Diego: Plural.

Kohnert, K. (2004) Language and learning disorders in the immersion classroom. Workshop presented at Meeting the Challenges of Immersion Education Summer Institute for Center for Advanced Research on Language Acquisition, University of Minnesota, Minneapolis.

Lindholm-Leary, K. (2001) *Dual Language Education*. Clevedon: Multilingual Matters.

Lindholm-Leary, K. and Howard, E. (2008) Language development and academic achievement in two-way immersion programs. In T.W. Fortune and D.J. Tedick (eds) *Pathways to Multilingualism: Evolving Perspectives on Immersion Education* (pp. 177–200). Clevedon: Multilingual Matters.

Peña, E.D., Iglesias, A. and Lidz, C.S. (2001) Reducing test bias through dynamic assessment of children's word learning ability. *American Journal of Speech-Language Pathology* 10, 138–154.

Petzold, A. (2006) Assessment of struggling elementary immersion learners: The St. Paul Public Schools Model. *The ACIE Newsletter* 9, 1–2, 10–11, 13.

Petzold, A. (2004) Accurate identification of struggling students in the immersion classroom. Workshop presented at Meeting the Challenges of Immersion Education Summer Institute for Center for Advanced Research on Language Acquisition, University of Minnesota, Minneapolis.

Sparks, R. (1995) Examining the linguistic coding difference hypothesis to explain individual differences in foreign language learning. *Annals of Dyslexia* 45, 187–214.

Swain, M. and Barik, H.C. (1976) A large scale program in French immersion: The Ottawa study through grade three. *ITL: A Review of Applied Linguistics* 33, 1–25.

Swain, M. and Lapkin, S. (1982) *Evaluating Bilingual Education: A Canadian Case Study*. Clevedon: Multilingual Matters.

Turnbull, M., Hart, D. and Lapkin, S. (2003) Grade 6 French immersion students' performance on large-scale reading, writing, and mathematics tests: Building explanations. *Alberta Journal of Education* 49, 6–23.

Turnbull, M., Lapkin, S. and Hart, D. (2001) Grade 3 immersion students' performance in literacy and mathematics: Province-wide results from Ontario (1998–99). *The Canadian Modern Language Review* 58, 9–26.

Woelber, K. (2003) Determining eligibility of special education services for immersion students with learning disabilities. Master's thesis, Hamline University, St Paul, MN.

Chapter 14

Reflecting on Possibilities for Immersion

F. GENESEE

The chapters in this volume provide a snapshot of the evolution of immersion since its inauguration in Canada in 1965 (Lambert & Tucker, 1972). Some chapters describe programs that are examples of immersion that have been developed in countries with policies of official bilingualism, as in Canada; for example, Björklund and Mård-Miettinen's chapter on Swedish immersion in Finland, Ó Duibhir's chapter on Irish immersion in Ireland, and Burger, Weinberg, Hall, Movassat and Hope's chapter on French immersion at the university level in Canada. At the same time, these authors illustrate how the original model has evolved to embrace different goals, populations and concerns. The Finnish programs, for example, have expanded the original application of immersion to include multiple languages (see also Cenoz & Genesee, 1998; Zehrbach, Chapter 4), an important addition in many areas of Europe and indeed around the world as globalization becomes a driving force in education. The Burger *et al.* chapter describes an innovative immersion project as a way of extending opportunities for bilingualism at the tertiary level of education. The Hawaiian immersion program discussed by Wilson and Kamanā is a unique immersion program in an official indigenous language, one of a growing number of programs that aim to promote individual bilingualism and, at the same time, revitalize indigenous languages and cultures (see also, Peter *et al.*, Chapter 10).

Yet other innovations to immersion are described by other authors. The Chinese immersion programs described by Lindholm-Leary involve typologically different languages (Chinese and English) with radically different orthographic systems. The two-way immersion (TWI) programs described by de Jong and Bearse, Dorner, Lindholm-Leary and Zehrbach extend the original immersion model by including both majority and minority language students in the same classrooms. de Jong and Bearse's chapter is an especially welcome contribution because of its discussion of two aspects that are seldom considered – immersion at the high school level and how second language (L2) learning in immersion is linked to issues of ethnic identity.

It is encouraging to see continuing evidence for the fundamental effectiveness of immersion in promoting bilingualism as the model evolves and takes on new forms. At the same time, the chapters in this volume highlight a wide range of issues that are gaining and deserve attention as immersion matures. Because of space limitations, I have chosen to focus on just the following four: (1) advocacy, (2) the role of parents, (3) assessment and (4) accessibility.

Advocacy

Immersion programs do not exist in a vacuum; they are shaped by multiple forces inside and, importantly, outside the classroom. Hoare's chapter on immersion in Hong Kong and Mainland China illustrates how even 'implementation of the [immersion] curriculum is in many respects a result of ... different policy contexts' (p. 212). He goes on to point out that 'schools' narrow focus on academic success' can result in programs with unofficial policies that emphasize academic achievement over linguistic competence. Indeed, an emerging and growing focus of concern among researchers and professionals who work in immersion programs elsewhere is how best to achieve a pedagogical balance between focus on meaning (i.e. academic content) and focus on form (i.e. language skills) in order to maximize students' L2 proficiency while also ensuring high levels of academic achievement (Lyster, 2007). Concerns about L2 outcomes are also expressed by de Jong and Bearse in their chapter on TWI Spanish–English at the high school level, Ó Duibhir in his chapter on elementary school Irish immersion, and Broner and Tedick in their chapter on early total Spanish immersion in the United States. While these authors discuss concerns about L2 proficiency in terms of pedagogy and curriculum, Hoare prompts us to also consider unofficial policies in the form of expectations about what really counts in immersion.

Policy-related issues are also raised by Wilson and Kamanā, who point out that 'increasingly the survival of minority autochthonous languages is supported through their recognition as "official languages" in their regions' (p. 37). Recognition of Hawaiian as an official state language affords immersion in Hawaii advantages that programs in other regions do not enjoy and, in particular, the possibility of extended use of Hawaiian as the primary language of instruction until the end of secondary school, much longer than in immersion programs elsewhere in the United States. At the same time, Wilson and Kamanā point out that status as an official language is not enough to ensure the viability and long-term impact of a program. They argue that sustained and strategic advocacy to create supportive policies for immersion is critical to achieve significant long-term goals, especially when one of the goals is to ensure the survival of a threatened language.

While this is a lesson of clear relevance to the somewhat unique context of indigenous language immersion programs, as in Hawaii or in the Cherokee nation (see also Chapter 10 by Peter *et al.*), it is arguably important in all communities that seek to initiate, maintain or expand immersion programs. Indeed, the St Lambert immersion program, which marked the beginnings of immersion 45 years ago, was instituted in the face of strenuous opposition from local educational authorities (Lambert & Tucker, 1972). It was only as a result of significant and persistent parental pressure that the program was initiated; maintenance and expansion of the program was ensured once empirical evidence documented its success. To this day, however, advocacy plays an important role.

What is the lesson to be taken from these experiences? Those who seek to begin new programs as well as those involved in existing programs, in my opinion, are well advised to create an advocacy group that is charged to monitor changes in existing policies and to promote the development of new policies at the school, local district and state/provincial levels that support immersion. Immersion programs often do not figure in the minds of policy makers and, as a result, they can become vulnerable when local politics, policies and circumstances change. A designated advocacy group or committee can safeguard programs from the effects of such change. To be effective, advocacy efforts must include a dedicated group of parents, local politicians, and businesspeople who take on the designated role of advocacy to ensure that policies that support the program are in place.

The Role of Parents

The success of immersion programs depends critically on parental support, as was pointed out earlier in the case of the St Lambert project. As Dorner explains, in the case of parents who speak a minority language at home, support depends on parents' understanding counterintuitive findings that their children will attain the same levels of competence in the majority language and in academic domains as students in non-immersion programs despite the fact that their children's initial schooling will take place in a minority language. In the case of indigenous language programs, such as the Cherokee immersion program described by Peter and her colleagues and the Hawaiian immersion program described by Wilson and Kamanā, parental involvement is particularly important for *revernacularization* (to use Wilson and Kamanā's term) and revitalization of endangered languages. To achieve these goals, parents themselves must learn and use the language at home and in the community; otherwise, the language is just another thing that is taught and used at school by their children. Parents are also important in one-way and two-way immersion programs. Parents must be convinced of the effectiveness of immersion to decide to enroll and retain their children in programs despite, in some cases, publicity and pressures against doing so and despite worries that arise if their children face learning challenges, an issue I shall return to later.

Concerns about the level of L2 competence that students achieve in immersion programs, referred to earlier, can be addressed, in part, by encouraging parents to expand their children's L2 learning opportunities outside school through family holidays in regions where the L2 is used, exchanges with same-age native speakers of the L2 and so on. While we do not yet fully know the full extent to which immersion students can master an L2 in immersion, it is probably safe to say that there are limits to the levels of L2 competence that students can achieve if their L2 learning and use are restricted to the immersion classroom. Our experience even in the bilingual community of Montreal has taught us this. It is reasonable to expect that involving parents as full partners in their children's L2 development by encouraging them to take steps to expose their children to the L2 outside school can result in enhanced levels of L2 competence.

In short, support from parents in multiple ways can help achieve the multiple goals of immersion education. Yet, as Dorner rightly points out, how best to work effectively with parents has received scant empirical attention. Dorner makes a number of useful suggestions for working with parents, including the provision of information sessions in contexts that are not traditional but are better suited to parents (family or neighborhood gatherings) and including language interpreters for minority language parents at information meetings – an obvious, but often overlooked, idea. Additional possibilities come to mind: school visits for parents (with the assistance of interpreters for minority language parents) might be considered on the assumption that 'seeing-is-believing', or testimonials during information sessions at school or community meetings from parents and students who have had first-hand experiences with immersion. The latter could be useful because it would broaden the sources of information that are made available to new parents and students.

Assessment

It is customary to distinguish between summative and formative forms of assessment (Marzano, 2006). Summative assessment is undertaken to evaluate the end results of an educational intervention, such as immersion, and is usually associated with high-stakes decisions at either the individual student level, such as grading students, or at the program level, such as deciding to continue to discontinue a program. The evaluation of the St Lambert French immersion program is an example of the power of summative assessment. The results of these evaluations were responsible, in part, for the spread of immersion because they gave immersion credibility (Johnson & Swain, 1997). Similar assessments have been carried out elsewhere, for example, in California (Lindholm-Leary, 2001) and Finland (Laurén, 1997). The chapters by Lindholm-Leary on Chinese TWI and by Björklund and Mård-Miettinen on multilingual immersion illustrate the value of summative assessments in evaluating innovative and evolving forms of immersion.

In addition to the summative assessments that are carried out by university-based researchers, there is a role for school-based summative assessments that document the success of local immersion programs. In the face of changes in district administration personnel, budgets and general education policies, immersion programs that are unable to demonstrate their effectiveness empirically can be vulnerable. Thus, locally managed summative assessments can be a useful part of local advocacy to ensure the continuance of immersion in the face of such threats.

Formative assessments occur while content is being taught and learned and continue throughout the period of learning. A primary objective of formative assessment is to inform teachers of what their students know or do not know and what they can or cannot do. Most importantly, classroom-based formative assessments allow teachers to monitor their instruction and make modifications to it based on student performance (Ainsworth & Viegut, 2006). There are few examples of the use of formative assessment for these purposes. The chapter by Peter, Sly and Hirata-Edds is a significant exception. Their chapter illustrates the multiple benefits of formative assessment with respect to curriculum development, instructional planning, individualizing instruction and identifying needs for professional development, among others.

Other chapters in this volume provide examples of research that could be carried out locally and serve the same goals of formative assessment, provided modifications were made. For example, the student questionnaires discussed by Burger and her colleagues working in immersion at the university level could realistically be planned, carried out and analyzed by school or district administrators and, subsequently, used to modify their programs. Similarly, Broner and Tedick's study, although conducted in a rigorous and systematic fashion characteristic of researchers, could be carried out by immersion teachers, with modifications of course. Other 'assessments' reported on in this volume could likewise be adapted and serve the goals of formative classroom assessment, to great benefit (e.g. de Jong & Bearse, Chapter 6; Ó Duibhir, Chapter 8).

Classroom- or school-based formative assessments lend themselves to examining diverse important aspects of immersion – including, teacher and student use of language to enhance L2 learning (Broner & Tedick, Chapter 9; Ó Duibhir, Chapter 8), students' views and attitudes of L2 learning (Ó Duibhir, Chapter 8; de Jong & Bearse, Chapter 6) and students' views of their instructors and the usefulness of specific components of their learning experiences (Burger *et al.*, Chapter 7). For formative assessment to be useful, it must be managed and 'owned' by teachers and other educational personnel working in the program. It is through direct management and ownership of formative assessment that teachers are able to eliminate the threat that often comes from externally managed, summative evaluations and, thus, to see and realize the direct educational benefits of formative assessment. For formative assessment to be beneficial, it must also be ongoing – an integral part of program implementation across grade levels. Formative assessments must be translated into modifications to the curriculum, instruction and materials if educational benefits are to result. And this should be done across grade levels to ensure coherence and maximize learning. Finally, for formative assessment to be used to the benefit of L2 teaching and learning, it must involve cooperation among immersion teachers across grade levels and between immersion and non-immersion teachers so that curriculum and instruction are coordinated across languages.

Accessibility

The wealth of evaluative research that has tracked the success of immersion since its inception leaves no doubt of its general effectiveness. In contrast, there is scant research on immersion students with special education needs or from disadvantaged backgrounds. This volume is unique in including two chapters on this topic. Zehrbach raises the issue of attracting students with special needs to TWI charter schools. Because participation in immersion programs is invariably voluntary and because there is often the erroneous perception that only the best students can learn effectively when taught through two languages, parents and educators often believe that students who are likely to struggle in school are not good candidates for immersion. The question is, 'Are they'?

There is some research on students who are at risk for academic difficulties in school because of low academic ability, disadvantaged socioeconomic backgrounds, and minority groups status who tend to underachieve in comparison with students without such challenges (see Fortune, Chapter 13; Genesee, 2007, for summaries). There is also some research on children from majority English language backgrounds with below average native language abilities who might be considered to have a language-learning disability (Bruck, 1978, 1982). These studies indicate that these students attain the same levels of native language and academic achievement as similarly challenged students in L1 programs. However, there are limitations to these studies that call for much more research into the suitability of immersion for at-risk learners. First, most of these studies were conducted in Canada and, in Montreal in particular. Further research is needed to document the generalizability of these findings in other settings and, in particular, in settings that do not provide the same high level of support for bilingualism as is evident in Canada. Second, most studies were conducted more than 20 years ago. Replications of early studies, especially those on students with language-learning impairment, using current operational definitions of disability or impairment, would be important to update existing empirical evidence.

Also, there is a need for studies of other at-risk groups, including students who are at risk for reading disabilities, a major reason for students leaving immersion. At present, there is virtually no research on such students. Much current research on L2 reading acquisition, among both minority language students (i.e. English Language Learners) who are learning to read in English as an L2 and majority language students who are learning to read in French as an L2, indicates that learning to read in an L2 is the same as learning to read in an L1 in some fundamental and important respects (see August & Shanahan, 2006; Genesee & Jared, 2008; Riches & Genesee, 2006). This is encouraging because it indicates that what we know about L1 reading acquisition can inform policy and practice with respect to L2 reading instruction. However, there are significant differences between learning to read in an L2 and an L1, and we have a long way to go to better understand the nature of these differences and how they affect learning, especially among students who have difficulty learning to read.

Fortune provides an excellent overview of the present research on such learners and suggests how findings from this research can be used to guide program policy and practice with respect to students who are likely to struggle in immersion. Concern about the accessibility of immersion for

ALL students raises not only policy and practical issues, but also ethical issues. On the one hand, ethical issues are implicated in decisions, official or unofficial, to exclude students from immersion because to do so is to exclude students from what is arguably the most effective method of promoting bilingualism that we currently have. This, in turn, reduces students' access to the cognitive (e.g. Bialystok, 2006) and job-related benefits that come from high levels of bilingual competence. In the case of children from minority language backgrounds, excluding struggling students from TWI programs not only reduces their opportunities to acquire bilingual proficiency, but also their access to an educational alternative that has been documented to be as effective and often more effective than mainstream education in promoting English language development and academic achievement (e.g. August & Shanahan, 2006; Genesee *et al.*, 2006). As Fortune rightly points out, although present empirical evidence is limited, we have enough empirical evidence at present to formulate reasonable and justifiable principles to guide policy and practice with respect to these learners. In other words, there is no reason to summarily exclude struggling students from immersion and, to the contrary, current evidence, albeit still evolving, indicates that such students can benefit from participation in immersion within the limits set by the learning challenges they face.

Conclusion

The chapters in this volume provide rich documentation on traditional and innovative forms of immersion education. At the same time, they sensitize us to ongoing and emerging issues that deserve our attention. The present chapter has focused on advocacy, the role of parents, assessment and accessibility, while ignoring other issues, such as professional development of immersion teachers, the development of curriculum and instruction materials and how best to enhance immersion students' L2 competence, because of space limitations. These other issues are equally important. It is encouraging to see from this collection continued evidence for the effectiveness of immersion in traditional and innovative formats and, at the same time, to read in depth critical analyses of such a broad range of important issues and such constructive suggestions and possibilities for moving forward.

References

Ainsworth, L. and Viegut, D. (2006) *Common Formative Assessments*. Thousand Oaks, CA: Corwin Press.

August, D. and Shanahan, T. (eds) (2006) *Developing Literacy in Second-Language Learners: Report of the National Literacy Panel on Language-Minority Children and Youth.* Mahwah, NJ: Erlbaum.

Bialystok, E. (2006) The impact of bilingualism on language and literacy development. In T.K. Bhatia and W.E. Ritchie (eds) *The Handbook of Bilingualism* (pp. 577–601). Malden, MA: Blackwell.

Bruck, M. (1978) The suitability of early French immersion programs for the language disabled child. *Canadian Journal of Education* 3, 51–72.

Bruck, M. (1982) Language disabled children: Performance in an additive bilingual education program. *Applied Psycholinguistics* 3, 45–60.

Cenoz, J. and Genesee, F. (eds) (1998) *Beyond Bilingualism: Multilingualism and Multilingual Education.* Clevedon: Multilingual Matters.

Genesee, F. (2007) French immersion and at-risk students: A review of research evidence. *The Canadian Modern Language Review* 63, 654–687.

Genesee, F. and Jared, D. (2008) Literacy development in early French immersion programs. *Canadian Psychology* 49, 140–147.

Genesee, F., Lindholm-Leary, K.J., Saunders, W. and Christian, D. (2006) *Educating English Language Learners.* New York: Cambridge University Press.

Johnson, R.K. and Swain, M. (1997) *Immersion Education: International Perspectives.* Cambridge: Cambridge University Press.

Lambert, W.E. and Tucker, G.R. (1972) *The Bilingual Education of Children: The St. Lambert Experiment.* Rowley, MA: Newbury House.

Laurén, C. (1997) Swedish immersion programs in Finland. In J. Cummins and D. Corso (eds) *Encyclopedia of Language Education, Vol. 5, Bilingual Education* (pp. 291–296). Dordrecht: Kluwer.

Lindholm-Leary, K.J. (2001) *Dual Language Education.* Clevedon: Multilingual Matters.

Lyster, R. (2007) *Learning and Teaching Languages through Content: A Counterbalanced Approach.* Amsterdam: John Benjamins.

Marzano, R.J. (2006) *Classroom Assessments and Grading that Work.* Alexandria, VA: Association for Supervision and Curriculum Development.

Riches, C. and Genesee, F. (2006) Cross-linguistic and cross-modal aspects of literacy development. In F. Genesee, K. Lindholm-Leary, W. Saunders and D. Christian (eds) *Educating English Language Learners: A Synthesis of Research Evidence* (pp. 64–108). New York: Cambridge University Press.

Index

Authors

Subjects